ACCLAIM for DENVERSKY5280

STANDING OVATION to DENVERSKY!! *Sturgeon Lake, Minnesota*

YOU ARE MY SECRET AGENT *from the other team! Florida*

EXCELLENT!...WITTY, FUN, INFORMATIVE. *Just like your posts! Maine*

YOUR ADVICE WAS AWESOME *and hilarious. Milwaukee, Wisconsin*

THANK YOU SO MUCH! *I had no idea so many of the common terms could actually be misunderstood or interpreted as red flags. Toronto, Canada*

YOUR ADVICE WAS EXACTLY WHAT I NEEDED! *Thanks so much! I know I'm not alone in this, but, I haven't been very good at selling myself in general. Bend, Oregon*

YOU MA'AM ARE A LIFESAVER! A MIRACLE WORKER! *Colorado Springs, Colorado*

IF YOU FOLLOW DENVERSKY'S ADVICE, you're GOLDEN! *Michigan*

FANTASTIC! THANKS DENVERSKY! I see where I was going wrong with the initial messages now. Birmingham, United Kingdom

WHEN I SEE SANTA NEXT, I'll put in a good word for ya! Pennsylvania

I DIDN'T REALIZE what my profile said vs what was written. I will tweak it...and work on some pictures. Thanks again. You are a sweetheart for sure! Illinois

I LOVE YOU, DENVERSKY! I promise I won't forget about you when I'm a billionaire! Los Angeles, California

I HAVE A DATE Sunday, Monday, Thursday, and Friday... if you're ever in Eastern Kentucky I definitely owe you one... I've been alone for 13 months, and I am definitely digging the attention. I owe you big time... Again thanks so much. Kentucky

THANKS! THANKS! THANKS! For the changes I made based upon your suggestions, things are finally working!!! Alberta, Canada

DENVERSKY HAS XRAY-LIKE VISION and is great at picking up on every last detail in a profile. Never underestimate her advice. It's highly recommended! Florida

AWESOME SECRETS
for MEN

~Catch Your Online Match~

**on Match.com®, Chemistry™
PlentyofFish™, eHarmony®
Perfect Match®, OkCupid™, DateHookup™**

& ALL INTERNET DATING SITES

~~~~~~~~~~~~~~~~~~~

TIPS & TRICKS! PROFILES!

FIRST FLIRTS!   FREE DATES!

Let us be your Tour Guide.

©2010 DenverSky5280 Denver CO USA

Dedication

This book is dedicated to you... because you are willing to explore and take a chance and reach out across the electronic universe.

Maybe you're searching for your BEST-FIRST-DATE. Maybe you're searching for your LAST-FIRST-DATE.

Whomever you're searching for, this book is for you. This is to help you find that special person... the one who makes you smile, the one who makes your heart pound, the one who turns on your mind, body, and soul.

May you find your special someone...

she's looking for you, too!

DenverSky5280

Denver, Colorado   April 7

AWESOME!

This is an extraordinary book.

You can start with dessert first.

That would be the **SEX Chapter**, **What Women Want**, **First Flirts**, **Free First Dates**, and a few other sextions... oops... make that sections.

Or... *You can start with Chapter 1 to know all the Awesome Secrets.*

Or... *you can WING IT and COPY from this book.* The book is laid out like a giant Thanksgiving buffet. Copy or imitate the examples to improve your Profile, your First Flirts, and your entire online dating experience.

If you decide to copy and WING IT, in 10 minutes you can write a good online Profile and send a good First Flirt email.

Here's how you do it: ➔➔➔➔➔

➔➔➔➔➔

➔➔➔➔➔

SUPER-QUICK
WAY to SUCCESS

1. ➔ **Choose** a User Name (see User Name Chapter for ideas).
2. ➔ **Choose** 1 Headline (use Headline Chapter/Appendix).
3. ➔ **Choose** 1 Opening Line (use Opening Line Chapter/Appx).
4. ➔ **Choose** or imitate 1 example from each of these Chapters or Appendix: *For Fun, My Job, Favorite Hot Spots, Favorite Things, Last Read, and 1st Date.*
5. ➔ **Choose** 1 Ending (use Endings Chapter/Appendix).
6. ➔ **Find** 2 photos of your smiling face & 1 full body photo.
7. ➔ **SUCCESS!** Post it on the Dating Site!
8. ➔ **Choose** 1 First Flirt (use 1st Flirt Chapter/Appendix)
9. ➔ **Email** the woman you like!

Now 1 question: **What's better than SEX?** Many men would answer the only thing better than sex is more sex. This book isn't about MORE SEX. It's about how to get more dates, better dates, and hopefully find "the One". *If this book helps you get more SEX... sssssh... she doesn't like it when you kiss and tell.*

SECRETS in this book are clearly labeled so you can't miss them. They look like this: **HUMONGOUS SECRET!**

Veteran or virgin, this book will work for you. You can start with the Super-Quick Way to success or read the whole book...but only if you want to be smarter than 99% of the men online.

Are there really that many AWESOME SECRETS?
In a word... YES! ➔➔➔➔➔

Hi and Welcome!

This book of *Awesome Secrets* is the result of helping thousands of online men and women. Over 40,000 online Profiles were read, and thousands were individually critiqued.

I still participate in the online Dating Forums. It's fun, and learning never stops! I always smile when men and women email me and share their wonderful success stories.

A huge thank you goes out to a special group of online Forum folks who offered encouragement and insight...*Rick, Ron, Billy, Tom, Andy, Marcelo, Cowboy, Doc, Jim, Ray, Kerry, Glen, Adam, Tallu, Tracy, Pam, Lynn, Lynette, Carol, Gloria, Jessica, Tina, Teri, and Sabrina.* You're a fun, funny, and smart, motley crew!

In this book are **little secrets** and **Big Secrets** and **HUMONGOUS SECRETS**. The book would have been shorter except for one thing: People kept saying, "***Don't just tell me, give me EXAMPLES. Give me something I can imitate.***" We did. This book gives you the Secrets, *and* it gives you pages and pages of examples to follow.

Whether you're looking for your BEST-FIRST-DATE-EVER or your LAST-FIRST-DATE, this book is for you. No matter if you're single, divorced, widowed, or separated, you've come to the right place. This advice has worked for men of all ages from the U.S. to Canada to the U.K. It can work for you, too.

Looking forward to hearing your success story!

Wishing you a wonderful journey, DenverSky

Awesome Secrets for Men
Table of Contents

Hi MysteryWoman!

This is John in Fairview. Welcome to Online Dating!

I liked your profile... especially your great story about 'fudge'. I'm a Snickers man!

Check out my profile, and see what you think. I play for entertainment purposes only (sort of like the lottery)... but you never know, you might win.

Have fun, John

Hi John,

Your profile made me LAUGH out loud! Someone should have snapped you up yesterday or at least by early this morning.

They had a whole extra hour since we turned the clocks back for Daylight Saving Time.

:Dee (MysteryWoman)

Hi Dee,

Thanks for the compliment. I saw your photos and liked what I saw.   I read your profile and liked what I read.

I guess no one's snapped me up yet because... I am looking for a GREAT woman, not just a nice woman.

I must have been waiting to meet you. ;-)

Tag, your turn... John

WOW!

It happens that quickly. Two people see each other's Profiles, and the flirting begins. If you're looking for a great date or "the One", the best place to look is online. If you're looking for a "meaningful, overnight relationship", the best place to look is online.

Romance isn't confined to the weekends anymore. You can reach out and touch someone 24/7. If you want a MATCH or a PERFECT MATCH, HARMONY or CHEMISTRY, a LITTLE FISH or a BIG FISH, or if you want to DATE A COUGAR, it's out there.

What dating site should you join? Ask 10 people, and you'll get 20 different answers. Dating sites come and go, and some of the most popular dating sites at the time of this writing are Match.com®, Chemistry™, PlentyofFish™, Perfect Match®, eHarmony®, DateHookup™, and LavaLife®. They're all fun, and over the years they've gotten quite similar.

What site is right for you? There's only 1 way to find out. Try it! Many sites charge a monthly membership but let you test drive it for free. If they don't, buy a short 1 to 3 month membership. You'll quickly see if the site is right for you.

If one of your favorite sayings is *"God, grant me patience and grant it to me now"*, you might prefer a site which allows you to search the database for potential dates. While most dating sites let you do your own searching, a few sites don't. Ask before you buy a membership.

All Internet Dating sites are entertaining, but they don't give you a Road Map when you join. There is no Travel Agent to guide you on your way. There is no Triple-A to tow you home if you get stuck. You can't click MapQuest to give you directions.

Awesome Secrets for Men is your dating map on steroids. It will guide you through the challenging and complex world of Internet Dating.

With this map, you won't end up stranded and alone and without water in the dreaded **Photo Flatlands.** You won't be hopelessly lost on **More-About-Me Mountain**. Why spend all your time at the proverbial Frog Pond, when you can be having fun in **First Flirt City.** Whether you're responding to the woman (yes, women will email you first if your Profile is good enough) or sending your own First Flirts, this book will guide you.

Awesome Secrets for Men has little secrets, BIG Secrets, and HUMONGOUS Secrets. The biggest secrets are clearly labeled like this: **BIG SECRET** or **HUMONGOUS SECRET.**

They work on all Internet Dating sites. Dating sites aren't identical twins yet, but the strong family resemblance is striking.

Dating sites let you flirt and chat and email. An Email on most sites is called... wait for it now... an *Email.* Other sites call it an *Ice Breaker; First Contact; First Flirt; Message; Smile; Encounter; Conversation; Correspondence.* No matter what you call it, it's an Email.

Who emails first, the man or the woman? YES! Internet Dating is an equal-opportunity world. The above email just as easily could have been initiated by the woman.

You say women rarely email you first, and those who do aren't usually your type? You say when you do email, you strike out more often than not? You say you're beginning to think that **"Read/Deleted"** or **"Not Read/Deleted"** is your new name?

If you want solutions to these problems, you've come to the right place. Your journey can be faster, more fun, cost less cash, and you, too, can find great dates. With a little luck, one of those dates will be the woman of your dreams.

Here's your **<u>FIRST HUMONGOUS SECRET:</u>**

- **Make sure your photos pass the KISSABILTY TEST!**

Uh? What? Huh? You haven't heard of the **Kissability Test**? The women looking at your photos have. Most men's *photos* fail the Kissability Test. The men don't fail, their *photos* do. Sorry guys, true fact. That's because... well, read the 2 chapters on photos. Any man can take good photos, but it's amazing how many fail and fall off the Kissability Cliff. *Awesome Secrets for Men* gives you a detailed photo checklist which immediately steps up your photo game from amateur to Pro.

PHOTOS get you in the door. The PROFILE keeps you there. Many attractive, successful, and confident men come across as Dull, Unappealing, or Desperate. That spells **DUD**.

Photos and Profiles are like Match play in golf... you have to win both challenges. This book shows you how to win both. It also shows you how to win the *First Flirt* challenge. If your Photos and Profile are good, but you bomb on the ***First Flirt email...***BUZZ! Next contestant, please.

Internet Dating looks darn easy when you're sitting on the sidelines watching your friends play. It's another thing when you're the one in the hot seat. A lot of men are driving in the dark with their headlights off. With this book of *Secrets*, you've got the high beams on and have the whole darn road map to success.

It's fun and educational (you can tell your friends and/or kids that 'cause it's true). If you're looking for a great date, you'll soon know the *Secrets* to playing better than the competition and getting that Best First Date. If you're looking for "the One", you will have the secrets to winning the Dating-Lottery and hopefully finding your Last-First-Date!

Enjoy the journey!

THERE ARE ONLY 2 THINGS WORSE THAN BAD PHOTOS & A BAD PROFILE

What's worse than bad Photos and a bad Profile?
NO PHOTOS & NO PROFILE.

If you don't have photos posted or if you have *bad* photos posted (most men do), read the 2 chapters which tell you how to take first-rate photos. **ANY man can take photos which work.** If you have no Profile or a short Profile (i.e., one or two short paragraphs), it's usually BAD no matter how good it is. As with other masculine things, 2 inches of Profile is usually too short.

One of the most popular dating sites tells its members this: You are **15 times** more likely to attract a woman *with* a photo than without a photo. Imagine what your income would be if you got 15 times more money. 'Fifteen times more' is a big number whether it's attracting more women or money in your paycheck.

If a woman can't see what you look like, she'll figure her dog probably looks better than you do. If you have no photo, she'll be apprehensive or turned off or uninterested and click right past you and on to the next man.

A novice woman who just joined an online dating site may read a "*No Photo*" Profile. Her inexperience of being a new member who reads *"No Photo"* Profiles won't last long. Women soon discover the little button on most search engines and dating sites which says: *"Eliminate No Photo Men"*.

You aren't interested in checking out the *"No Photo"* and faceless women, are you? Women like men with faces. Even Frankenstein and Phantom of the Opera had a face. Surely you don't look that scary?

If you have no photos, too bad, so sad. One CLICK, and you're eliminated. If you think you can get away with saying "I have a high profile job, and I'll be happy to send you photos if you ask", think again. Too many guys use that flimsy excuse. Guys who say they're 39 and are really 59 use it. Married guys pretending to be single use it.

Post photos. Don't be eliminated by her hitting the "No Photo" selection button. Post photos that work. *Awesome Secrets* tells you how.

Your Primary Photo gets you to **first base**. The rest of your photos get you to second base. Photos get you only so far. You're going to be stuck on second base *unless* your written Profile works as well as your photos.

Your written Profile gets you to third base. Why do some men's Profiles fly and others fizzle? Why do some merit a kiss, and others are a catastrophic miss? Sound the gong please. That's what this book is all about.

Awesome Secrets for Men takes you step by step through writing your Profile. Lots of examples are given. Examples of what _not to do_ and what _to do_ are given. You get to read the Good, the Bad, and the Ugly. You'll know how to make yourself shine when you talk about what you do FOR FUN, your FAVORITE PLACES, your JOB, where you'd like to go on that FIRST DATE, and much more.

Model your Profile from the many, good examples. Take a sentence here and a sentence there, change a few words to personalize it to your city or situation. BINGO! You win! You've got your own unique and classy Profile.

If you want a more awesome Profile, use one of the 7 Recipes (aka Formulas for you scientific men). If you can make easy Mac and Cheese, you can make a good Profile.

If you have no Profile or a teeny-tiny one, you send the message that all your parts are teeny-tiny including a teeny-tiny brain. Almost worse than no Profile is writing only 1 or 2 short paragraphs. Now you're shouting: "Hey ladies, I'm not serious about dating" or "I don't know what to say" or "I don't have much to offer" or "I'm kinda shy" or "I'm hiding something"... yada, yada, yada.

If a woman sees you don't take the time to write a Profile which will let her get to know you better, your chances online are somewhere close to ZERO. If your Profile and Photos are "eh" or "Ho-Hum", that's the kind of dates you're going to get. You gotta step up your game if you want more.

Men... Start your engines!

8 RULES

OF THE ROAD

The best way not to F-UP online is to follow the Rules of the Road. _Knowing the rules is the tip of the iceberg. The hard part is turning them into action._ Each of these rules and how to turn them into action is covered in detail in the upcoming chapters.

You may be the one driving, but we're alongside you as your experienced co-pilot and navigator. We've been down these roads before and know the territory well. 40,000+ Profiles were raked over the coals in preparation for writing this book.

What?...You thought we winged it? If we were as wise as you thought, people would be raving about our advice. Oh wait, maybe they are.

On several well-known Dating Forums, we've helped thousands of people with the _exact same advice_ that's in this book. Here's what some of those men had to say...

**Thank you for all your help.** I have a date Sunday, Monday, Thursday, and Friday. I was only looking for one woman to date, but I've been alone for 13 months, and I am definitely digging the attention. Again thanks so much. Kentucky

**Awesome suggestions!** I can't thank you enough for your help. Illinois

You go girl! I found all your comments illuminating and will incorporate them in the upcoming rewrite.   YOU ROCK! :-) United Kingdom

2 or 3 days ago I sent out 12 e-mails... 10 were read. NO response. *The 2 e-mails that weren't read have now been read AFTER I made the suggested changes. Both of them replied and said: "Yes, let's talk." Phone numbers have been exchanged. I don't know if it's a coincidence, but more than likely the changes really did help me out a lot. Thanks! Los Angeles, CA*

I changed my profile and I admit I stole a few things from you which seemed like me and voila, two ladies emailing me! Bing bang! Canada

We know these roads well, and soon you will, too. The 8 Biggest Secrets will make your journey quicker and more successful:

1. **<u>PHOTOS COUNT</u>: ANY man can take photos that work**. Most men (even attractive men) post photos that either don't work well or turn off women. This book will teach you the secrets to avoiding photos that flop.

2. **<u>SPELLING COUNTS</u>:** If you write you are "*successfull*", chances are you won't be. If you write you are "*intellagent*" and looking for your "*sole mate*", you'll have better luck finding the missing shoe under your bed than finding your soul mate.

3. **<u>COMPLETENESS COUNTS</u>: LAZY LOSES.** Men who are too lazy to write something about themselves and the woman they're looking to date send a very negative message. Women view you as: (A) a man who isn't serious about dating or having a relationship and/or (B) a man who isn't willing to open up and share.

4. **LIARS LOSE:** **Be who you say you are.** If you "fudge" too much about age, height, weight, education, or anything else, sooner or later you're going to have to come clean.

5. **BE POSITIVE and AVOID SARCASM:** **Focus on the positive not the negative.** Be positive in your Profile and emails. Avoid the words "**NOT**" and the word "**NO**" in your Profile. We all have baggage, and hopefully yours is just a carry-on. Avoid sarcasm. Many men think they're being funny, but their sarcasm falls flat. Read the chapter on differentiating humor and sarcasm.

6. **BE PROACTIVE:** **Just like in the real world, women like you to make the first move.** She likes confident men. If you're unwilling to ask for directions, she expects you to buy the map (or in this case the book).

7. **BE CLASSY:** The man who emails, "*Ask me about my TALENTED TONGUE*" won't get a lot of dates on most dating sites. There are plenty of casual and intimate sex sites which cater specifically to talented tongues. The tongue action in this book concentrates on putting classy first flirts in your mouth not tacky, pick-up lines.

8. **DON'T BURN YOUR BRIDGES:** **Politeness counts.** Sometimes you email a woman, and she's not interested. Sometimes a woman emails you, and you're the one not interested in her. Other times you're dating someone and want to see how it works out.

    Smart men know you always send a polite response. Smart men don't burn bridges. *The toes you step on today might be attached to the ass you may have to kiss tomorrow.*

PHOTO-OP SECRETS!

You only get 1 Chance to make

A GOOD FIRST IMPRESSION

Does your photo pass or fail the Kissability Test?

What is the Kissability Test? It's this: Each woman either consciously or subconsciously asks herself, *"Would I kiss this man?"*

Some women ask it a lot more candidly (or horizontally), but the bottom line is... too many men post too many bad photos. The photos are too dark, too blurry, or taken from too far away. If she can't see what you look like, your photo fails.

She doesn't want to go out with a man who owns a red, 1957 Corvette in mint condition... and later finds out he's the original owner. What she can't see, she avoids. She wants to see who she may be kissing in the future. She wants to see you don't make your living posing for Halloween masks. She's looking for chemistry. NO photo spells toxic waste.

If you don't take the time to post clear, close-up photos, you send the message you're not serious about dating. You send the message you're lazy and sloppy.

It's easy to clear the Kissability hurdle. Your primary photo (that's the photo which shows up when she's searching) must be close up, clear, and you must be *smiling* and looking neat and clean.

Smiling faces in photos are more approachable, and you want her to approach, right? Don't worry if you don't look like Brad Pitt or Danish model Mathias Lauridsen. Don't worry if you think you're not as good-looking as you were 5 or 10 years ago. That's true of practically everyone on the planet.

She's looking for a real man, not a movie star. Real men come in all shapes and sizes and faces.

Will she find you kissable? Only she can say for sure, but one thing is certain: If she can't see what you look like, she is not going to give you a chance.

What next? She's going to look at your **other** photos of course. You do have other photos of yourself posted, don't you? Some sites let you post 25 photos.

BIG SECRET: Do <u>not</u> post 25 photos. Post 8 to 10 photos. More than 10 photos sends this message: "Look at me, I'm desperate" or "Look at me, oooh I'm hot!" or "I'm a legend in my own mirror."

BIG SECRET: Women like getting photos which you haven't posted for all the other women to see. Save your extra photos for personally emailing her in the future. It's one of those awww moments that's a winner.

Ya say ya don't take a good photo? Ya say you always look like you just rolled out of bed? Ya say you look like something the dog dragged in? Ya say you look like the dog?

Even men who always take bad photos can manage to take a few good ones if you take enough of them. Take 50 or 100 or 200 photos with your digital camera. You will be able to come up with a few good ones.

Taking *lots* of photos works wonders. Male models do it. You should, too. *You're the model here.* Put on several different styles of clothing from casual to business to sportswear. Good haircuts score extra points. Eight inch comb-overs don't work. If you're a billionaire, any hair style works.

You can do a photo shoot in 1 day or spread it out over several days. Use the self-timer on the camera to take photos of yourself. You could ask a friend, but he'll probably spend more time laughing and ripping you to shreds than taking the photos. If you get a friend to help, don't be surprised if he asks you to return the favor when he sees the success you're having.

If this is too much work, no problem. Camp out in First-Flirt-City until you're ready for something else. First-Flirt-City can be a lot of fun. It's more fun if you've got kissable photos. If you're looking to get to Best-First-Date-Ever and graduate to Last-First-Date, you won't get there with crummy photos.

Most women prefer clean-shaven men. Bummer! If she doesn't shave her legs, she probably won't complain about your beard or mustache. If you have a beard and/or mustache and you're brave enough to shave, it will dramatically increase the number of women who find you kissable. Facial hair often makes a man look older, especially if it's a salt-and-pepper beard.

Natural daylight can work wonders in photos. When you're indoors, the camera flash can make your skin look greasy. Blot off the extra moisture or use what many male, news anchors use: face make-up or face powder to make you look natural, not greasy.

The camera flash can cast dark shadows under your eyes. You can use concealer or makeup to overcome the shadows so you look like you do in real life. If the camera flash makes you look like an oily Caesar salad with dark bags under your eyes, you'll make an impression, but probably not the one you want to make.

POST CURRENT PHOTOS. Current means photos taken in the last 1-12 MONTHS, not the last 1-12 years. Photos must be of you. If you start cheating with old photos or photos not of you, what are you going to do when she wants to meet you?

If you can't manage to take a good photo, go to a photo place. It's not very costly, and it's worth it. Good photos are an investment in yourself and your happiness. Get 8 or 10 photos taken. Women want to see more than one photo.

Photo places will get the angle right to highlight your best features. They'll get the light right so it flatters your face. Pay attention to what techniques and poses they use. Duplicate those techniques at home with your camera. The next chapter has all the specifics you need to take kissable photos. Use it as a checklist, and you'll be golden!

PHOTO

CHECKLIST

Love is blind... but online dating is a real eye-opener. It always helps to post first-rate photos.

Are you blurry in real life? Then don't be blurry online. Duh! Obviously that little secret isn't obvious enough. Too many men post blurry photos, badly-lit photos, photos of themselves taken at arm's length with a camera, and photos taken in the mirror. If you can't take the time to look your best and post good photos, she thinks this is the same kind of effort you'll put into dating her.

You don't need to be a male model to succeed with your photos. You do need to follow the Photo Checklist in this chapter. If you look like "Brad Clooney" or "Matt Depp" and are male, you don't have to follow this checklist. If you're one of the rest of the 6 billion people on the planet, follow the checklist. Put a little time and effort into your photos, and you'll look like a movie star compared to the other online men.

This is a long chapter for good reason. The amount of online, crummy, male photos is ridiculous. The man's dog often has a better smile than the man. She doesn't want to date your dog. She doesn't want to buy your motorcycle. Use this photo checklist to win the Photo challenge.

1) **<u>Your primary photo and most of your photos should be close up where she can see what you look like.</u>** If she can't see what you look like, she's not going to take a chance with you. Make sure she'll be able to recognize you from your photos. *Do not take a photo of yourself in the mirror or by holding your camera at arm's length. You need good quality photos, not mirror shots or web cam shots.*

2) **<u>All photos should be current</u>**. Current means in the last 1 to 12 months. Don't post photos from years earlier. Don't inadvertently make yourself your own competition by shouting, *"Look!...I'm a lot older now, and I have more wrinkles, too!"*

3) **<u>Ideally you should be the only one in the photo.</u>** Women don't want to see you with other women by your side, even if that other woman is your mom, your sister, or your 21 yr. old daughter. Even if you explain it in your Profile, her first impression is that you're dating someone much younger than you are. She's wondering if you slept with the other woman. Why did you break up? Why hasn't the woman fixed you up with one of her friends? It's okay to have people in the background, but ideally you should be the only one in the foreground. This is not a hard and fast rule, but it is a 90% smart rule.

4) **<u>Don't post photos where you've "cropped" some other woman out of the shot</u>**. Women don't want to see body parts of ex-wives or girlfriends. A cropped hand draped over your shoulder and looking like "Thing" from Addams Family is spooky. Women don't want to see a picture of you with a fourth of a woman's cut-off face next to yours. Eewww!

5) **<u>Besides not having other women in your photos, do not have male friends (or parts of male friends) in the shot.</u>**

You're adding competition that doesn't need to be there. Why give yourself competition? Your male friend may be taller or have better hair or be more her type. Women may find him more attractive. Or, he may be shorter, have terrible hair, and she'll wonder if all your friends look like that. She'll be looking at your friends and wondering if she'll fit in, wondering if she'll like them and vice versa. Avoid these problems by being the only one in the photo.

If you want to show you're very social, post photos of social activities, but make sure that your friends are not next to you as your competition. Have your friends in the far background or cropped out of the photo. For example, if you're at a birthday party or at a wedding of a friend, use the setting to convey the social activity. Stand next to the festive, party decorations, and take a few photos. It's easy to convey you're social and have friends without including them as your competition.

6) **Include 3 full face shots.** The 1st of the 3 is your primary photo. You should be smiling. All 3 face shots should be slightly different: straight-on face photo, a 7/8 face shot, a profile if that's a flattering pose for you. All 3 should be in different clothes. Wear casual clothes, business attire, sports gear, dressy, etc. The goal is to show her you look good in the daytime, the nighttime, work time, play time, any time.

Do not have a "come-hither" look on your face. Don't be running your hands through your hair, throwing a kiss at her, or mimicking the photos in XXX magazines. Male pouty, male sultry, or male slutty won't cut it. If you'd be embarrassed if your mom or dad or boss saw the photo, don't use it.

But ya say you have great abs and great biceps and a great chest. Congratulations! Leave something to the woman's imagination. Anticipation is always fun... for both of you. If you bare it from the beginning, she sees shallow not sexy. Tease her imagination. A well-fitting polo will show off the nice pecs and arms. You've turned on her imagination, and she wants to find out more. To find out more, she'll have to date you.

7) **Prove it with photos.** You can blab and write in your Profile how great you "clean up" or how athletic and toned you are, but pictures prove it. Use your photos to prove what you say in your Profile. A photo of you "all cleaned up" is a winner.

8) **Your 3 full face shots should show your eyes.** No sunglasses in your 3 full face photos. Women like to see your eyes. If you wear sunglasses, it spells *"this guy is trying to hide something"*. If you wear regular glasses all the time, include at least one <u>without</u> glasses. Why? You take showers with your glasses off, don't you? You go to bed with your glasses off, don't you? Nuff said.

9) **Besides showing your eyes in your 3 full face shots, show your entire face and head and that includes hair.** That means unless it's a terrific photo *and she can see your face clearly*, no hats, no helmets, no ball caps. Save the hat shots for your other photos.

10) **Hair today, gone tomorrow.** If you have super-short hair now, but used to have longer hair a few months back, post photos with and without the extra hair. If you have a beard and/or mustache, it's a good idea to include photos with and *without* the facial hair. Different looks appeal to different women. Clean hair is appealing. She might actually want to run her fingers through it.

11) **Longer hair can be attractive, but make sure your hair style is not out-of-date.** Long doesn't mean stylish. If you have the same hair style you had 10 years ago, check out the

male fashion magazines. Make sure you look current not clueless.

12) **<u>Include 2 full body shots.</u>** Full body means from the tip of your head to the tip of your toes. Naked doesn't work and neither does bundled up in your winter coat. Wear casual or dressy or sporty clothing. Show your head, your middle section, and your legs.

If you say you are athletic and toned in your Profile, make sure your full bod photos prove it. If you say you are average or a few pounds over, ditto. Everyone has a different idea of what "average" or a "few pounds over" means. Let her judge for herself by posting full body photos.

13) **<u>Location, location, location!</u> Where you pose for your full body shots is important.** Take one of your full body photos *<u>INSIDE</u>* your home. 'Inside' means the living room or family room or kitchen, not the bedroom or bathroom. Take another full body shot *<u>OUTSIDE</u>* your home in the front or backyard. She wants to see where you live and how you live. It's a reflection of who you are.

A man's home is his castle. What kind of castle will she be visiting if she dates you? If the outside is a dump, paint it, repair it, or stand by a tree where you can't see it. If you can't afford to fix it up, think about including something in your Profile that you just moved into a new place. There are lots of Ms. Fix-its out there who garden and landscape and know which end of a paint brush to use.

By taking one photo inside your home and one photo outside, you're sharing yourself with her. Women like that. Smart women look closely at the background in your photos. They are looking for inconsistencies between what you say in your Profile and what your photos reveal.

14) Yes to puppies, dogs, kittens, cats, and other warm-bodied pets. Ideally you should be in the photo with your cute critter. Some clever men pose their pet typing on the computer, surfing the web for cute dogs, catching Frisbees, paddling on a surf board. Clever pictures are good conversation starters.

Other warm-blooded pets are usually okay. If you are in doubt if your exotic pet is acceptable, leave it out.

Include only one pet shot. She doesn't want to date Fluffy or Fido. Make sure your pet looks well-groomed, friendly, and housebroken. Including a photo of Bosco lifting his leg and filling up the swimming pool may be hysterical, but it's a photo better shared later not sooner. You did know that, right?

15) No photos of snakes or crocodiles or other amphibians. Save those for the other guys who don't know any better. A giant boa constrictor coiling around your neck isn't romantic to most women. Can't-wait-long-enough-to-never-date-you is what most women are thinking. If you're looking to attract a kinky gal or a female herpetologist, go for it.

16) No photos of pet spiders such as tarantulas or other creepy crawlers on your head or shoulder. If you don't know why, reread the above paragraph.

17) No photos of you drinking or eating. This is not attractive. Even super-hot, male models don't look good stuffing their face. You may think a photo of you holding up a glass of wine and giving a toast is okay, but she may wonder if it's true you only drink occasionally. Maybe you only say you do.

Don't post any pictures which may cause her to have doubts and think worrisome thoughts. Don't post pictures that seem to be contradicted by what you say in your Profile. Some men list themselves as non-smokers, but oops! How did that cigarette get in your hand?

18) **No photos of you in your itsy, bitsy, teenie-weenie, yellow, polka-dot Speedo** unless you are much younger than 40, super-buff, and look better than Brad did in Troy. Even then, rethink it. Any time you take your shirt or pants off, you're sending a message you may not want to send.

When most women see lots of skin, they think "serial dater" or "superficial man" or "vain man". Use classy ways to show you have a nice physique: a semi-tight polo and jeans; bicycle gear; skiing photos.

Leaving something for the imagination is often a whole lot sexier than baring it all. If you're over 65, show skin if you must. You've got enough experience to handle those ladies who only want you for your bod.

BIG SECRET: Be cautious of the woman who poses with lots of skin. Too much skin is a Red Flag which should cause you to slow down vs. speed up. Is she so desperate she has to bare it all?

19) **No photos of you on your Harley unless your name is Fonzie.** You love your Harley; you live on your Harley; you want a motorcycle mama. If that's the case, post the motorcycle photo.

However, *if* you're not having the success you'd like, try leaving it out of your photos. Your bike stereotypes you as a "Biker-man". Being stereotyped limits your potential matches. Wait till she gets to know you better. Women who don't like motorcycles often like them *if they like you.* Let her get to know you first.

20) **Photos of you in your 2-seater, sleek, ultra-fast, sports car are "iffy".** She might wonder if you're a daredevil or careless with your cash. Do you splurge all your money on your car and other toys? Are cars and status all you care about?

Or she might be looking for a Sugar-Daddy, and your car shows her how deep your pockets are. If you want a woman who says to her friends, "*He's got Bank*", a good way to catch her is to dazzle the cash in front of her eyes.

Save your fancy, sleek car for impressing her in person. If you must have your slick car in your Profile, have the car off to the side rather than a solo photo of the car. She won't fail to see it. If you haven't figured it out by now, *subtlety works.*

21) **No photos of you in plaids, horizontal stripes, or loud Hawaiian shirts** (unless you live in Hawaii, and even then, rethink it). Wear solid colors in your photos. Your goal isn't to look like the living room sofa. Your goal is join her on the sofa.

22) **No scary Halloween faces or Cap and Gown.** Classy, cute, funny costumes… go for it. No Halloween costumes that will give her nightmares, no cross-dressing, no graduation cap and gown. Scary costumes and cross-dressing can easily raise unfounded doubts in her mind. The cap and gown photo may make you feel proud, but she'll be wondering if you have lots of student loans to pay off.

23) **No crazy smiles like you've had electro-shock therapy.** Smile naturally, and show your teeth so she knows you have some (and they're real and look good). All people including itty-bitty babies are more attracted to smiles than any other facial expression.

Smiling makes you look younger and friendly. If your teeth are stained, yellow, or in bad shape, get them fixed. Bad teeth make you look older than you are.

24) **No dead stuff.** No big dead fish, no dead deer on the hood of the car (even if it's a Ferrari), no stuffed, animal heads on the wall. The woman might like to eat turkey, but she doesn't want

to see the big, dead turkey in the photo with you. If you post a photo like that, take a close look at the photo. You'll see 2 dead turkeys instead of one.

25) **Should you show ink?** While many women like tattoos, many more do not. Women who don't generally like tattoos often like them *if they like you*. If you're not having the success online that you'd like, let her get to know you before she gets to know your body art.

If you follow these secrets, you will have taken KISSABLE photos. Let's count them up, and see what you need:

- **3 CLOSE-UP FACE PHOTOS**
- **2 FULL BODY PHOTOS**
- **1 PET PHOTO** *(optional)*

That's 5 shots (6 if you used a pet shot). If you don't have a pet, don't borrow one. Many women prefer that you're pet-free. Ideally, one of these 5 should be a photo of you *indoors* in your home and another *outdoors* in your yard, on the deck, by the garden, pool, etc.

Indoor and outdoor home photos convey your lifestyle and what appeals to you. While opposites can and do attract, most women are looking for synergy and "rhyme" in a date, partner, and mate. Your indoor and outdoor photos tell her a lot about who you are. The same is true of her photos. Look at them carefully.

Since you should have 8-10 photos, add 3-5 more. Is it absolutely necessary to post 8-10 photos? No, but these photos are the "can't miss" ones. You're bound to have photos showing another side of you. You on the beach, you sightseeing, you skiing, you-you-you having fun in fun places. If you're well-traveled, you'll have photos of places she's never been: the Eiffel Tower, the Coliseum, the Pyramids, the Great Wall of China, Africa, Australia, Brazil.

Pictures like these are great conversation starters. Other pictures that hit home runs are great views from your deck, a rainbow you caught just right in the desert, a great picture of your megacity. If you're an artist, post a photo of you next to your favorite piece. If you're a gardener, post a photo of your yard or a giant pumpkin you grew. If you work in an office, take a picture at your desk. You may want to clean it up first.

Your 3-5 FUN photos set your Profile apart from other men. They make you MEMORABLE. Memorable is good. She's going to be looking at many Profiles. You need to stand out in a good way. Add captions to your photos if your dating site allows captions. *Witty captions* can turn a good photo into a great photo.

ROTATE your photos. That doesn't mean turn them upside down or sideways. Some men do that, and most women find it annoying not clever. "Rotate" means to alternate your primary photo every few weeks. Different photos appeal to different women. Rotating your photos lets you appeal to a wider range of women.

Avoid putting family photos in your online photos. Keep your kids out of the photos, especially if they're minors. Nothing like getting the "ex" riled. Even if your ex approves, many online women do not. Furthermore, the focus needs to be on you, not your children.

Pay attention to which photos women say they like. If you start with a Primary Photo of you in a business shirt, you may discover the one with the casual shirt is the one women find most appealing. If that's the case, switch photos.

REMEMBER THESE 3 SECRETS ABOUT YOUR PHOTOS, and you will win the photo challenge:

- **KEEP THEM KISSABLE**
- **KEEP THEM CURRENT**
- **ROTATE YOUR PHOTOS**

BREAKING NEWS…one other BIG SECRET: A few sites now allow you to change the colors and background themes of your Profile. Other dating sites will likely follow suit. **Many women are color-sensitive. This doesn't just apply to your clothing in the photos, it also applies to the color of your Profile.**

If your site allows you to change the colors of the text and background or use your own or their graphics, make sure the end result of your creative efforts is **easily legible**. While few women are colorblind (.5% compared to 8% of men), green lettering on a red background isn't very legible. A black background with blue lettering is near impossible to read. Also, it's not cheerful and upbeat. Experiment and have fun with colors and graphics, but aim for cheerful, inviting, and legible colors.

NEVER USE THESE WORDS!

EVER!

I like to have fun, and *I look younger than I am. I'm a glass half-full kind of man. I'm comfortable in jeans and clean up well, too. I enjoy life and am looking for an attractive woman who's beautiful inside and out. I always put the toilet seat down...*

Except for the toilet seat part, join the billions of other men on the planet. Every other man has sentences exactly like those in his Profile, and he wonders why he's striking out. If you're one of those men, NIX those sentences now! They are Turn-Offs not Turn-Ons.

Clichés are snoring and boring. They are *100% meaningless* because every other man says the exact same thing. It's like they all copied off each other in class. If you're going to copy, take the time to copy something original and appealing, and tweak it, and make it yours. The man who says, "I like going out and staying in and dancing like no one is watching" is a dime a dozen. Cliché City!

Here are the most often used clichés in Profiles. If you have them in yours, remove them ASAP!

28

CLICHÉS TO NEVER EVER USE:

- **I am attractive...** or **I'm good-looking** or **I'm handsome** (Post photos and let her judge for herself.)

- **I look young for my age...** or **I look 10 years younger** or **I'm 42 but don't look it** or **People think I look younger than I am...** (Post photos and let her judge for herself. Many men who say this, look exactly their age or usually older.)

- **I enjoy life...** ("**I enjoy life**" is obvious. We haven't seen a Profile yet that says "**I enjoy death.**" Obviously, don't waste your words saying the obvious because it's obviously boring like this obviously repetitious sentence.)

- **I like to have fun...** (Many men use this to refer to SEX.)

- **I'm open-minded...** (Many men use this to refer to SEX.)

- **I clean up well...** or **I'm comfy in jeans or a suit and tie...** (Don't say it, use photos and prove it.)

- **My friends say...** or **I'm considered by many to be...** (Speak for yourself. She wants to know what you have to say. She wants to date you, not your friends.)

- **I'm looking for a woman who knows who she is...** or **I'm looking for a woman who is comfortable with who she is...** (This is a great way to offend a lot of women. Can you remember the last time a woman said to you, *"Gee, I wonder who I am?"*)

- **I'm looking for a great girl.** (She's a *woman* or a *lady*, not a girl.)

- **I always put the toilet seat down...** (Avoid potty talk. The visual picture you convey is a toilet and a guy peeing. Many men put this in their Profile which might explain why they're still looking for "the One".)

29

- **I'm not looking for games or drama...** (Who is?)

- **I'm looking for an attractive woman...** (You and everyone else. How many men say, "I want an ugly woman who is so big that when she sits around the house, she sits AROUND the house?" Everyone wants attractive dates. Most women have inner and outer qualities that can be described as attractive. Describe specific INNER qualities that mean "*attractive*". As far as outer beauty goes, make that determination by looking at her photos. Using the word "attractive" to find a date will lose you more points than it will gain you.)

- **I am not sure how to describe myself...** (This portrays a lack of confidence. A man who says "I don't know what to say here" comes across as an insecure man, a clueless man, or a man who can't find words because there's not a lot of good to describe. None of that is attractive.)

- **I'm shy until you get to know me...** (Women like confident men. Don't make excuses, and don't list your less desirable qualities. Focus on the positive.)

- **I work hard and play hard** or **I like to enjoy each and every day** or **I live life to the fullest...** (So does most everyone else. Don't waste your words saying the obvious. Be specific and give details how you live life to the fullest.)

- **I can make you laugh**... (So can reruns of Frasier and Seinfeld. Millions of men say they are funny, but their Profiles are boring. If you say you're funny, have some humor in your Profile.)

- **I'm looking for someone beautiful inside and out...** (So is most everyone else. Avoid talking about outer beauty, and describe some of the specific qualities that mean INNER beauty to you. As far as outer beauty goes, make that determination by looking at her photos.)

- **Sorry for the bad pictures...** (If you can't post decent photos now when you're trying to attract her, when will you ever put your best foot forward?)

- **I joined because I don't meet many women in my line of work...** (There are lots of other ways to meet women other than work. This is a wimpy excuse.)

- **I do not look and do not act anywhere near my age...** (Most women want men who act like adults, not teenagers. Women like men who have the wisdom that age can bring. Being young in mind and body and spirit is wonderful, but make sure your Profile doesn't convey immaturity. Most women are not looking to be your babysitter or your mommy.)

- **I'll fill this section out later...** (If you can't take the time to attract a woman now with your words, she knows you won't take time to attract her later with your actions.)

- **I'm not a paying member so I can't email you...** (If you're not willing to pay to email, she figures you're not serious about finding a date or a relationship. She wonders if you're cheap or insolvent.)

- **I'm sarcastic...** (Haven't seen a woman yet advertising for a sarcastic aka derisive aka cynical man.)

- **I don't know what to say here** or **It's not easy talking about yourself...**

If your Profile is bombing, clichés like those used above are often the cause. Check out the **APPENDIX** for more examples of clichés which will make her want to flush you even if you do put the toilet seat down.

SECRETS ABOUT SPELLLING

...oops, make that SPELLING

I'm honest, intellagent, sucessfull, hard working, responsable and i'm easy to get along with.   I hope to meet my match here...

If the man can't spell *"successful"*, how likely is it he'll be successful meeting his match online?   Your Profile is your ad. Good ads don't have misspellings.

If you don't take the time to spell and punctuate correctly, she views you as a sloppy man. Not too many women are looking for sloppy men.

Although most Dating Sites do not have spell check, you can write your Profile and emails in a word processing program. Spell check it there, and cut and paste it into your dating software. If you can't spell, avoid Instant Messaging, or your Instant Messages are going to spell Instant Misery.

Proof whatever you write so you don't go POOF! Misspellings in your Profile are like big globs of green spinach between your teeth. The more misspelled words, the more globs of spinach. Misspellings are a quick way to turn a good-looking man into an unattractive man.

Misspellings expose you *may* have fudged on your education. Somebody had to graduate last in your class, and a sloppy Profile will make her think that somebody was you.

Poor spelling and poor grammar are great ways to differentiate the "sneaky" and "less-than-honest" men from the legitimate men. Many women look closely at your spelling to see if you're as smart as your Profile says you are. When you list a good education and your spelling doesn't match, BUZZ! Next contestant, please.

When you read a woman's Profile, pay attention to her spelling. If her educational level is high and her Profile is sloppy with typos, it's a huge clue she may not be who she makes herself out to be. The Spelling Secret should be obvious, but obviously it isn't, or Profiles wouldn't be rampant with typos and *alot* of *spellling misstakes*.

You are cute, u r sexy, you're fantastic, you are gorgeous, *your profile is very interesting, you look great, how are you tonight, tell me about you, I'm intrigued, can I take you to dinner tonight, you are wonderful, yummy!, how are you!*

Hi, I have a cabin in the woods, ur quite appealing, I am a European and sexy and open-minded, Jackpot!!!, verrry nice, wow you are hawt!!, hi cutie, hello, mmm...gorgeous, you are truly hot, you're sexy, let's learn more about each other, oh my my my, very exciting, you are really attractive...

Those are the actual Instant Messages one woman received during 1 HOUR on one of the top Internet Dating sites. She also heard these in the first 60 minutes: *Are you open to a 3-some, are you open to bi-men, do you like to watch men, I'll make you happy, wanna play, let's play, I love to cuddle!*

*You are sooo sensual, want to play truth or dare, want some company, do you like women too, are you into domination, I am curious, I'm doing the back stroke, I have some more pictures if you're interested....*and many more which the editor deleted from this section.

This wasn't a "sex" site. It was one of the top dating sites. The woman wasn't a super-hot chick, and she didn't have cleavage or booty photos. She was 5'3", average build...and she was **57**. She didn't do anything to initiate the contacts. She sat and watched as the IM's surged in like a tsunami. In 60 minutes, she received 87 instant messages from men of all ages.

There are lots of online players of both sexes looking for action. If you want action, it's out there on all dating sites, and some of those "flirts" might net you a date. Some dating sites are known for their fast action. You can have a lot of fun and will learn a lot in the Instant Messaging world of Internet Dating.

If you're not interested in competing with the hot, horny, mostly short-term men, avoid IM's. Focus on regular email messages. Those usually net better results especially for long-term dating and/or relationships.

If your site allows Instant Messages, you can set your account to "No Instant Messages". Women find this especially helpful. They also find it illuminating to occasionally turn on the IM's. IM chatting helps keep them grounded. As one blonde woman said, *"IM Men can't get Mad Cow Disease because they're all pigs."* She was a little harsh, but maybe there were a few pigs mixed in with the wolves.

You need to have a thick skin and a strong self-image to play with IM's. Have your eyes wide open. There are great people IM'ing, but their counterparts include lots of non-responders and lots of players. Don't let your heart skip a beat if you miss an

Instant Message or if your IM's are turned off. Women who are serious about dating will send a regular email if they are interested.

If you're looking for action, many IM women are looking for action, too. A woman will be IM'ing and flirting with you, and you'll be on top of the world. She says you're attractive and witty and really sexy. She thinks you're oh sooo desirable! You're hawt!

What you don't know is Miss IM is chatting up 3 or 4 other men at the same time, looking for some evening fun. POOF! Suddenly she's gone. Miss IM got the offer she was looking for. She disappears into the night, never to be heard from again. Who got lucky? Hard to say...maybe it was you.

Disappearing women happens with regular emailing, but not like it does in the IM world. If you like getting flattered and then dumped (or totally ignored), IM'ing is often good at granting your wish.

BEING FUNNY

& WITTY

Better to love a short man, than never to have loved a tall.

Get a new car for your date. It'll be a great trade!

Hard work has a future payoff. Laziness pays off now.

Give me ambiguity or give me something else.

What's the difference between a lawyer and a prostitute? The prostitute quits after you're dead!

He who laughs last thinks slowest.

A doctor and lawyer walk into a bar... The doctor is here to examine you and see if you have a funny bone in your body. The lawyer is gonna sue the pants off you if you don't. If your Profile is like most male Profiles, you might want to start running!

Examinations of 40,000 Profiles reveal the funny bone is missing from 95% of them. Or the men are temporarily delusional. Or both. There is an easy solution.

Don't say you are funny... *Write* **Funny.**

Don't say you are witty... *Write* **Witty.**

BIG SECRET: There is a fine line between being funny and being sarcastic. It's like pornography. You usually know it when you see it. If you're not sure if she'll find it funny, don't use it. Read the following examples to better differentiate humor from sarcasm.

- HUMOR: **I wonder if this really works? Maybe we should prove it?? Quick, read my profile and send me an email so I know that it works!**

- HUMOR: **My ideal match likes setting and achieving her goals, knows how to talk as well as listen, has high values, and... and she gives good hugs!**

- HUMOR: **This action figure comes with his own wardrobe and car. He's in like-new condition, too!**

- HUMOR: **Here I am. Now you get 2 more wishes... email me and let me know what they are.**

- HUMOR: **If you're college-educated and own a castle in France, email me today. Oh, wait... if you're college-educated, email me. I have tons of FF miles. We'll find a castle in France.**

- HUMOR: **WARNING: SURGEON GENERAL reports that dating this down-to-earth, smart and nice man may cause you to be dizzy, breathless, and slightly disorientated...**

Here are some examples which are too over the top for most women:

- TOO MUCH SARCASM: I am sorta stupid. Lazy, too. I can't hold a job because they expect me to show up on time. I'm looking for a really ugly girl so that I can look good when I stand next to you. I hope you know a lot of farting jokes because I need some new ones to tell my friends. I hope you don't like to drink beer, because then there's more for me. I hope you don't have a lot of baggage because I live in my car, and the trunk isn't very big. I know I'm picky, but a man has to have some standards.

- <u>TOO MUCH SARCASM</u>: If you're good at trauma/drama and like to fight, that's great! My new 52" TV got repossessed, and I miss my reality TV shows. We can do our own! I'm really good at shouting and throwing stuff.

- <u>TOO MUCH SARCASM</u>: I hope you're at least 50 to 100 lbs. overweight so I can look thin when I stand next to you. I hope you're on good terms with your mom so you can get her to clean my house so I don't have to. If you do meth or cocaine, we probably won't get along because your addictions would interfere with spending money on mine.

Humor and wit work exceptionally well in Profiles. Humor adds life and interest and smiles to a Profile. Your Profile goes up by a full letter grade if it gets the woman smiling.

If you get her saying, "*OMG, I can't believe he said that*", your sarcasm might be sinking the Love Boat. You don't have to totally abandon ship, but tweak it down to less than half-throttle. Reduce the vrrrooom, or you're liable to go kaboom.

FUDGERS, LIARS,

AND PREVARICATORS

"I just dated my mother," said the 40 year old man. *"She said she was my age, but showed up looking 20 years older and just like my mother. The hair, the face, everything! It was terrible!"*

True story! And funny, especially because it didn't happen to you. Men who fudge often find they've shot themselves in the foot. If you *write* that you're 40, and then *post pictures* of yourself at 30, and *show up* looking your real age of 50, you won't get a great reception from your date.

Even if you are a young-looking 50, the fact you "fudged" so much will make her doubt your honesty and character. You have a serious uphill battle. Don't be surprised if you lose the battle on the first date.

Being who you say you are scores big points in online dating. One way to start out on the right foot is to make sure your Profile is not hidden.

Women are gun-shy when a man with a hidden Profile contacts her. Women immediately wonder what you're hiding. Too many women have had the unpleasant experience of being contacted by a man with a hidden Profile who says he's "single" or "divorced" but later turns out to be married.

A second more obvious reason not to hide your Profile is so women can find you. Women search for men. Give them every opportunity to find you. A third reason not to hide your Profile is because a number of dating sites give you extra months free if you don't hide your Profile. A fourth reason not to hide your Profile is because if it's hidden, women won't know you've looked at them.

When you click on a woman's Profile, she'll know you've checked her out if your Profile is not hidden. On most sites, you appear in the woman's *"Who's Viewed Me"* section.

On most Internet Dating sites, there's a *"Who's Viewed Me"* section. Some sites call it *"Visitors"* or *"Lookers"*. That's where you can see which women have looked at you (provided the woman isn't viewing her matches in Stealth/Hidden Mode).

Women look in their own *"Who's Viewed Me"* section to see which men have been looking at them. While most women wait for you to initiate contact, women who find you appealing will write to you first.

Occasionally it is helpful to hide your Profile. If you're going on vacation for a week or two, you may wish to hide your Profile. If you're dating a woman and the dating is moving into "relationship" territory, you might want to hide your Profile. If she's as serious about you as you are about her, hiding your Profile will send good vibes her way and score you bonus points.

GOOD, BETTER, BEST

USER NAMES

Hi! Call me Dick!

If your name is Dick, it's probably best to avoid using your real name as your online User Name. If your name is Richard, it's probably best not to use RicHard as your User Name. You might think it's funny. She won't...until she meets you and finds out you're extremely honest...and modest.

A good User Name is unique and attractive. It's easy to be unique and *un*attractive. You're not trying to impress the guys with your name. You're trying to impress women.

Many men use their initials as part of their User Name. Some add the month and day they were born. You see names like this:

ST1207   LS715   JWFxyz   DPG_1184
BRL002   RGB404   Rlt1003   RMN_0490

Those work, but why settle for okay when better is a few keystrokes away. Your User Name may become her new "pet name" for you. It would be nice if she could pronounce it.

Here are names that are descriptive, easier to remember, and pronounceable:

Lance_Austin	**ChicagoMan**	**JimfromCA**
Ocean2Desert	**LifesAbeach**	**UrbanMan425**
TrappedTX	**SamBlueEyes**	**LivinATthelake**

Professions as part of your User Name work well, especially if you have a profession women find attractive:

Teacher4U	**CPAinLA**	**StLouisDoc**
JonAbc	**IT_Man32**	**SmilesNewYork**
VetMichigan	**Engineer2**	**WebWriter**

You can incorporate a hobby or activity or ideology into your User Name. If your hobby or activity or ideology defines who you are, by all means use it. If it's only part of who you are, think the whole box instead of one flap of the box. Names which convey specific interests are:

ParSaver4U	**Cowboy4u**	**Yankee_Fan3**
CyclistNY	**Fitforever1**	**SailandSurf**
PA_Pacifist	**GOPLarry**	**Recycled_likeNew**

If you're a romantic man, you might want a more touchy-feely user name. You have to walk a fine line with romantic names. A few of the following names will limit the women who will be attracted to you. If it's not your intent to be so limiting, tone it down. Some of these names can work, but for many women, they'll be too touchy-feely:

Spirit5	**WishUHere**	**Hugggs**
Chemistry4U	**HiXOX**	**RomanticMan**
Tonite4us	**Affectionate1**	**MaineSqueeze**

You can invent intellectual or cerebral or witty user names. Don't be so esoteric and obscure that you come off as a snob. Many men write they are "*Rennaissance*" men or "*Renaisance*" men or "*Renissance*" men. If you're a "*Renaissance*" man, it helps if you spell your name right. Here are some intellectual and witty names:

Intelligent2	**Eclectic_Man**	**JuxtaposeMe**
RSVP2Adam	**VoteforMe**	**LifeTraveler4U**
Multifaceted	**MrRight0625**	**NotJunkMale**
WinHere	**NuanceMan**	**Limited_Edition**

Pick a name you relate to. Avoid forgettable names, snobby names, unpronounceable names, and turnoff names. Here are examples of *names to avoid*:

- **Fdjizeo** – Too hard to remember.

- **Xxxtralovin** – If you're not getting the kind of classy women you want to attract, it's because you're advertising for XXX-Rated ones.

- **GnosisCity** – Too obscure.

- **Looking4Dulcinea** – Most women will have no clue what you are talking about. Most have not read Don Quixote and do not know she was his "idealized love".

- **Floppy44** – Your nickname in school might have been Floppy due to your floppy jeans or floppy ball cap. There is no Internet Law which says you have to use your school nickname. Invent an attractive User Name, not one that's sure to flop.

- **Panther234** – Avoid any animal image that is violent or snarly or wild unless that's what you're looking for.

- **Clueless911** – Nobody wants clueless.

- **HandsomeRobert** – Too egotistical.

- **ReReturnee** – Shows you struck out, and you're back.

- **JohnLonely002** – Shows you're desperate.

- **MrLoveCuddles** – Gag.

Invent a name which represents you. Later on if you decide another name suits you better, most sites allow you to change your name.

Although Shakespeare said, "*A rose by any other name would smell as sweet*," he wasn't in marketing. A smart person in marketing said, "*First impressions count.*" Take that into account when choosing your User Name.

BE

A HEADLINER

Time for a 2 second quiz. The following Headlines were written by three different women. Which woman would you want to date just by reading the first 3 words of her Headline?

> **Woman_1:** I'm sorta picky...

> Woman_2: Make me laugh...

> **Woman_3: Smiles, Romance, Travel**

Headlines matter. A few words can convey volumes. On most dating sites when a woman views her matches, she sees:

- Your PRIMARY PHOTO
- Your USER NAME
- Your HEADLINE
- The first few sentences of your PROFILE

Good Headlines are like good headlines in magazines and newspapers. They capture your interest and get you to read the entire article.

It's easy to write a bad Headline. Bad Headlines fail for many reasons. If your current Headline looks like one of these bad ones, *hurry* and imitate a good one. Examples of Good Headlines can be found in the next chapter and in the Appendix.

BAD HEADLINES:

- **Hi...** (Ugh..any man can do better than this)

- **92675...** (Can you say "failure to communicate"?)

- **LessBS** (There are nicer/classier ways to say this.)

- **Please excuse my photo...** (Don't make excuses.)

- **I'll get some pictures up soon.** (No excuses; post photos.)

- **R U A Hi-IQ SWF** (You're not paying by the letter.)

- **My heart is lonely...** (Desperate men strike out. Confident and positive work better than sad and whiny.)

- **I'm looking for someone to make me happy...** (Most women think it takes 2 to make a relationship.)

- **I thought I'd give this a try...**

- **I thought I'd try this again...** (He won't do much better this time until he changes his bait.)

- **Grrrr....I bite, but gently...**

- **Smart and sensuous for you!**

- **I'm open-minded and fun!**

- **Help make me a better man!**

- **Single, 39, never married...** (If you're over 35 and never married, don't advertise it in your headline.)

- **Child at heart** (She's looking for date, not a child.)

- **I'm handsome and in great shape.** (Use photos instead.)

- **Pay attention here please**... (Can you say 'controlling'?)

- **Ven Volar conmigo** (If you're going to use foreign phrases, translate them immediately after you use them.)

HUMONGOUS SECRET: The purpose of a good Name, good Headline, good Profile, and good photos is *not* to find your perfect mate.

What? What? What did you say?? The purpose is not to find the perfect mate. That's like trying to become CEO without doing the work to get there. That's like trying to bed the lady before you've kissed her. You won't know if the woman is right for you and vice versa until you meet.

Your goal is to GET THE DATE! Aim for the date. You gotta start with the date to catch the mate.

Check out these two newspaper headlines:

Red Tape Holds Up New Bridges

Panda Mating Fails --Veterinarian Takes Over

Did you catch the accidental and funny, double meanings in those headlines? If not, reread them.

Visualize the new bridge being held together with red duct tape. You probably don't want to drive under that one. As far as the panda headline goes, if you don't get that one, ask your vet to explain it to you.

Your Headline needs to work better than a bridge being held together with red duct tape. Your Headline isn't a pick up line. It isn't... "Are you going to kiss me or do I have to lie to my friends" or "Your pants are like Windex, I can see myself in them."

A good Headline whets her appetite and gets her to read more about you... not less. Your Headline is the teaser to get her to click on your Profile and see why she should date you. Good Headlines often put the focus on the woman, and tell her what you are offering her in the relationship. Those are much more effective

49

than the "I want" Headlines.   Here are examples of good Headlines. Check out the APPENDIX for more.

GOOD HEADLINES:

- **Enjoying the Journey...want to join me?**
- **Took a while to get it. Now want to share it.**
- **10 Reasons You Should Date Me**
- **10 Reasons You Shouldn't Date Me**
- **Want to live together or should we meet first?**
- **Meet me at Trader Joe's?**
- **Knock, knock?** (A clever knock-knock joke came next.)
- **I was wondering when you'd get here!**
- **I'm good at catching falling stars**
- **Happy but looking for happiest!**
- **Washington, we need a solution**
- **Is your passport ready?**
- **The magic word is ....TODAY!**
- **I'm here for the interview**
- **Brilliant Billionaire** (Money and humor always work)
- **Pssst...over here**
- **Toto, we're not in Kansas anymore**
- **Anything is possible...**
- **Made in Italy**
- **Tarzan looking for Jane**
- **What do you mean today's not your birthday?**
- **I got you a present and a cake!**
- **Single Brit, sexy accent included! :)**
- **Want to know a secret?**
- **Do you believe in Chivalry? How about Chicago?**
- **Pick me! Pick me!**
- **Snoopy is my favorite. How about you?**
- **You WIN! You WIN!**

YOUR FIRST SENTENCE COUNTS DOUBLE!

GOOD vs. BAD OPENING LINES

The man rubbed the lamp, and wonder of wonders, a genie appeared and said...

Opening lines are critical. The opening line above makes you wonder what happened when the genie appeared. Did the genie grant the man 3 wishes? You want to find out more. (Somewhere in this chapter *is* the end of that story. If our opening line was successful, you'll be anxious to read what the genie said.)

That's your goal, too... to get the woman to read more. Your Opening Line of "*The Profile*" section needs to GRAB her interest. *The Profile* goes by various names depending on your dating site. You'll see names like: *About Me and What I'm Looking For; A Personal Statement; An Introduction; Self Summary; In My Own Words; The Skinny.* The bottom line is... it's your Profile. It tells potential dates who you are and who you want to date.

The Profile section is *critical*. The first line of the Profile section is the most critical. It counts DOUBLE. Your Opening Line of the Profile needs to be good or great because typically that line shows up when women search or view their matches.

Are you a little unsure what to write? Are you a lot unsure? Do you feel like you're climbing Mt. Everest naked and without oxygen? Join the club!

This dangerous area is known as More-About-Me Mountain. It's easy to fall off the mountain or get buried in an avalanche of TMI (Too Much Information). You have to be original and make yourself stand out without appearing egotistical.   You can't be boring, or negative, or full of feeble excuses, or arrogant, or big-headed, or pig-headed.

Here's the good news… the vast majority of men's Opening Lines and Profiles are terrible. That's bad news for them, but good news for you. They are your competition. With a little practice, you will be able to stand out from those men who have B.O. What's B.O.? **B**ad **O**pening Line. As you might have guessed, Bad Opening Lines stink.

The kinds of mistakes most men make in their Opening Lines usually fall into one of the following 3 B.O. (Bad Opening) categories:

1) **Boring and Unoriginal and Cliché:** Women ignore these men. Their opening lines are 100% meaningless since 2,000,000+ other men said almost the exact same thing.

2) **Red Flags that turn women off:** It's easy to avoid Red Flags when you know how. If you've been losing yardage or warming the bench instead of going out on great dates, pay special attention to the chapter on Red Flags.

3) **<u>Bad Deal Makers/Deal Breakers:</u>** Instead of pissing off every woman on the planet, check out the chapter on Deal Makers and Deal Breakers. Read and apply.

Let's get started with some boring, unoriginal, forgettable Opening Lines. Some of these lines could be used in the body of the Profile, but not as an Opening Line.

Most every person on the planet could have said what these men said: *they like life, they like beaches, they like travel, movies, music, going out to eat.*

One of these days some bright man is going to satirize this and start his Profile with, "**I like to breathe air and hope you do, too.**"

HUMONGOUS SECRET: Try not to begin your Profile with the word "**I**" or "**My**". There are millions of other words which are better for capturing her interest.

HUMONGOUS SECRET: *Minimize* the amount of sentences in your Profile that begin with "**I**" or "**My**". Too many "I's" in a Profile make you sound egotistical and stuck on yourself. It's extremely easy to switch around the order of your words once you know the trick.

Here's the trick:
Instead of saying *"I like to ski,"* say "**Skiing is a sport I enjoy.**" Instead of saying *"I like to eat out,"* say "**Going out for Italian food is always fun.**"

BAD OPENING LINES (B.O.):

- **(B.O.):** I enjoy living life to the fullest. I always enjoy laughing and having fun.

- **(B.O.):** I enjoy going out to nice restaurants, music and dancing. I like movies and DVDS, and some TV.

- **(B.O.):** I am handsome, intelligent, honest, considerate, and articulate.

- **(B.O.):** I work hard and play hard. I like to dine out whether I'm here at home or when I travel.

- **(B.O.):** I look younger than I am. I enjoy live music, dancing, restaurants, and all kinds of music.

- **(B.O.):** I am looking for someone who is very comfortable with herself, not afraid to be who she is. (If you want to annoy a woman, write what this man did.)

- **(B.O.):** I'm funny, smart, athletic, and romantic.

- **(B.O.):** I like sunny beaches and warm weather.

- **(B.O.):** My friends convinced me to try this. I've been single for too long, I guess or maybe my friends are getting tired of putting up with me.

- **(B.O.):** My kids convinced me to try this. They have some strange ideas sometimes.

Yawwwn. Those are a good representation of what women read in the Opening Lines of many Profiles.

The ones around the next curve are worse. Get your air-sickness bag out now. Men who write lines like the ones in the next chapter don't have to worry about getting lost with a woman on Destiny Drive. She isn't going to get in his car any time soon.

Now it's time for the genie to reappear…**The man rubbed the lamp,** and wonder of wonders, a genie appeared and said…"I will grant you 3 wishes, but for every wish I give you, your Ex-wife will get double."

The man thought a moment and said, "I'd like 10 million dollars." In a blink of an eye, 10 million dollars appeared in his bank account, and 20 million appeared in his Ex-wife's bank account.

The man thought again and said, "I'd like a brand new, red Ferrari." In 2 blinks of an eye, a brand new, red Ferrari appeared in his driveway, and 2 red Ferraris appeared in his Ex-wife's driveway.

"You now have 1 more wish," the genie exclaimed. The man thought again and said, "I'd like you to scare me half to death."

SUPER-BAD

OPENING LINES

My magical watch says you aren't wearing any panties. Oh, you are? It must be an hour fast!

The word of the day is legs. Let's go back to my place and spread the word.

I think it is time I tell you what people are saying behind your back...! Nice Ass.

Try not to laugh too hard at these Super-Bad Opening Lines. Most men (but not all) are smart enough to avoid crude or rude or too-much-too-soon in their Opening Lines. However, they often aren't smart enough to avoid boring and cliché and lonely and desperate opening lines.

The Opening Lines and misspellings below are typical of many Profiles. The misspellings were included to remind you to spell check and proofread everything. You don't want her to see a ton of misspellings in your Profile and have her say, *"If he can't put his best foot forward here, where can he?"*

Some Opening Lines have so many eliminators they eliminate all the women on this planet and in the 3 nearest galaxies. If your Opening Line sounds *anything* like that, it's why you're striking out. Many men also have lines like these next ones throughout their Profiles. Make sure you're not one of them.

- (B.O.): **I find describing myself very hard to do.**

- (B.O.): **It's tricky describing yourself to strangers and then everyone says the same thing...** (Many men say what this man says which is that everyone says the same thing. No joke.)

- (B.O.): **I know a picture is important, and I'm really sorry I don't have one yet.** (Excuses don't cut it. She knows men like these are very sorry dating prospects. They usually never get around to posting a photo.)

- (B.O.): **I'll fill this in later.** (If he can't fill it out now, chances are he never will get around to it.)

- (B.O.): **House is gone, dog is gone, last wife is gone.** (~Sniffle~ He just crashed on Too-Much-Information Highway.)

- (B.O.): **IF YOU HAVE NO PICTURES, DON'T EMAIL! I WON'T REPLY.** (Don't use all CAPS. It means you are shouting. Also… rude never works.)

- (B.O.): **I am new to online dating and feel very uncomfortable and at a loss for words.**

- (B.O.): **My NON-negotiables in a date are….** (A man who starts with a dictatorial checklist spells loser. The section on Deal Makers/Deal Breakers shows how to get across your "must-haves" without sounding like a control freak.)

- (B.O.): **I have a lot to offer. I'm not desperate.**

- <u>(B.O.):</u> I don't consider myself perfect. To begin with, I'm divorced so that didn't go so good. I've learned a lot and am willing to try and do better this time.

- <u>(B.O.):</u> IF YOU STILL HAVE ISSUES WITH YOUR FATHER or MOTHER, GET SOME THERAPY.

- <u>(B.O.):</u> I work long hours and hate coming home to an empty, dark house.

- <u>(B.O.):</u> I'm shy, but once you get to know me you'll like me. (LOTS of men are shy. Don't advertise your shyness. Women like confident men. Talk about your positive qualities, not your negative ones.)

- <u>(B.O.):</u> This section says I need to put in at least 200 words. This section says I need to put in at least 200 words. This section says ...

Any man can do better than the last example, but you'd be surprised how many men (and women) think they're being clever writing exactly what that man did.

~LOUD WHISTLE SOUNDS~

False Start!

Holding!

Pass Interference!   Sixty seconds ago you started writing your Opening Line. Already 3 penalties have been called on you.

Time Out!   Time to get familiar with the secret penalties! There are penalties in Online Dating similar to those in American football. The online penalty flags are **Red Flags** instead of yellow. You can lose a little yardage, a lot of yardage, and some men get ejected from the game.   Some men have so many Red Flags in their Profiles, you can't see if the field is real or artificial.

The sport of Dating requires intelligence, stamina, and good information. If you want to outdo your competition, learn from the mistakes he's making and avoid them. Play the game better than he does.

The officials in this game are sexy women with whistles who cut you very little slack. Many good men get ejected from the game and are dumbfounded as to why.   It's because they're playing at a huge disadvantage. The penalty whistles can only be heard by women and guard dogs. The Red Flags are invisible. You need superpowers to play this game.

Luckily for you, this chapter can give you superpowers. You will develop the uncanny ability to hear at ultra-high frequency. You'll be able to see those dastardly, invisible Red Flags.

There is no test at the end of this chapter to see if you've learned the penalties to avoid. That's the good news. The bad news is you may have already taken the test. Check out your online Profile. Make sure the invisible Red Flags listed in this section don't have you sidelined on the bench and missing all the action.

Here are the most common Red Flag Penalties which can lose you lots of yardage or take you out of the dating game:

TOO MANY PLAYERS ON THE FIELD: **ONE (1) man is allowed on the field at any one time. Penalties are always called on the following men:**

- **My friends say that I'm smart, well-traveled, athletic and have ...** (Don't put what your friends say. Lots of men do, and it's cliché and boring. She doesn't want to date your friends. She doesn't know your friends, and she wants to hear what *you* have to say about you before she wants to hear what your friends have to say. Most importantly, she wants a man who is confident and who can make statements without putting them in the mouth of a friend.)

    IMPORTANT NOTE: If you want to show you're very social, use photos from a social gathering, but don't include your friends in the photo unless they're in the far background. For example, if it's a birthday party, use a photo of you standing by the cake or by the huge stack of presents. There are many ways to show you're social without including your friends as competition.

- **My mother and sister set a high standard.** (She's wondering if you're a Momma's boy or if she's going to have to compete with your Mom and sister for your attention. She's wondering how hard she'll have to work to please 3 people, not just one: your Momma, your sister, and you. Too many Red Flags on the field for her to be interested. See *Pass Interference Penalty*.)

PASS INTERFERENCE: **Your work, family, or friends may interfere with having enough time to spend with her. Examples:**

- **I have a demanding job because I just started my own business.** (It's great you're ambitious and started your own business. If the business is brand new, she's wondering 2 things: 1) Is it going to be successful? 2) Do you have time for her? Address those concerns.)

- **My life is very busy with activities, two jobs, family and friends, neighborhood volunteer...** (She's wondering if you have time for her and her needs/wants.)

- **I work hard.** (Working hard isn't the penalty. The penalty is when your Profile conveys all work and no play. She needs to know you'll make time to play with her.)

- **My kids are my life and mean the world to me.** (Of course they do, and that should go without saying. She wants to know there's room for her in that world.)

WHINING: This penalty is rarely seen in other contact sports, but it's often seen in this sport. In other contact sports, real men don't whine and rarely make excuses. Penalties were called on these whiny men:

- As with most of our generation, I was road kill on the highway of marriage. I have my degree in dating and romance from the School of Hard Knocks.

- I signed up on a lonely night...you probably did, too.

- My pictures aren't that good, but I'll post some better ones later.

- I'm told I'm better looking in person, so please excuse the photos.

We told you this wasn't an easy game to win. Shall we go over the rest of the RED FLAGS, or would you prefer to chicken out right now and have a good cry? Here are other common penalties:

HOLDING: He's too clingy or will smother her. Examples:

- I am very romantic and love to give. Just being with the other person is enough for me.

- Making sure you're happy is the most important thing to me.

- Whatever you like to do, I like to do, too.

HOLDING YOURSELF: These men are too Me-Me-Me or Superficial. Examples:

- I am attractive and looking for an attractive woman.

- Yes, I want to know how much you weigh. Too many women post pictures that don't show her whole body.

- I would describe myself as a rare special gift. I am a handsome man (some say very handsome) looking for an attractive, affectionate, giving, and loving woman. Yes, I'm picky.

FALSE START: Unable To Commit or Not Ready For A Relationship. **Examples:**

- **I am trying this because I have been out of the dating scene for over 5 years because of school and work and would like to meet someone...** (Someone who hasn't dated for 5 years sounds like someone unable to commit or find good balance in his life. Don't talk about the past, focus on the present.)

- **I'm new at this. I separated last month after a long and difficult marriage. I'm looking for a woman for friendship and more.** (Stay off Too-Much-Information Highway. Talk about the present, not the unpleasant past.)

- **I'm not really sure what I'm doing here, but figured I'd give it a chance and see what's out there.**

- **I was married most of my life. I purposely chose to not date for the past few years. I'm just now starting to date.**

UNSPORTSMANLIKE CONDUCT: This includes lying, fudging, and unpleasant personality traits. This penalty can get you ejected from the game. **Examples:**

63

- **I'm really 5 years older than listed. I'm not sure how I selected the wrong year, but I tried to change it but the site won't let me.** (Sites often don't let you change your age, but it's curious that men never err on being older. If you think she's going to believe anything in your Profile, think again.)

- **I'm a happy person most of the time, not into trauma drama.** (He's happy "most of the time". What happens the rest of the time? Does he yell or sulk?)

- **I guess most women out there would rather find someone who's not quite as sarcastic as me.**

- **My ex will tell you: "He's a nice guy with a good heart and is easy-going."** (If you've got such a good heart and are so nice, why do you have an "Ex"? That's what your potential date is wondering. Leave off everything your Ex says about you.)

- **I'm an intelligant man who appresiates the finer things. I like to go first class. I'll spoil you with pleanty of complements.** (The man's spelling is inconsistent with his listed education. If he's lying about his education, she won't believe him about anything else.)

ILLEGAL CONTACT: If you're married and are posing as single, you get ejected from the game. Other men who often get ejected are men who want babysitters, or Mommies, or Sugar Mommas. Examples:

- **I am a little boy at heart.**

- **I've never grown up. I like to play and have fun.**

- **I miss you when I laugh. I miss you when I cry. You are the one who will make my tears disappear.**

- I'd like to find someone who is ambitious and driven. I don't want to have to push someone to excel...

- I WOULD LIKE A SPECIAL WOMAN. ONE WHO IS ATTRACTIVE AND FINANCIALLY SECURE. SHE SHOULD HAVE A WIDE CIRCLE OF FRIENDS. (This man starts out with I want and never says what he brings to the relationship. All CAPS is akin to shouting.)

ILLEGAL PROCEDURE: Too much info or... spooky:

- I don't wear pajamas.

- I'm 2 people in one...

- Do you have fantasies of being disciplined by a man who loves and adores you...

- I like the lakes, and I like milkshakes, cupcakes, clambakes, sweepstakes, snowflakes. I don't like earthquakes or snakes. Before I'm through, in 25 words or less, I'll tell you why I like you. (Poetry is tricky. Avoid poetry unless your name is Shakespeare or Robert Frost. Then your odds of getting a touchdown or hitting a home run are much better.)

- Let us join as twin sparks and life forces of knowledge and destiny.

Avoid the Red Flags, and you'll have much better success! We can't guarantee how long your new superpowers will last, but reading the next chapter will make them last twice as long.

SUCCESSFULLY CLIMB

MORE-ABOUT-ME MOUNTAIN

RING. . .RING. . . ...
Hello!   Welcome to Select-a-Hot-Date Hotline.
Please listen to all the options before making
your selection:

> *If you want a woman who isn't obsessive-compulsive, please press 1 repeatedly.*
>
> *If you want a woman who won't be co-dependent, please ask someone to press 2.*
>
> *If you want a woman who doesn't have multiple personalities, please press 3, 4, 5, and 6.*
>
> *If you want a woman who isn't paranoid-delusional, we know who are and what you want.   Stay on the line so we can trace the call.*
>
> *If you want a woman who is psychic, listen carefully and a little voice will tell you which number to press.*
>
> *If you want a woman who never gets PMS, it doesn't matter which number you press. No one will answer.*

While you're deciding what type of woman you want to date (or not want to date), you first need to tell her something about you. You need to talk about who you are *before* you start listing what you want her to be like.

The 1st step is a doozy. You need a Good Opening Line. Many men not only litter More-About-Me Mountain with Bad

Opening Lines and Red Flags, they fall off. Many men get ticketed for DUI (Disclosing Unattractive Information).

Don't confuse the Opening Line with the Headline. The Headline comes first, and the Opening Line comes after it. Usually both show up when she views potential matches or searches for men.

Your Opening Line counts DOUBLE. It's your bait to catch her attention and get her to click on your picture. After she clicks, she sees the rest of your Profile and photos.

Good Opening (G.O.) lines often convey <u>what you bring to a relationship</u>. Here are examples for you to imitate. In some cases, the whole opening paragraph was included. Many more are lurking in the APPENDIX.

- (G.O.): **WOW! You're finally here. I KNEW you existed. If I knew I was going to be this lucky today, I would have bought a lottery ticket.**

- (G.O.): **I'm R cubed: Ready to date with Resources in Rhode Island. I have plenty of time to travel, and I am looking for a traveling partner not just through Rhode Island but through life.** (You can make this any 3 R-words: Really smart, Really athletic, Really well-read.)

- (G.O.): **Ringgg. Ringgg... Hi, I'm at work trying to solve the financial crisis, bring world peace, and get the zoning maps done for the city. I can't come to the phone right now, so please leave a message at the tone, and I'll get back to you as soon as I can. Beeep....**

- (G.O.): **My idea of camping and roughing it is staying at a hotel that doesn't have room service.**

- <u>(G.O.)</u>: Do you laugh at horoscopes and read them anyways? Every sign sounds like it could apply. How do they do that?

- <u>(G.O.)</u>: Frankenstein looks at my photos to make him feel more secure. But I think I have a better smile. What do you think?

- <u>(G.O.)</u>: Yesss! It's Summer!! Don't let all this good weather go to waste. Let's ride bikes, go to concerts, check out the best movies, see who has good food and good art festivals! Ready, Set...Wink or Email!

- <u>(G.O.)</u>: Socrates said, "The unexamined life is not worth living." What do you think? I like interesting conversations about philosophy...or funosophy (the art of having fun). What's fun to you? (Quotes work well. See chapter on quotes.)

- <u>(G.O.)</u>: Limited Edition! Like new, with very low mileage. Comes with a lifetime warranty, and quantity limited to 1 per household. Tax deduction included, and this is not a cash-for-clunkers offer. Disclaimer: No TARP funds were used in preparing this offer.

- <u>(G.O.)</u>: Who built that snowman in the front yard? I confess. I occasionally build snowmen complete with carrot nose and winter hat. I think the adults enjoy it as much as the kids! Rainy weekends find me in front of the fireplace sipping hot tea or a glass of red wine. Sunny summer weekends find me in the garden or going for a walk or bike ride. Weekdays usually mean putting together a business deal and evenings mean...

- <u>(G.O.)</u>: Want to go window shopping (or real shopping) down Pearl Street Mall? Want to see all the Best Picture Movie Nominees? Want to rail about Republicans? Me, too.

DEAL MAKERS / DEAL BREAKERS: SECRETS of USING GOOD QUALIFIERS & ELIMINATORS

One man's idea of an ideal woman: *She would be allergic to jewelry and credit cards and never ask, "Does this dress make me look fat?" Her favorite hobbies would be cooking, cleaning, and shoveling snow. She would be very affectionate and give great back rubs.*

Another man's ideal woman: *She would be nice and have a nice truck. Please post picture of truck.*

Every man has Deal Makers and Deal Breakers when he's dating. Good qualifiers and eliminators help define who you'd like to date. A common Deal Maker/Breaker is smoking. Many men say "*no way*" to smoking and won't date someone who smokes.

Qualifiers are good to use, but too many is like too much salt on your food. It ruins the meal and will ruin your Profile.

If you lock yourself into an extensive and inflexible checklist, no woman on the planet will fit. Even if she does meet every criteria of your long list, what are the odds you're going to fare equally as well on her extensive and inflexible checklist? Here's a **BIG HINT: BE FLEXIBLE!**

If you're getting NO dates, often it's because you have too many qualifiers. She reads your Profile and says to herself, *"That's Mission Impossible!"* The opposite is also true. If you're getting few or no dates, often it's because you have NO qualifiers. She says to herself, *"That sounds like every woman on the planet."*

HUMONGOUS SECRET: **You've got a winning Profile if the woman you're looking for says to herself, *"Hey, that sounds like me!"***

Use qualifiers and eliminators like you would use salt. A pinch or two, not the whole darn shaker. Using them crassly and rudely defeats the whole purpose of using them. She might fit your qualifiers, but one of *her* Deal Breakers is quite likely no rude or crude men.

If it's 100% crucial the woman of your dreams shares certain activities with you, convey that in your Profile. Be flexible. As one man put it, *"The secret to our long marriage is that we both like to golf. I go on Tuesday, she goes on Thursday."*

Phrasing your Deal Makers and Deal Breakers with delicacy and a light hand is one of the hardest things to do in a Profile. That's why you'll find plenty of examples in this chapter.

They include Deal Makers/Breakers on Relationships, Children, Looks, Fitness, Activities, Hobbies, Intelligence, and more. If you're a Separated man, read how to mitigate the woman's objection to dating a Separated man.

Wording your "qualifiers" isn't easy, but it will help you get more and better dates. Use these examples to get you started. If you need more ideas, there are many more examples in the APPENDIX.

RELATIONSHIPS:

I'm looking forward to marrying and having kids, but let's wait till after the 1st date.

I'm looking for someone to enjoy this journey called life...and to travel with me.

I'm looking for friendship first that will hopefully develop into something more.

I'm looking for my last first date.

I'm someone who enjoys being one half of a couple. I make it a priority to spend time together, but I also enjoy having our own quiet time.

I'm not looking for a pen pal, I'm looking for a life partner.

I'm looking for my Last-First-Date. Maybe it will start with a Best-First-Date. Want to see?

Although I've never been married, my last relationship lasted longer than most people's marriages. I'm looking for a long-term relationship that will lead to marriage.

Emailing is fun, but I'd much rather take you to dinner, go dancing, check out a museum.

ATHLETICS:

I enjoy skiing in the winter and hope you do, too.

I'm very athletic and hope you are, too.

I'm someone who likes to be active and enjoys working out. Care to join me?

I hike on the weekends and look forward to you joining me.

I mountain climb on some weekends, but I don't expect you to accompany me (but, of course, you're welcome to join me!).

I hope you like sailing because I have my own boat.

Socializing and athleticism is a big plus. Terrific if you're a woman who likes to get dressed up in that little black dress and ski black diamonds (probably not at the same time)....if that sounds like you, we need to talk.

POLITICS:

Politically I vote Liberal and get along best with women who vote that way, too.

I'm a conservative and mesh best with conservatives.

COUNTRY LIFE:

I live in the country and am looking for someone who likes the wide open spaces.

I have my own horses and ride in the country every weekend.

CITY LIFE:

I live in the city and enjoy live theater. I hope you do too.

I live in NYC and love the variety of activities, especially Broadway and off-Broadway venues.

READING:

I've always loved to read and enjoy going to book groups.

I always have at least one or two books going. Want to exchange bestsellers?

COOKING:

I hope you like to cook as much as I do. I'm handy at chopping and slicing and dicing, and pretty good as the head cook, too, especially if it involves outdoor grills.

My cooking repertoire is limited, so if you like to cook or want to take classes with me, let's go!

GOLF:

I like to golf once or twice a week. It would be great if you do, too.

I like to golf once or twice a week. If you don't, that's not a deal breaker.

OUTDOORS:

You'll find me outdoors in the summer, but winter finds me inside by the fireplace!

I work indoors during the week, and my weekends are spent outdoors...working in the garden, hiking in the desert, or driving down to the ocean.

Being outdoors energizes me. Climbing 14ers with the guys is my idea of fun. Skiing in the winter time is even more fun, and it would be great if you liked skiing!

DANCING and MUSIC:

Music inspires me. Dancing energizes me.

If you can't dance, I'm a good dancer and a good teacher.

CHILDREN:

I have 2 children in grade school and am looking for someone who enjoys kids or has their own young children. I share custody, and the kids are with me every other week.

I'm a single dad, and I have one daughter in high school who will soon be off to college. Balancing family and a relationship is important to me.

I share custody of my son, and he starts high school next year. If you have kids, that's great, and if not, you can borrow mine!

I was a single parent to my 3 sons (yes, like the old TV sitcom). They are now grown and successful. Big sigh of relief!

My kids are well-launched and independent. I'm not averse to making room for more.

I think kids are GREAT, and I have 2 of my own (ages 2 and 4) and see them several times a month. If you have kids that would be a plus. Especially if they are older than mine. You can clue me in on what to expect next!

I was married but didn't have kids. My nieces and nephews sometimes think I'm smarter than they are (don't tell them otherwise). I have a sense of humor children seem to enjoy. These days I'm trading "blonde joke emails" with my 10 year old niece.

My grown children are my pride and joy. They visit me, or I visit them a few times a year.

One day let's have the house, one or two kids, and a dog!

Thanks for stopping by…. Nest is empty… kids are away at University. I have a long list of fun things to catch up on. Care to help me check them off my to-do list?

TRAVELING:

It would be nice if you could travel a few weeks a year. I get 4 weeks vacation!

I'm looking for someone who enjoys travel. I travel on business frequently and would enjoy it if you could join me sometimes.

Like to go new places, explore new cultures? Me, too! I don't want to run away for the weekend, I'm looking for someone who wants to run away for a lifetime of good company, good conversation, great adventure.

BAGGAGE:

I travel light. I have a golf bag that I've had for 10 years. That's the only baggage I'm attached to.

I learned a long time ago that emotional and social baggage gets heavy. And it costs a fortune to store! I've gotten rid of mine, and hope you've gotten rid of yours, too!

If you're under 40 or never been married, we're probably not a good match. I like women with some mileage and some baggage. I usually forget to pack an umbrella, and maybe you could share yours.

SEPARATED:

I've been separated for over a year, and there is no chance of reconciliation. I've been told separated is "the kiss of death" when you're trying to date, but I hope you don't stereotype me that easily.

I'm separated, but soon to be divorced. There is no chance of reconciliation, but we are friends and share joint custody of the kids.

I won't technically be divorced till later this year. My ex and I live in different states, and that's slowed down the paperwork considerably.

My divorce is due to be finalized in the next 3 months.

I still haven't figured out why people label "separated" as the "kiss of death". Maybe I'm just luckier than most…we parted as friends and used the same attorney.

Papers won't be signed for a few more months, so if you want to wait until then to meet me, that's great! In the meantime, how about I get to know YOU, and then you'll have a head start on getting to know me in 2 months.

EXERCISE and DIET:

Fitness is important to me, and I hope to you, too.

I'm physically attracted to fit and healthy ladies. Long hikes in the mountain are my thing.

You don't have to be one of those obsessive compulsive have-to-work-out-7-days-a-week types, but it would be nice if you like to work out and join me for walking or weights at the gym.

I'm a vegetarian and it would be nice but not essential if you are. I try to keep fit, but still haven't figured out how to stop that clock from ticking. It would sure improve my marathon times.

My only vices are coffee and good chocolate and working out! Oh, and champagne on birthdays and special occasions!

ATTRACTIVE AND FIT:

It is important I stay in shape…that means hitting the gym a few times a week. I hope staying in shape is important to you, too.

I'm not looking for Barbie (I'm not Ken, but I do have a dream house). A woman with a great smile and who is "easy on the eyes" is always welcome. And, yes, I admit it, I'm a leg-man. I'm 6' 4", and I like tall women. (Be very careful when talking about looks. Even a light hand like this and mentioning "easy on the eyes" can cause women to consider you too superficial. Avoid any mention of models.)

Genetics and workouts! I was fortunate on the 1st and work out regularly. I'm attracted to women who like to work out and eat a healthy diet.

SMARTS:

Long hair optional, brains mandatory.

I enjoy having long conversations about philosophy and current events.

I'm looking for someone who is interested in all kinds of different things from art to politics to classical music.

RELIGION:

I get along best with people who are more spiritual than religious.

I go to church regularly and hope you'll accompany me.

I'm eclectic in my religious attendance…..I go to churches, temples, and mosques.

I like animals, but I'm ~ah~ah~choo!....allergic to dogs and cats.

I hope you like dogs....I have a Golden Lab who likes people.

SKIN COLOR or ETHNICITY:

I'm color appreciative....I'm not into PINK or Purple hair, but all other colors of hair or skin are beautiful to me. (If you're open to dating people of other ethnicities, mentioning that fact expands the possibilities. On the other hand, if you *prefer* a certain hair color or skin color, mentioning it in your Profile usually reduces the possibilities. Many women see you as superficial.)

I'm open to dating women of all colors and ethnicities. I don't stereotype people and hope you don't either.

DISABILITY or MEDICAL ISSUE:

A disability or medical issue is not easy to discuss in person or in your Profile. Many professional organizations which assist people with disabilities and medical conditions have helpful dating tips on their websites. If you haven't taken advantage of their real world advice, that's a good place to start.

A general consensus seems to be this: If your disability or medical issue is one which is not noticeable when you first meet someone, it's usually best to wait until you get to know the person before bringing up the subject. For example, if you had cancer and it was successfully treated, it's usually best not to include that in your Profile. On the other hand, if your condition is readily apparent when you meet someone for the first time, address it in your Profile. Here are some examples:

We all have our challenges to overcome. Mine involved a motorcycle accident a few years ago. Not only did I survive, it gave me a whole different outlook on the world. I went back to school and will finish up my degree this summer. Now I talk a bit slower than I used to, but I think more clearly. For example, I always wear my helmet while biking. Like I said, I got lucky.

Many ladies ask me how I communicate online since I'm blind. I have a special computer and special software. Yes, technology is wonderful. It enabled me to go to school, get a good education, and find a job to support myself. I'm a full-time teacher.

Now that you've read some Deal Makers and Breakers, think about what your own are. The 3 key areas in most relationships are SEX and MONEY and RELIGION.

Although you need to stay off Too-Much-Information Highway, you also need to give prospective dates an idea of what you're looking for.

Your goal in using Qualifiers and Eliminators is to "narrow" the field to women who are more compatible with you and to accomplish it with class. Using too many qualifiers isn't good, not using enough isn't good either.

HUMONGOUS SECRET: If you've been using the "attractive" word in your Profile as a qualifier…nix it now! "**Attractive**" is a subjective word. If you use the word "**attractive**" as a qualifier, women think you are looking for Angelina Jolie or Beyonce or Jessica Alba or the girlfriend of the latest James Bond. Most women conclude you're a shallow man if you focus on looks (even if you focus on other non-physical things in your Profile). It isn't necessary to use "attractive" as a Deal Maker in your Profile. It's a given!

When you see her Profile and photos, you can decide for yourself if she fits your vision of "attractive". There's no reason to include it in your Profile as a qualifier unless you want to help out the rest of the online guys.

WARNING: Specifics are good when talking about traveling, music, activities, reading material, spirituality, hobbies, athletics, fitness, interests, work, children, and lots more. BUT... specifics are terrible when talking about sex in your Profile.

You do not know her well enough to do that (yet). Your goal is to get the date. If you skip the DATE and try to go directly to getting the MATE, you're usually going to bomb, big time.

Avoid sex specifics and graphic detail unless you want to scare away most women. However, totally ignoring sex isn't the solution. SEX is such an important matching criteria that it's the next sextion... oops make that section.

SEX and SEX and SEX SEX SEX

What to say!   How to say it!

What not to say!

After a chapter title like that, I can hardly wait to read what I'm going to write next.

Press down....More.....Ok more...WOW yes ahh ohh yes....almost there....oh good...ummm.... harder....faster! FEELS GOOD...oh gooooddd! I just love playing with the TV remote control, don't you?

Sex stuff in your Profile can easily be misunderstood. If you press her buttons wrong, you're going to turn her off, not on. HOT SEX in your Profile rarely works. Most women will click right by you. Those who do respond often send something like this:

"Hi Guy! Please turn your computer screen upside down now!!! Hurry.... 370HSSV 0773H"

In your Profile, there are ways to convey *"I'm interested in you-know-what"* without the woman thinking you need sex 3 times a day and 6 times on Sundays.   You need to be realistic. Somebody's gotta get out of bed and make the meals...or at least answer the door and tip the pizza delivery guy.

81

Subtlety is the key. Saying **"Mine is bigger than his"** or **"I just got a prescription for Viagra. Wanna help me try it out?"** isn't subtle.

If you try to bypass the foreplay, don't sit by your computer waiting for the women to email you first. It ain't gonna happen. If it does, watch out. Urban legend has it that more than one man has received this email: *"Hurry, come on over, honey. I live with my roommate, but right now there's no one home."* When he got there, nobody was home.

You have to woo women. Showing up naked with a case of beer isn't enough to get her in the mood. Champagne and fresh strawberries work better. So does taking her out for a nice dinner, and you know... hand-holding, and hugging, and kissing. Bummer!

Give her a chance to meet you before you show her all the tricks your tongue can do. In your Profile, think hand-holding not French kissing.

Women can get away with talking about physical affection in their Profiles much easier than men can. Just because she can, doesn't mean you can. It doesn't work in reverse. If she mentions physical affection, it's flirty and cute. If you mention it too much, it's abusive and crude. If it's in her Profile, that doesn't mean you can ask for sex on the 1st date. All it means is that she likes it... not that she likes it on the 1st or 2nd date. She usually wants to see if she likes you before she starts peeking under the hood. Women are funny like that.

Some men try to include a sexual compatibility checklist in their Profile. They want women who like "**lots of hugging and kissing**". Men who do that would be smart if they included a "**No Way**" check box at the end of their list. Telling her you'll throw in a pair of black, French panties and bra, tastefully soaked in the finest of Paris perfumes, will make sure you don't get the date. The same is true of emails… too much too soon is going to land you at the Dog Pound or the Frog Pond.

Let's say you put this in your Profile: "**Looking for a sensual woman who is comfortable with her body.**" The sentence is so open to interpretation, a woman doesn't know what you have in mind. For all she knows, you may want her to dance semi-naked on the kitchen table not only for you but also for six of your closest male friends.

If you put "**nothing kinky**", that makes it worse. Kinkiness is far more open to interpretation than "*sensual*" or "*comfortable with her body*". If you're online looking for sex, sex, and more sex, these words might be appropriate.

If you're wanting more than sex, how do you get across the idea you're a man who ***enjoys romance***? Just like that. The mushy cards in the supermarket or card stores do this especially well. You don't have to be blatant. Be understated and tasteful.

Subtle and classy ways to talk about Sex and Intimacy:

- GOOD SEX TALK: **I'm looking for a woman who I can share a morning cup of coffee with and a glass of wine at night.**

- GOOD SEX TALK: **Since I can slay dragons, she should be addicted to candlelight and knights in shining armor.**

- GOOD SEX TALK: **My astrological chart says that Romance is my sign, and my best astrological match is someone clever who reads my profile today...Hey, that's you! Maybe we can discuss it over lunch?**

- GOOD SEX TALK: **I'm taking a survey. Are you for or against candle-lit bubble baths with champagne on the 1st date?** (This type of tongue-in-cheek humor will work best if most of your Profile is humorous.)

- GOOD SEX TALK: **There are many differences between infatuation and love. There's attraction and affection and caring and passion and loyalty. Many roads but it all starts with the road to friendship.**

- GOOD SEX TALK: **I'm romantic. Starting the day with a warm hug and a kiss makes any day better.**

- GOOD SEX TALK: **Affection is effective!**

- GOOD SEX TALK: **"Have I told you lately that I love you?" Of course not, I haven't even met you. But...what are you doing for lunch? ;-)**

- GOOD SEX TALK: **I'm an affectionate man who isn't afraid to say he likes to cuddle. I know they might revoke my MAN-card for saying that, but I'm willing to take that chance.**

- <u>GOOD SEX TALK</u>: **Are you comfortable expressing warmth and affection? Send me your best pick-up line, and I'll let you know if it worked!**

- <u>GOOD SEX TALK</u>: **There is nothing more romantic than.......**

- <u>GOOD SEX TALK</u>: **My idea of a romantic evening is ...**

On those last two, fill in the blank with something tasteful and understated. It will get your point across, and you won't risk turning her off. If you find out you're turning off more women with your sex talk than you're turning on, here's a **BIG SECRET**: Turn down the sexual volume of your Profile.

Spitting hot, hot fire often works, but rarely does it work *before* the 1st date. The following men were spitting hot, hot fire in their Profiles. If you're striking out, turn down the scorching fire to low or nix it altogether. Wait until you get to know her before you say, *"I like your style, you got sheer class, but babe, my god, I WANT YOUR ASS!"*

TOO MUCH HOT FIRE TOO SOON:

- <u>UH-OH SEX</u>: **I want the six S's....Someone who is Smart, Sensuous, Successful and Sexy Sexy Sexy.**

- <u>UH-OH SEX</u>: **Do you know the difference between sex and conversation? Would you like to go upstairs and talk? ;-D**

- <u>UH-OH SEX</u>: Do you like short love affairs? I hate them. I've got all weekend.

- <u>UH-OH SEX</u>: If I gave you a sexy negligee, would there be anything in it for me?

- <u>UH-OH SEX</u>: Dating is a lot like fishing, you can either mount it, keep it, eat it, or throw it back!

- <u>UH-OH SEX</u>: I love to give massages!

- <u>UH-OH SEX</u>: I know when we meet you'll be wondering what I look like under my clothes. That's okay, I'll be wondering what you look like, too.

- <u>UH-OH SEX</u>: My motto is, "Life is like an ice cream cone. You have to learn to lick it."

- <u>UH-OH SEX</u>: Read my whole profile before responding. I'm DARING and OPEN-MINDED and CONFIDENT. You may think you are, but 99% OF YOU AREN'T! Especially about YOU KNOW WHAT!....:-)

- <u>UH-OH SEX</u>: I'm more dangerous than the average man. I don't nibble, I bite! GRRRRR!

- <u>UH-OH SEX</u>: Edible oils are my fave...low cal and climatic!

- <u>UH-OH SEX</u>: No kinky games unless we both get to play them.

If you do not open the romance topic at all in your Profile, she may wonder if you're a warm and affectionate man and "if your equipment still works".

The words *"romance"* and *"affection"* are tasteful words to convey your interest in the physical aspect of love and intimacy. Use them wisely. Don't flood your profile and interests with cootchie-cootchie-coo. Easy does it.

Other tasteful words which convey your sensual nature are: *affectionate, caring, thoughtful, loving, warm, demonstrative, warmhearted, tender, intimate, cozy, snuggle, sensitive, devoted, receptive, romantic, amorous, cuddling, sentimental, hug, kiss, candlelight, embrace, hold, cherish, etc.*

If you find your "sex" words aren't working as you hoped, you can change them, delete them, or add to them in seconds. For example, if you're the man who ended your Profile with **"Bye for now sweet lips. Can't wait to meet you! Xoxo"**, you can change it anytime you want. When is the best time to change it? Now would be about right.

LITTLE CHECK BOXES

CAN SINK YOUR SHIP

"You must be a twin," said the lovely young woman. *"No one person could be that wonderful."*

You want to convey your "wonderfulness" in your Profile. Focusing on your positive traits in a modest way puts you on the right path.

While you're merrily going down the right road, you might want to check what you're carrying with you. We're talking about those little "check boxes" you filled out when you joined your dating site. Your Check Box answers can make women think the results of your IQ test were negative. Fortunately, it's easy to retake the test and redo your Check Box answers.

Remember those Check Boxes on Age, Height, Body Type, Hair Color, Education, Politics, Occupation, Kids, Religion, Income, and more? These check boxes determine if you'll be selected when women are searching for men or when they're sent matches. On many sites, she'll also see what you'd like *her* age, height, body type, education, location, and other criteria to be.

Your Check Box answers can easily turn off women you don't want to exclude. NEVER EVER put *"Prefer Not to Say"* as an answer. *"Prefer Not to Say"* or *"Didn't Say"* is a sure way to strike out immediately. *"Undecided"* or *"Not Sure"* is a much better choice.

Being too picky or not picky enough can land you in Check Box Gulch. Here's a real life example: The man selected preferred height for his date as a woman between 3 feet and 8 feet tall, age between 30 and 50, distance within 50 miles. He had no preference about education or smoking or much of anything else.

Some would say he is an open-minded man who isn't stuck on dating one kind of woman. If she's 12 inches shorter than he is or 12 inches taller than he is, he's going to consider her.

On the other hand, the man's Check Box answers would lead many women to think he's brain dead, or a con artist/gold digger, or desperate, or only out for sex. Women who are serious about having a relationship will look at everything you filled out in your Profile including the Check Boxes.

HUMONGOUS SECRET: Gold Digging is an equal opportunity occupation. She's going to be looking at your Check Box answers to make sure you're not a con artist.

You should do the same thing. Look at her Check Boxes. Be on the alert for women who have check boxes with huge parameters.

If she doesn't care if you're 3 feet tall or 8 feet tall, if she doesn't care if you're 30 years old or 60, if she doesn't care about body type or politics or religion, she might be open-minded. She might also be single-minded.

THE AGE RANGE CHECK BOX:

Reality check time! If you're 50 and are looking to date a 30 year old, unless you bring enough to the table to collapse said table, you're going to be paddling in the Frog Pond for a long time. If you're 40 and are looking to date a 20 year old, ditto.

While you can find women much younger than you are to date, most women are looking to date men fairly close to their own age. The majority of women aren't looking for the "manther" (aka much older man). Similarly, most women aren't cougars looking for the young stud.

HUMONGOUS SECRET: The biggest mistake men make in their Age Range check boxes is turning off women who are IN their age range. Yes, IN their desired age range.

For example, let's say you put an age range 1 to 10 years younger than you are. You may think you're enhancing your chances of finding the woman of your dreams by choosing such a wide range. Instead, you'll end up pissing off most of the women who are in your mid and upper age range. She figures you'll date her until a younger woman comes along and catches your eye. Don't make the mistake of alienating 80% of the women who are looking for you.

You can still search for the sweet, young thing, but it's best not to display it in your Check Boxes. A good poker player doesn't show all his cards.

A good Age range to DISPLAY in your Profile is this:

1) Select a **<u>Lower Age range 3-5 years YOUNGER</u>** than you are.

2) Select an **<u>Upper Age range 3-5 years OLDER</u>** than you are.

3) **If your site allows, <u>it's often best not to put any restrictions on age if you're over 30.</u>**

The above age parameters are a good place to start. If your Check Boxes shout, *"Older guy looking for sweet, young thing"*, you'll be alienating a lot of potential dates. Women close in age to you won't give you the time of day.

But ya say you're a good-looking man and very young-looking for your age? You're highly successful! Financially independent! Tons of energy! Congratulations! There's just one thing... you're not the only one going on the date. That isn't to say you can't and won't find a woman who's much younger and who's mutually interested in you.

You can. If you search on young women who are 5 or 10 or 20 years younger than you are, you will find some looking for the older man. You'll find some who are looking for a *"Manther"* or a *"Sugar-Daddy"* or *"Father-Figure"* or a man who's *"Got Bank"*.

Be careful what you're advertising for in your Profile. As one experienced man wrote in his Profile: *"If you're 6 to 10 years YOUNGER than I am, don't contact me. If you ignore my wishes, please wait until the first date to ask me for money."*

MEN... Check out what the women are looking for in terms of age. You'll soon know if a wishful thinker showed up the day she or you filled out your check boxes.

RELATIONSHIP CHECK BOX:

Dating/ Long Term/ Friends/ Hang Out/ Activity Partner/ Intimate Encounter/ Marriage

---

Most people who join dating sites are looking for Dating or Long Term or Marriage. Some dating sites have a Check Box which lets you specify what relationship you prefer. If you can't decide if you should put "Dating" or "Long Term" or "Marriage", it's usually best to choose "Dating" or "Long Term". Marriage as a Check Box selection can be intimidating to many women, even women who are eventually looking for marriage.

Many men change their Relationship Check Box from Dating to Long Term every few weeks. Alternating between them lets you target the best of both worlds. If your site doesn't have a "Relationship" Check Box, include something in your Profile to tell her what type of relationship you'd like to find.

On most conventional dating sites, if you choose "Intimate Encounter" or "Friends" or "Hang Out" or "Email" or "Activity

Partner", you'll get fewer dates. Most people on conventional dating sites are there for dating.

Also, everyone's definition of "Friends" and "Hang Out" is different. While you may think "Friends" means "a friendship that can progress into dating", many women view friendship as an activity with no hugging, no kissing, and no sex.

"Intimate Encounter" and "Activity Partner" work better on some sites than others. Many sites cater specifically to the "Intimate Encounter". Other sites cater to the "Activity Partner".

Before you pay money to join a site, make sure it's a site which has enough members who are looking for the same thing you are.

RELATIONSHIP STATUS CHECK BOX:
Single/Never Married

If you're over 35 and you've never been married, telling a woman you were *"born that way"* is a good start, but you've got to do more than that. While some women would call you smart or lucky, as one 40-something, single man put it, *"It's usually the KISS of DEATH."*

The good news is that it doesn't have to be. However, you need to address it in your Profile or it will be.

Here are the many *Kiss-of-Death* thoughts which surface when she sees you're over 35 and single: *Are you a man who wouldn't commit and now you're desperate? Are you an eternal momma's boy? Are you so picky that nobody was ever good enough for you? Are you a man who's never grown up? Have you just decided having kids is important to you, and you're looking for a baby carrier?*

None of those things may be true, but she doesn't know your history. You can't change the facts of your Never-Been-Married status. However, you can address it in your Profile and greatly mitigate the stereotype.

Heartfelt honesty always helps. Give her a short explanation so she'll give you the benefit of the doubt. If you're looking for a long-term relationship or commitment or marriage, address it briefly. Briefly means 1 or 2 sentences.

The best way to defuse the over-35 and never-been-married is if you have been in a committed relationship in the past. Include something like this in your Profile:

- **I've been in one, long-term relationship that lasted 10 years.**

- **I've been in love a time or two, and I'm looking for my last first date.**

- **I've been in one long-term relationship that lasted longer than most people's marriages.**

- **I'm looking for my last first date. In case you're too shy to ask... my last relationship lasted 11 years. We were better friends than lovers, and I'm looking for the whole enchilada.**

- **We were better lovers than friends, and I'm looking for the whole enchilada.**

- My last relationship lasted longer than most people's marriages….but see…what happened is that the day we went to get the rings, this bus went zooming by….now I always make sure I walk between you and traffic. I'm jesting of course, and I hope my profile depicts me as the kind of man who will be there for you. So when do you want to go looking at rings…??

Most women would say a 6 month relationship is not a long-term commitment. It's not wise to use a 6 month relationship as an example of what great, dating material you are.

RELATIONSHIP STATUS CHECK BOX: Separated

The Separated status is another **"KISS of DEATH"** situation. Many women won't have anything to do with you until your divorce papers are signed.

Women don't like getting involved in uncomfortable situations, and divorces aren't picnics in the park. There are problems to solve, decisions and divisions to be made, custody issues to work out, legal papers to sign.

Women are concerned your "*Separated*" status may be temporary. Here's what she's worried about: *Maybe you'll reconcile with your spouse. Maybe you'll ping-pong back and forth between dating your ex and dating her. Are you carrying too much baggage? Are you ready for a new relationship? Is she going to be the rebound-woman whose shoulder you cry on and who you dump after the divorce is finalized?*

All this spells uncomfortable. On the other hand, many other women will not stereotype the Separated man. She'll hear you out and see if you're worth dating. She views you as the "New Kid" on the block. She realizes some woman out there didn't appreciate you.

Be on the lookout for those women. Also be on the lookout for con women who see you as easy pickings. You're lonely or sad or upset or in need of a friendly ear and a good hug. They're happy to tell you whatever you want to hear.

If you are Separated, include a line in your Profile which gives her an idea when your divorce will be finalized. She doesn't want to ask. Address it matter-of-factly and without anger or recrimination. Just the facts, man. Check out the Deal Makers/ Deal Breakers chapter and Appendix for more ways to write a tasteful line or two about being Separated.

RELATIONSHIP STATUS CHECK BOX: Widower

Sometimes the widower unintentionally shoots himself in the foot. If the widower states in his Profile, *"No one can ever replace her but..."* or *"She was my shining star,"* most women aren't going star-gazing with you any time soon. No woman can compete with a memory, and she's not about to try.

Loving and respecting a past relationship is wonderful, but if you're looking for a new relationship, make certain the old one doesn't cloud the search. A good way to handle this is to state something like this in your Profile:

- **I've been dating for a year and am looking forward to finding a committed relationship.**

- **I became a widower a few years ago and am looking forward to enjoying the company of a woman who is active and has time to travel.**

- **I had a good marriage and am looking forward to starting a new relationship with someone who has the same kind of values and interests.**

Widowers have to keep their eyes open for the con women, too. In this regard, the Widower is much like the Separated man. They can be viewed as "easy pickings". A good way to avoid this is to avoid mentioning you are a _recent_ widower.

HAVE KIDS CHECK BOX:

Many men have kids. Some have kids who live with them part or full time. If you have young kids, address the custody situation in your Profile. She doesn't want to write and ask you. What she doesn't know, she avoids.

If you're open to dating women with children, put a line in your Profile to let her know. If you're open to dating single moms, that will deepen your dating pool.

Do not talk about your kids in your first sentence or your first few paragraphs. She wants to date you, not your kids. One of these years your kids will be grown and out of the nest. She wants to hear about you first.

If you begin your Profile with *"My kids mean the world to me"* or *"I have great kids and I love them"* or *"I love my kids and like to spend time with them",* you are conveying kids first, her second.

It's a given that you love your kids and like to spend time with them. What isn't a given is how many kids you have and how old they are. Address this in your Profile. There's a big difference between having one child who's 14 and having three kids who are 3, 5, and 8. Good ways to write about kids can be found in the Deal Makers/Deal Breakers chapter.

INCOME CHECK BOXES:

Your income is a sticky area. Many men display their income because it shows they are financially successful, and fiscal success is attractive to many women.

Many financially successful women are looking for a man who is as fiscally sound as she is. If she views a man's Profile and sees no income listed, she doesn't know what to think. She may think you have a high income and don't want to post it publicly. She may think you don't want to attract "Gold Diggers". That's why some very successful men (and women) leave their income Check Box blank. They don't want dates looking at their income first and their Profile second.

BIG SECRET: "Gold Diggers" will find you no matter what is displayed in your income Check Box. That's their job! Listing no income won't protect you from the Gold Diggers. It can backfire on you instead. If you have no income listed, many financially secure women conclude you're not financially secure or successful. If you're highly educated, she thinks you weren't motivated to achieve financial success.

There's another important reason you should consider filling out the income box. If you leave the box blank, on many sites there is NOT an option for women to search on "no income". The only way you will appear on her searches is if she selects "ANY" for income. Many women don't do that. They're not interested in finding a man who earns less than $25,000 a year.

She can't read your mind or your W-2. If you're not getting the kind or amount of contacts and replies you think you should be, it may be because you have no income in the Income Check Box.

If you're not comfortable including your income on your Profile, by all means do not include it. You might be excluded when women search, but you can overcome this by doing more searching of your own.

On the other hand, you may have your true income listed and you may be getting contacts you do not want. You may be 50 and have an income of $100,000+ listed. You may find you're getting 25 year old women contacting you. While this may be flattering and attractive to some men, other men find it annoying. If you've already raised your kids and are not looking to raise another one, you can set your Age Range preferences to reflect this.

It's fine to be flattered by the "young gals" who wink at you and email. Being fooled is another matter. Some men lower their income to avoid getting this kind of attention. That has the drawback of making you look less successful than you are. Alternatively, you can reply to the youngsters that you're not enough of a match or reply, *"I have cowboy boots older than you are"* or *"If I decide to adopt any more children, I'll let you know."*

HER INCOME CHECK BOX:

On some dating sites, you select what kind of income you want the woman to have. She'll see your selections when she reads your Profile.

As with your Income Check Box, her Income Check Box can be treacherous territory. Consider this scenario. You earn a good income but list NO income for yourself. You select a HIGH income for her. HIGH Income men who don't list their income and put a high income for the woman send this message: **"I'm a Taker."**

Oops! Not the message you thought you were sending? Many low income men fill out their check boxes exactly as you did. Their income box is blank, and they put a high income for the woman. You don't look any different than they do.

Here's how to avoid looking like a taker. Make sure your written Profile and your photos convey your financial success. Otherwise, you're going to be the one who looks like a Gold Digger. She wants a man who wants her for herself, not her bank account.

Put the shoe on the other foot. You appreciate knowing the financial status of the woman you're looking to date, and it's no different for her. Many men check the same income boxes for themselves as they do for the woman. Many other men leave both income boxes blank but this has the downside that you're going to attract women who don't have the financial success you prefer.

When you search for women, you're going to have the same problem with the darn income box. Many successful women are proud of their accomplishments and readily list their income. Other women are concerned about male Gold Diggers and list no income.

On many sites when you search, the only way you will find women who have NO income listed is to select "ANY" as her income. For example, in real life she might earn over $75,000, but if she has no income listed, the only way you'll include her in your search is to select "ANY" as her income.

There is a good way to find women with good incomes but who leave the income box blank.

Do this when you search:

> - In the Income box choose "ANY".
>
> - In the Education box, choose Bachelors and Masters and PhD/Advanced Degrees. Statistically, the higher the education, the higher the income.
>
> - You can narrow your search further by only searching for women who have Masters and PhD/Advanced Degrees.

You're going to have to read the woman's Profile to see what she did with her great education. At least you'll know the woman made it through school. Probably.

Probably?? There are fudgers and liars in the Internet Dating World just like in the real world. Like the real world, the best con artists are the ones who appear the most honest.

We know you're smart, but so were the thousands of people who got conned by Bernie Madoff. As you probably recall, Madoff made off with *billions* of dollars from some very smart people. He was caught by the SEC and sentenced to 150 years in prison in 2009. That didn't do much for his victims. The bottom line is this: If those rich and bright people can be conned, you can be, too.

HUMONGOUS SECRET: **READ BETWEEN THE LINES.**
Read a lot of Profiles. You'll get better at *reading between the lines*. **Look for what's NOT in the Profile as well as what is.** Also ask yourself if the "lady doth protest too much". Often

women who say **"things in the material world aren't important to me"** are protesting too much.

Be careful including lines like those in your own Profile. Women know men without jobs and with little financial resources find it easy to say, **"Worldly things aren't important to me. It's what's in your heart that matters."**

PHYSICAL QUALITIES CHECK BOXES:
Body Type, Hair, Eyes, etc.

Your written Profile conveys you are looking for a woman with *inner* beauty. Your Profile says you're looking for a long-term, committed relationship. Your Check Boxes show you prefer a woman with blue eyes and blonde hair.

~~WHISTLE sounds!~~ Even a blue-eyed blonde will see the contradiction. You may prefer to date blue-eyed blondes or dark-haired brunettes, but don't convey that in your Check Boxes. You'll come across as superficial. Even gorgeous women with blonde hair know their looks fade in time. If she dates you, she's wondering what's going to happen 5 or 10 or 15 years down the road when her hair starts to gray and those smile lines deepen.

Check Boxes which indicate superficiality of hair color and eye color won't look good no matter how good-looking you are and no matter how much money you make.

Any discussion of physical qualities would be incomplete without talking about Body Type. In online dating, AVERAGE as a Body Type means many things. On many sites, people who are 20 or 40 or 60 pounds overweight put "Average" or "Needs-to-lose-a-few pounds". Everyone's interpretation is different. That's why it's critical you include 2 full body photos.

If you're unsure if you're average or needs-to-lose-a-few or big and beautiful, here's how the "Body Type" game is played. Most people err on the side of being more appealing rather than less. In other words, they might be 15 or 20 pounds over, but they put average.

Do not put you're athletic and toned *unless you look like you work out regularly.* Having a little extra to hug is not the kiss of death. Women like having something to squeeze, but most aren't looking to squeeze a guy who's delusional about body type.

OTHER CHECK BOXES: Butts and Erotica

Check Boxes which are here today may be gone tomorrow. New ones may appear in their place. A recent change on a very popular dating site was the elimination of the Best Feature Check Box. Many men checked "Butt" as best feature. Many checked "Erotica" as a turn-on.

Although these Check Boxes recently disappeared on that site, they may reappear at any time. If Check Boxes like these reappear, think twice before you advertise your butt. It's a good way to land on your butt.

Your Profile isn't the place to boast about Erotica. Erotica conjures up all kinds of images from kinky to candlelight. Erotica ranges from playful to painful, from sensual to strange. She has no clue where you fall on the Erotica continuum.

Erotica is a topic best saved for after you get to know her. Read the Sex chapter for classy ways to convey sexuality and intimacy in your Profile.

Most women who are serious about dating and quality relationships read your whole Profile including the Check Boxes. Don't make the mistake of thinking Check Boxes aren't important. They are very important. If you're on a site which has comparison information as to how you two mesh, women pay attention to this information.

Review and edit your Check Boxes if necessary. Pay special attention to the INCOME Check Boxes and the AGE Check Boxes. You may not be a diplomat, but your Check Boxes need to be diplomatic.

WRITING A GOOD PROFILE

PART ONE:

Avoid Boring & Cliché & Cookie-Cutter

Always remember you're unique, just like everyone else. If you feel like you're diagonally parked in a parallel Universe, join the 6 billion member club known as Humanity.

Everyone on the planet is unique and special. Here's the challenge when writing Your Profile: You need to convey you're unique and special WITHOUT using those words! You've got to get her interested. At the same time you don't want her to think you've deprived some village of its idiot or its egocentric fool.

The Profile section is where you get dressed for the contest. You put on your best pair of jeans, or business suit, or Knight-in-shining-armor suit, or your fool's hat.

On some sites, the Profile section is called....wait for it now... the *Profile*. On other sites, it's called: *About Me and Who I'm Looking For; A Personal Statement; An Introduction; A Self Summary; The Skinny;* or *In My Own Words.*

Some Dating Sites break down the Big-Box Profile section into smaller sections or individual questions. They do this because so many people fail miserably at filling out the Big-Box Profile section. The smaller sections and questions usually encompass the following 10 topics:

1. **FOR FUN**
2. **MY JOB**
3. **MY ETHNICITY**
4. **MY RELIGION**
5. **MY EDUCATION**
6. **MY FAVORITE HOT SPOTS**
7. **MY FAVORITE THINGS**
8. **WHAT I READ LAST**
9. **MY PETS**
10. **FIRST DATE**

If your dating site uses questions to help you fill out your Profile, the questions fall into the same categories as listed above. You might see questions such as the following:

- Where do you like to go on a 1st date?
- List 1 or 2 of your biggest accomplishments.
- What 5 things can't you live without?
- What cheers you up when you've had a bad day?
- What leisure activity are you most enthused about?

Regardless if your Internet Dating site has one big section for your Profile or lots of little sections or questions, the rules are the same. You need to be interesting, specific, and NOT cookie-cutter and cliché.

Each of the above 10 sections has a separate Chapter in this book, and the Appendix contains many examples of what to do and what not to do in filling out those questions or topics.

HUMONGOUS SECRET: One of the best ways to avoid being cookie-cutter and cliché is to use specifics and details. For example, if you say you like *"traveling"*, she can't see *"traveling"*. She can see **"traveling in Italy and photographing the Parthenon."**

- If you say you're *"nice"*, she can't see *"nice"*. She can see **"I always will remember your Birthday, and Valentine's Day, and Just Because You're You Day…..that's the day you wrote me first. You are going to write me first, aren't you?"** Humor always works when it's done well.

- She can't see *"I like reading."* She can see **"I like anything from the latest fictional bestseller to reading Dr. Seuss to my kids at bedtime."**

- She can't see *"I like music."* She can see **"I like classical music. You know… the Beatles, the Stones, and maybe a little Mozart thrown in for good measure."**

Let's look at some actual Profiles. Some of these Profiles are a cut above the usual bad or okay Profiles which appear over and over again. Men who write Profiles like these think they've written good Profiles because they're better than the bad Profiles. That doesn't make them good. It only makes them less bad.

We call these Profiles "Could Be Much Better" Profiles. The 3 main reasons Profiles "Could Be Much Better" are because they are usually either:

- **Too short**
- **Too boring**
- **Too cookie-cutter and cliché**

COULD BE MUCH BETTER PROFILE:

> I am seeking a woman with a gentle blend of chemistry and personality. Having fun and trust and honesty and romance are important to me. I like a woman who likes to talk about anything and everything. I'm looking to enjoy the company of someone who shares my interests and has interests of her own. Is that you?

Too short?...Yes. Too boring?...Yes. Too cookie-cutter?...Yes. Is it forgettable? Huh?? Is what forgettable??

§ § § § § § § § § § §

Let's try another. In the following Profile, the freeform prose after the intro makes it stand out. Then why is it designated as "Could Be Much Better"?

First, the intro is cookie-cutter and boring and sounds like 2,000,000 other Profiles. Second, freeform prose is too much like poetry. Poetry doesn't appeal to many women. Third, the sexual innuendo of the poem is too much too soon.

MEN... if you overwhelm a woman with your passionate nature before you meet her, odds are you will never meet her. If you're aiming for the bedroom in your Profile, you'll probably end up shooting yourself in the foot. Chances are she won't volunteer to be your nurse.

Lighter Profiles work better than super-serious ones. She's online to find a great date. She's not here to read a manifesto or get a peek at your Prenuptial Agreement.

It's good to be original and stand out and have fun with your Profile... BUT... **while many of the BEST Profiles are super-original and break all of the normal Profile rules, so do most of the WORST ones.** If your originality comes across as more spooky than spellbinding... Buzz! Next contestant please.

<u>COULD BE MUCH BETTER PROFILE</u>:

I am a fit, glass half-full, intelligent and athletic man who enjoys life. I am monogamous and kind. I like to cook and like to eat out. I am emotionally and mentally available. My only vice is chocolate. I am healthy and emotionally available. You are fit and stay in shape with a healthy lifestyle. I will write you poetry and let you know that you are treasured. I'm thinking about you:

Your deep eyes sparkled and embraced me.
I caressed your hair, and you smiled.
I sighed as you kissed my waiting lips.
My body is yearning for yours.
Our souls unite. Bliss.

Time for a cold shower? This is too much too soon for most women. Most women don't like poetry and combining poetry with passion usually flops online. Few women will rush to email you or get your number. Instead, she'll think about unlisting her number.

§§§§§§§§§§§§§

The next Profile is cookie-cutter. Every man on the planet wants what this man wants. Writing a Profile which sounds like everyone else's isn't a good way to find a good match. This man also makes the mistake of *perseverating* in the sexual arena.

Perseverating? Hey, we saw it in a Profile and had to use it. "Perseverating" means "to repeat something insistently or redundantly". HINT: Don't use the word "perseverating" in your Profile unless you use it humorously.

As he perseverates, note the many sexual words he uses: fantasies, passionate, massage, touch, camera-shy, tactile, etc. We've underlined them to call them to your attention. This man also has enough "**I's**" in his Profile for 4 or 5 Profiles. Not good. Women like men who put the focus on her not only on themselves.

HUMONGOUS SECRET: Make sure all the sentences in your Profile do not start with "**I**". You'll sound less egotistical, and you'll sound smarter. For example, rather than saying *"I like to hike,"* say **"Hiking is something I enjoy."** Rather than saying *"I like to read,"* say **"Reading the latest bestseller is always fun."**

Rather than saying *"I like to travel,"* say **"Last year I went to Australia."**

COULD BE MUCH BETTER PROFILE:

I think good communication and trust are important. I like to share anything and everything. I like to listen and I want a woman who listens as well as shares her day with me.

I want someone to be there for the good times as well as the bad times. I want to share our desires, hurts, and our fantasies. I am financially secure, intelligent, and I'm also passionate, affectionate, amorous, fun, and playful.

I love to cuddle and give and get massages. I'm in good shape and exercise most days. I believe in chemistry. I love to travel and love to take pictures when I travel or just around the house. I hope you are not camera-shy.

People would describe me as adventurous, open-minded, tactile, kind, and loyal. I am looking for someone who shares my interests and I would like to share hers, too.

§ § § § § § § § § § §

The next Profile is cookie-cutter once again. It's articulate but forgettable. The "**code word**" in the latter part of his Profile will turn off a lot of women.

If you're one of the many men using a "code word" in your Profile, NIX it. Testing her ability to respond with the code word isn't intelligent unless you make your code test fun and humorous.

COULD BE MUCH BETTER PROFILE:

I'm a glass half-full man and have a good sense of humor. I'm not into trauma-drama, and I have good balance in my life. I like to think of myself as calm and emotionally available.

Things I like: the beach, traveling, biking, hiking, and just sitting around watching a good DVD. I'm a laid back, kind person with a good heart looking for a long-term relationship. Starting with a friend and a traveling companion is a good first step.

Hopefully, you're intelligent, educated, fun, confident, goal-oriented, and ready for a relationship. I like confident women who like nice restaurants and quiet out-of-the-way cafes. I like exploring off the beaten path.

Tell me about you and what 3 things you get the most compliments on. And if you've gotten this far in my profile, thanks for reading.

Respond back with the code word so I know you actually read my entire profile. The code word is Bravo007. Please mention this. If you are just average and not as Matchificent as your profile says you are, no letters of rejection are required.

§ § § § § § § § § § §

The next Profile also has a lot of cookie-cutter jargon. Are you shocked? Most Profiles make the major mistake of being cookie-cutter, cliché, and boring. They sound like everyone else's. Many men write long lists of adjectives describing themselves and what they are looking for in a date/mate.

HUMONGOUS SECRET: People do NOT remember lists of words and adjectives and clichés. They remember STORIES. Stories give her a "*conversation hook*" to email and chat with you.

HUMONGOUS SECRET: Focus on the POSITIVE in your Profile. The following Profile makes another mistake many men make. The man talks about his **negative** qualities. Do NOT bring up your less-attractive qualities. There's plenty of time for her to get to know your foibles. No one is perfect, but hopefully your good stuff outweighs the bad. If it doesn't, work on it.

This next man has plenty of Red Flags and negatives in his Profile. He has an extremely long list of qualifiers which makes him come across as picky and demanding. His big, final no-no is his last paragraph. At the end, he admits he lied about his age.

COULD BE MUCH BETTER PROFILE:

I've been very lucky and have had a great life so far. I have a good family and lots of friends. Now I'm looking for a great relationship.

I am a positive person, very attractive, look younger than I am, am fit, successful, well-traveled, and have a great sense of humor.

On the negative side, I am Type A and tend to be a perfectionist. I like a clean house but am not obsessed with it. I'm sometimes stubborn and impatient, but I'm getting better. There are some things I will compromise on, but others I won't.

I'm looking to meet an attractive, professional woman who is fit or slim. Long hair is a plus. She must be financially secure, like to travel and have a good sense of humor.

She should also be: educated, smart, kind, sensitive, a giver, open-minded, have interests of her own, and share some of my interests including golf and skiing.

She would watch little TV and like to read, especially non-fiction. And last but not least, she can't wait to meet me. Don't want much, do I?

I must admit that I fudged a bit. I'm on the other side of 40, but my pictures are current and people tell me I look years younger than my real age!

§ § § § § § § § § § §

The next Profile is much better than the ones above. It's good, but could easily be great. Removing some of the cookie-cutter jargon and adding specifics and details would have kicked it up to great.

You don't learn the man is Italian until the middle of the profile. He easily could have capitalized on this unique quality early on by saying, *"For fun you should read this with your best Italian accent. I was born in Italy and lived there until I was 21."*

One of the secrets to writing a good Profile is to capitalize on what makes you interesting and unique and special. Doing that also makes you MEMORABLE. In an ocean of millions of people, memorable in a good way… is good!

GOOD BUT COULD BE MUCH BETTER PROFILE:

I am fairly tall for a man (6'2"), athletic, and attractive (if you squint slightly). I'm a good listener and funny and smart and caring and romantic.

At least that's how my friends would describe me (but, hey, that's why they're my friends). Life has been great, and even when I run into the rough spots, I try to find the amusing side of the situation.

My job has taken me to many different countries including my home country of Italy. Meeting people from all walks of life has given me a much bigger view of the world than I otherwise would have been able to achieve.

I believe in soul mates and chemistry (don't most people?). Healthy mind, body, and spirit are essential for me, and I'm looking for the same in a mate. I'm looking for someone who is looking to be together for the entire journey.

I'm not a hopeless romantic, more like a hopeful one. I like kisses for no reason, candlelight dinners for two, impromptu adventures, and, of course, an intimate relationship.

> I want someone I can share my life with and someone who wants to share hers. I'm out-going and mesh well with out-going women.
>
> What do you think? Maybe we should get started and see if we make a good combination of personalities. Even if we don't fall head over heels, I'll bet we have a great time, and you'll get to meet a new friend with an Italian accent.

§ § § § § § § § § § § §

The next Profile is original and fun but too short. Some women may find the answers he gives to the questions he poses a bit too edgy, irreverent, and sarcastic.

A common error men make in Profiles is they think they are funny but come across as too sarcastic. If you've written a Profile that isn't getting you the kind of feedback you want, don't hesitate to "tweak" it. Rewriting this Profile with "softer" funny answers (see below for the rewrite) would attract a wider range of women and most likely the kind of women he's hoping to attract.

GOOD BUT COULD BE MUCH BETTER PROFILE:

> I know you've got your list of questions, so I'd like to answer some of them before we meet such as:
> 1) Will he mind if I'm not a morning person?
> 2) Does he have a lot of baggage?
> 3) Is he romantic and sexy?
> 4) Is he intelligent?
> 5) Is he fit and athletic?
> 6) Is he funny?

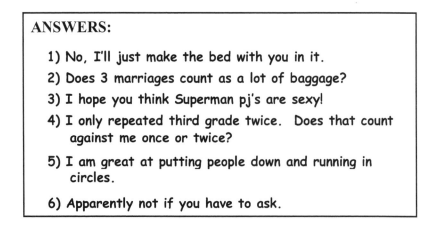

ANSWERS:

1) No, I'll just make the bed with you in it.
2) Does 3 marriages count as a lot of baggage?
3) I hope you think Superman pj's are sexy!
4) I only repeated third grade twice. Does that count against me once or twice?
5) I am great at putting people down and running in circles.
6) Apparently not if you have to ask.

If he's not getting the kind of responses he likes, here are some NEW answers he could try which are less edgy and less sarcastic:

ALTERNATIVE ANSWERS:

1) No, I like to sleep and cuddle in the mornings, too.

2) Only a small Coach wallet.

3) You'll have to kiss me to find out.

4) Yes, I'm very smart. I will always remember your birthday, Valentine's Day, Xmas and will spend MORE on your presents than I spend on mine.

5) If I'm running in circles, it's usually at the gym.

6) Email me and let me know how I did!

§ § § § § § § § § § §

Those last 2 Profiles were much better than most. If you already have a Profile, and it has some good parts, keep those and tweak the rest. If it's really lousy, trash it, and start again. The sooner you figure out you've fallen behind, the sooner you'll be able to catch up!

WRITING A GOOD PROFILE

PART TWO: 7 Recipes for Success

Good Profiles are like good sex. Too short is not good. Longer is better than too short. But too long is too much.

If you remember the above **HUMONGOUS SECRET**, you'll hit a home run. Take time to write a Profile that is "just right" in length. Too short and you're out of the game. Too long and she's rolling her eyes and thinking, *"When is this ever gonna end?"*

Writing a good Profile isn't as much fun as having sex. It's not as much fun as going out on a date. However... writing the Profile will get you the date. As for the sex... you're on your own.

If you read the Foreword to this book, you already know the *easiest* way to write your Profile... you use the examples in this book. The Foreword has a **Super-Quick Recipe** for coming up with a good Profile. You pick and choose examples from the various Chapters and the APPENDIX to "fit you".

If you want an even better Profile, keep reading. There are 7 Man-Friendly Recipes to help you write a good Profile. If you're a Macho Man, call these recipes 'Formulas'. With a little thinking and tweaking, you can write a great Profile.

The first Formula is the ***"Ask-a-Question Profile"*** (aka ***"Fill-in-the-Blank Profile")***. It's almost faster than baking a frozen pizza. Other formulas include a *"TOP 10 List Profile"* and a *"Make Your Own Pizza from Scratch Profile"*. The Pizza Profile is an easy recipe once you learn the "trick" to doing it.

But how do you get your Profile to sound intelligent or humorous or classy? Easy! There are examples to use as inspiration or to copy. A word about "copying". Copying works, but it's best to *personalize* it to you. Some people copy good sections from this book. Then they piece it together to make a Profile. That will work, but only if the things you copy are truly "you" or if you tweak them and personalize them to you.

You can always pay someone to write your Profile. One dating site charges $39 to write your Profile for you. That gets a little pricey if you want to change your Profile now and again. If you pay someone to write your Profile for you, you're going to have to gather your personal information and details. Without that, your Profile will look like all the other Cookie-Cutter-Boring-Gingerbread Men out there. Once you gather your info, you're halfway to writing your own great Profile so you might as well give it a go.

If you recall the literary hero Cyrano de Bergerac, you'll immediately know why you want to create your own Profile. To refresh your memory, Cyrano is the romantic hero with the big nose. Cyrano and his friend Christian love Roxanne. Cyrano helps his friend out, writes love letters for him to Roxanne, and signs Christian's name. Roxanne falls for Christian based on the letters he wrote her. There's only 1 thing, Cyrano wrote the letters.

Your lady doesn't want to be the current version of Roxanne. She wants to date the person behind the written Profile, and you want to make sure that person is you. Even if you pay someone to write your Profile for you, use some of the suggestions below and add your own touch to make it yours. Your next date might say, *"I loved your Profile. Did you write it yourself?"* You want to be able to say, *"YES, I did."*

There are many other ways to write Profiles other than the 7 Formulas in this book. There's the Interview Formula where you write questions and interview yourself. That's similar to the Ask-a-Question/Fill-in-the-Blank format but the question and answer parts are longer.

There's the Blog Format where your Profile is a weekly or monthly blog about you. Those are hard to write unless you have a very interesting life. If you have a "normal" life, witty writing can make it shine (think Seinfeld).

There's the Never-Been-Done-Before Profile. That's a Profile which breaks most of the conventional rules of good Profiles. Examples of Never-Been-Done-Before Profiles are 'Genre Profiles'. Pick a theme like King Arthur or the Wild West or Pirates of the Caribbean or Star Wars. Write your Profile from the perspective of being in that past or future time period.

One warning about Never-Been-Done-Before Profiles. The worst Profiles are usually the Never-Been-Done-Before kind.

How do you know if yours is EXCEPTIONALLY GOOD or Exceptionally Bad? If it's good, it's working and attracting the women you want to attract. If it's bad, it ain't workin, hun.

Profiles are works in progress. The one you post today might be great and attract the kind of woman you want to attract. On the other hand, if you find out it's not working exactly as you thought it might, **tweak it,** and make some minor or even major changes.

LITTLE HUMONGOUS SECRET: Keep a word processing file of your Profile. It helps you keep track of what you wrote. You may have a few Profiles you alternate between. You may find a previous version or part of a previous version worked better for you. You can cut and paste your Profile directly from your word processing file to the online Profile box. You'll be able to spell check it before you post it. Nice to know!

The 7 MAN-FRIENDLY FORMULAS are:

1) **ASK-A-QUESTION (Fill-in-the-Blank)**
2) **TOP 10 LIST**
3) **DEAL MAKERS / DEAL BREAKERS**
4) **MAKE YOUR OWN PIZZA**
5) **RIDDLE-ME-THIS**
6) **HUMOROUS**
7) **QUOTE SOMEBODY FAMOUS**

Each of the above Formulas is explained in detail in the next chapters.

SECRET RECIPE #1:

ASK-A-QUESTION PROFILE

Judge a man by his questions rather than his answers.

The Ask-A-Question Profile lets you pick the questions you want to answer. Pick the questions *which make you look good.* Skip the ones that don't. That's the best way to ace a test! This is also known as the Fill-in-the-Blank Profile because you need to include ANSWERS after your questions.

This is a super-easy Profile to write. Start with a short, introductory paragraph. That's a longer version of the Good Opening lines we talked about earlier. If you are drawing a blank, look at the samples in the chapter on Good Opening lines.

If you've had a long day and are too tired to flip back to that chapter, kick back and relax and imitate the ones below. They are longer versions of a Good Opening line. The additional sentences expand on the thought of the Opening Line by being SPECIFIC.

Check out the Chapters on FUN, JOB, EDUCATION, and FAVORITE PLACES for more examples which could be added on after the Opening Line. The Appendix has lots more, too. Here are some examples of good beginnings:

- <u>GOOD OPENING:</u> **Hi there! Thanks for stopping by my little corner of cyberspace. I'm looking for friendship first and hopefully a friendship that will develop into something more. I'd like you to know more about me, so I've included this compatibility questionnaire.**

- <u>GOOD OPENING:</u> **WOW! There you are....you finally found me! I don't just want an "okay" match, I want a really terrific match. I bet you do, too. We haven't met, and here's the amazing news....there are already tests! Tests?? Yes, I've taken the test. I've posted it below to help you get to know me better. Let me know if I pass muster.**

- <u>GOOD OPENING:</u> **Hello from Minnesota where all the women are attractive and intelligent, the men are smart and handsome, and all the children are above average. Welcome to my profile and thanks for wanting to learn more about me. After reading my profile, if you're interested in getting to know me better, it's best to send me a wink or an email. I'm still working on reading minds, but the only one I've mastered reading so far is my own.**

- <u>GOOD OPENING:</u> **YOU WIN! YOU WIN!! Our compatibility criteria must have lined up nicely for you to have landed here. This profile isn't available to the average lady. You have been specially selected to participate in the beta-test of the latest and greatest version of Find-a-Great-Date.**

- <u>GOOD OPENING:</u> **Hi from Dave....welcome to my world. I figured you wanted to know more about me, so I picked 10 questions I'm almost certain you want to know the answers to. And after reading my questions, if you want to know more.....for a limited time only, I will answer any question from you. Yes, I am as brave as I look. You need to know**

you get double extra points or a free pizza if you make it an easy question. Okay, let's get started…

After your intro paragraph, choose 10 to 20 questions below to include in your Profile. A combination of EASY questions and the HARDER ones works best. Ask the question, and fill in the blank after the question with your answer. More easy and hard questions as well as good opening paragraphs are in the APPENDIX.

<u>EASY QUESTIONS</u>

- Favorite movies or TV shows?
- Favorite books/authors?
- What's your favorite magazine?
- Favorite comedians?
- Favorite musical artists?
- Favorite Actors or Actresses?
- Favorite items of clothing?
- Item of clothing you wouldn't be caught dead in?
- 3 Websites you visit frequently?
- I own too many items from:
- What's the last gift you bought for yourself?
- What do you do for fun?
- Where do you like to eat out?
- What Myers-Briggs Personality type are you?
- What do you like to do on a day off?
- During a typical week, what physical activities do you do?
- What interests do you hope a partner would share with you?
- What's your idea of a romantic evening with someone you've just met?

HARDER QUESTIONS:

- If you won $10,000 in the Lottery and weren't allowed to invest or save it, what would you spend it on?

- If you had a year off with pay, what would you do?

- The blizzard hit, and you're stuck at home for 2 days. What would you do?

- What do your best friends know about you that casual acquaintances don't?

- Name 2 or 3 things that you're really good at:

- Name 2 or 3 things you're really lousy at: (Don't be negative… make it humorous.)

- What's your best memory and why?

- What would you do if you got next Friday off with pay?

- If you had 3 wishes, what would they be?

- The 1 question I'd most like a date to ask me is:

- The 1 question I'd most like to ask my date is:

- If your house was on fire, what 3 inanimate things would you save first?

- What 5 things can't you live without?

- What 2 or 3 accomplishments are you most proud of in your life?

- What perks you up when you've had a bad day?

- What is the one dream or goal you'd like to come true?

- What is one dream or goal that did come true?

- How do you measure being a successful parent?

- What hobby or leisure activity are you most enthused about?

- 5 to 10 words that would best describe my personality are:

- 5 to 10 words that would describe who I'm looking for:

- If you could spend a day with any 2 famous people who are alive today, who would you pick and why?

- Other than your parents, who has influenced you the most in your life and how?

- What 2 or 3 things are the most valuable lessons your parents taught you?

- What 2 or 3 things are the most valuable lessons your kids (or friends, etc.) have taught you?

- My idea of a great second date is:

Last but not least, at the end of your questions, write a good "Ending" and "Closing Paragraph". Here are a few examples, but check out the entire chapter on good Endings and the APPENDIX for many more examples.

- GOOD ENDING: **Play this backwards on your computer. I think it says, "Email him now." Let me know.**

- GOOD ENDING: **Thanks for reading. Hope you got to know me better, and hope you found some things of interest. I confess I'm not psychic and not a mind-reader, so if you think we might "click", a wink or email will work best.**

- GOOD ENDING: **Are we having fun yet? If so, wink or email! I didn't used to like winks, but I'll take a wink as a sign of flattery that you're interested and want me to read your profile!**

- GOOD ENDING: **How did I do? Did I pass? Are you ready to send me your own questions? I'd enjoy hearing more about you if you think we might click!**

- GOOD ENDING: **Okay, is your world shaking? Or was that a mild California earthquake? Either way, did I merit a smile or two? Hope so, and hope you'll let me know if I did.**

- <u>GOOD ENDING:</u>   Wow….this is amazing. One click of your mouse and our lives could change for the better. On your mark, get set…..GO!

- <u>GOOD ENDING:</u> I've been in like, in love and know the difference.   I am looking for my last and best relationship. If you are, too, let's email, chat, or meet. You choose.

- <u>GOOD ENDING:</u> What is Chemistry? I think it's the ability to turn on the Mind. Not just for a date but for a lifetime. If that's what you think, I'd love to hear from you. Email or email. Pick one!

- <u>GOOD ENDING:</u>   I'm younger than my age would indicate.   That's probably because I was born in the afternoon. I am not perfect, but I still believe there can be a perfect match. We just have to find each other!   If you're out there, emails work wonders.

- <u>GOOD ENDING:</u> So tell me, what's going on in your world?   And are you daring enough to send me your own test questions? Operators are standing by!

SECRET RECIPE #2:

TOP 10 LIST PROFILE

The Top 10 Reason for writing a Top 10 List is because they work, and they can be amazing. Oh wait, that's 2 reasons! Top Tens stand out because few people use them. Those who do use them, often don't use them well. Lists typically fail because they're too boring or too cliché or too sarcastic. Hmm…those are the exact same reasons most Profiles fail.

The good Top 10 List is timeless. It worked yesterday, it works today, and it will work tomorrow. It works far better than people who say *"I'm funny"* or *"I make my friends laugh all the time."* A ton of men say that in their Profiles. Usually there is little to nothing in their Profile which is funny or humorous.

If you have a good sense of humor, show it off. Put together your own Top 10 List. Women love "humor" as much or more than the "awwww" moments in Profiles.

If you're the more serious type, don't automatically discount writing a Top 10 List. Many serious men have a dry-humor edginess. Write a Top 10 List that is *serious*. Then go back and lighten it up with some of your slightly irreverent humor.

A touch of dry humor goes a long way. Not all of your Top 10 items need to be funny, but at least a few should be. Check out some of David Letterman's Top 10 Lists to get your brain cells pumping or do an Internet search for "Top 10 Lists". You'll find many entries to tickle your imagination. Below are suggestions for topics for your Top 10 Lists. Check out the APPENDIX where more examples are waiting.

TOP 10 LISTS:

- WHY YOU SHOULD MEET ME
- WHY YOU SHOULD DATE ME
- WHY YOU SHOULDN'T DATE ME
- 10 THINGS I CAN TEACH YOU
- 10 THINGS YOU COULD TEACH ME
- 10 PLACES I WOULD HATE TO GO ON A DATE
- 10 PLACES I WOULD LIKE TO TAKE YOU ON A DATE
- 10 MOST IMPORTANT THINGS I'VE LEARNED
- 10 MOST WORTHLESS THINGS I'VE LEARNED
- MY TOP 10 PET PEEVES
- 10 WAYS TO GET ME TO SAY YES TO THE 1st DATE
- 10 WAYS I'LL USE TO GET YOU TO SAY YES TO THE 1st DATE
- 10 BEST PICKUP LINES OF ALL TIME THAT I'VE NEVER EVER USED

Start your TOP 10 Profile with an intro paragraph if you so choose. Always end your Top 10 List with a good Ending. Check out the Chapter on Endings and the APPENDIX. Here's an example of a Top 10 List which concludes with a good ending:

THE TOP TEN REASONS to MEET ME

10. Halloween is my favorite holiday, and I do have to wear a mask 'cause in normal life I come pretty close to putting Brad Pitt to shame. Or maybe that's Bart Simpson?? I keep getting those 2 guys confused.

9. I am 5'11" tall, but look at least 6' on my tall days. I can get things from the top cabinets without a ladder.

8. I sing on key and won't embarrass you at family get-togethers.

7. I didn't vote for Bush in either election.

6. My dog likes me and will vouch for my good character.

5. I would be your very best friend in every way.

4. I will always remember your birthday, and I promise I won't get you a matching electric sander or tickets to the Giants game. Maybe a cordless drill and hockey tickets?

3. I also remember half-birthdays and just-because-I-care-about-you days.

2. I am possibly the man of your dreams (but only if you like cute, smart men).

1. I will make you smile every time you see me!!

If you don't smile on our 1st date, I'll pay for the whole date. Oh wait, I was gonna do that anyways. I am fun and loving as well as fun-loving. I value intellectual and emotional and physical health.

> **If you do, too, and are looking for that "right man", I am looking for you. I am looking for that one of a kind connection that begins with friendship and grows into more. I like to email first and get to know each other, but there's no substitute for meeting and finding out.**
>
> **If you've found my profile before I've found yours, you absolutely must be kind and email me to let me know you're out there. Would "now" be too soon?**

§ § § § § § § § § § § §

Top 10 List Profiles look like "Lists". Some women like the look of Lists because they're visually easier to read. Other women prefer prose (paragraphs) to Lists. Many women have seen so many lousy Lists, they hate Lists. Others have seen so many lousy prose Profiles, they welcome a good List.

Personal preference varies, but one thing is certain... if it's well written, she'll love it. If it's good or great, you'll get the date!

SECRET RECIPE #3:

DEAL MAKERS & DEAL BREAKERS

PROFILE

The last woman in the country who is 36-24-36, who has a face like an angel, who is a devil in the bedroom, who has season tickets to the NBA and NFL games, and who just won the Powerball Lottery got married last week. Guess you'll have to revise your list of Deal Makers and Deal Breakers.

Deal Makers and Breakers is a fun Profile to write. For the best results, throw in some semi-serious Deal Makers and Deal Breakers with the humorous ones.

As usual, start your Profile with a good Opening Line and intro paragraph like we used in the Ask-a-Question Profile. Conclude your Profile with a short Ending like we used in Ask-a-Question and the Top 10 List Profile. The chapters on "Opening Lines" and "Endings" as well as the APPENDIX are filled with examples so you can begin and end your Profile on a high note.

Put your Deal Makers and Deal Breakers in separate paragraphs in your Profile. Label them so she knows which are Turn-Ons and which are Turn-Offs. There's not much worse than attracting your worst nightmare and the absolute opposite of who you want to date.

Here are some Deal Makers and Deal Breakers for you to choose from. Use them to inspire you to create your own. The earlier chapter on using good Deal Makers/Deal Breakers has many more suggestions as does the APPENDIX. Choose about 8-10 of each to include in your Profile.

DEAL MAKERS and DEAL BREAKERS:

- **Your favorite place to have coffee is Starbucks....in Maui.**

- **Your favorite color is my favorite color (now you have to email me to see if you're right).**

- **You have to have a drink to calm your nerves before you head to your AA meeting.**

- **You like confident men who email rather than wink!**

- **You can find Chicago on a map.**

- **You can find Afghanistan on a map.**

- **You know the difference between two, too, and to.**

- **You think Bush was a good President.**

- **You think Bush was never present as President.**

- **You love to play tennis (golf, ski, swim, hike, etc.).**

- **You can kick my butt on the ski slopes (tennis, etc.).**

- **You are on a first name basis in 2 or more bars.**

- **You have Credit Counseling as #1 on your speed dial.**

- You think Dom Perignon is a Mafia leader.

- Your friends come to you for bankruptcy advice due to your vast experience.

- You are cuter than I am.

Here's what a Profile of Deal Makers and Deal Breakers might look like. It can easily be shortened or lengthened by changing the amount of Deal Maker/Breaker criteria.

GOOD SAMPLE PROFILE (DEAL MAKERS/BREAKERS):

YOU WIN!! The following Profile is not available to the average woman. YOU have been specially selected to participate in this NEW Beta-Test feature.

T-DOTS are the new Turn-On and Turn-Off criteria and were designed for the discriminating and choosy woman.

T-Dots are more accurate than the GREEN Dots of Match.com®. You will know in a few minutes if you REALLY click with this man. His photos are current, age is accurate, and he has a sense of humor (but you already figured that out... didn't you?).

TURN-ONS: Score a (+1) for every TURN-ON you possess:

**Smart and well-educated

**Playful or dry sense of humor (i.e., doesn't act 12 more than once a month)

**Affectionate, likes to kiss, cuddle, and you know...

**Knows that DJI isn't a Disc Jockey organization

**Has at least 3 things in her cooking repertoire

**2 of the 3 aren't coffee and toast

**Remembers bdays, Xmas, and "just because I care about you" days

**Knows what's going on in the world

***PLEASE ADD UP YOUR SCORE. Now for the 2nd part... Score (-1) for every Turn-OFF you possess.

**Bad teeth (or has more toes than teeth)

**Has Credit Help line as #1 on speed dial

**On a first name basis in 2 or more bars

**Prefers sleeping bags to comfy beds

**If you have kids, you have to get their permission to date on a school night.

**Last thing read was a street sign

**Talks more to your cat, motorcycle, or mom than to the man in your life

**Thinks mud wrestling qualifies as live theater

Okay... add up your score! Are we having fun yet? How do the 2 scores compare? LOTS of Turn-ONS? Only a few Turn-OFFS?

WOW!! If you're as Matchificent as your profile says you are, hurry... send this man an email and tell him how lucky he would be to date you! :D

SECRET RECIPE #4:

MAKE YOUR OWN PIZZA

FROM SCRATCH PROFILE

Waiter: Ladies, would you like your pizza cut into 8 or 12 slices?

Blonde: Oh, 8 please. We couldn't eat 12 slices.

No matter if your Pizza has 8 slices or 12, you know a good Pizza when you bite into it. Profiles are like Pizzas. When you read a good Profile, you know it.

Just like a good Pizza, they're yummy! Usually they're descriptive, and you get a good sense of who the woman is.

In an earlier chapter, you read some Profiles which could be better. In some of those Profiles, they forgot the cheese. Some forgot the pepperoni or sausage or veggies. Worse yet, some added heaping handfuls of jalapeños peppers and armfuls of anchovies.

All good PIZZA PROFILES follow this easy 1-2-3 Recipe:

1) INCLUDE SECRET INGREDIENTS

2) PAINT A PICTURE SHE CAN VISUALIZE

3) INVITE THE WOMAN TO CONTACT YOU

Even if you're a lousy cook and need detailed instructions to boil a 4-minute egg, you'll be able to follow this Pizza recipe and create your own intriguing Pizza Profile.

If you can write "funny", that's a bonus, but **sincere and honest work.** Humor works, but don't be so sarcastic that you turn her off. If you show too much "bite", she may not "write".

It takes a little bit of work to write a good, custom Pizza Profile. The GOOD NEWS is if you're not up to writing a Pizza Profile from scratch, here's the quick but delicious Frozen Pizza version.

Pick ONE word. Told ya you could do it! In the following Custom Profile, the word chosen was "Cuddling". It could have been Chemistry or Candlelight or hundreds of other 'debatable' words. The 'debate' in the following Profile could take place anywhere: at work, out to eat with a friend, in an online Forum.

GOOD SAMPLE PROFILE (QUICK PIZZA PROFILE):

> **Hi! Hope you'll give me your .02 and help settle a debate that's going on in the Profile Review Forum. I need a woman's point of view.**
>
> **There's a heated debate going on about the "C" word in Profiles. No, not the "Commitment" word, the OTHER "C" word… "Cuddling".**
>
> **I'm interested in your opinion. The young guys under 40 are saying that a man should NEVER put something like this in their profile (or we risk getting our MAN-card revoked):**

"I enjoy watching most kinds of movies (Lord of the Rings, Twilight, Shrek, JFK) and holding hands and cuddling on the sofa is great."

One well-respected female reviewer says that guys my age can get away with the "C" word (cuddling) in their profile provided it's done in good taste. She says most ladies like to know we older guys still like some spice in our life.

So, what do you think? Should I avoid the "C" word, or is it Okay to use it?

TEXT your vote via email to MichiganMan5000. Operators are standing by.
    Text 1 for YES (okay to use the C word).
    Text 2 for NO (not okay to use the C word).
    Text 3 for "I'm not sure….Let's chat about it over coffee or a drink."

Oh…and here's a bit more about me just in case you're thinking about texting 3…
(Now write a short paragraph or 2 about you. If you need some examples, check out the Chapters on Fun, Job, First Date, etc. as well as the APPENDICES.)

Your **Secret Ingredient** in this case was the "C" word. You used a Secret Ingredient, painted a picture she could visualize, and humorously asked her to email you.

Here's a second example of a delicious Pizza. This time the word used was "**Chemistry**".

GOOD SAMPLE PROFILE (QUICK PIZZA PROFILE):

Chemistry Shmemistry…

Hi! Glad you stopped by. I need a lady's opinion. My friends and I were having a debate after the Super Bowl. A woman's point of view is badly needed.

We were sitting in a restaurant and recounting all the great action, and one of the older guys brought up the "C" word. Not the "Commitment" word, the OTHER "C" word…"Chemistry". We were talking about football team chemistry, but one thing led to another, and we started talking about women. Who would have thought!

He said real men should never ever use the word Chemistry in their online profiles. He's threatening to revoke my Man-card if I use it. Good thing I'm younger and can run faster than he can!

His girlfriend disagreed and said that men can use the Chemistry word… but only if our name is Fermi or Nobel or Curie. She says women can get away with using it, but men…not so much.

What do you think? Is it okay if I use the C word in this Profile?

TEXT your vote via email to LouisianaCPA.
Operators are standing by.

Text 1 for YES (okay to use the C word).

Text 2 for NO (not okay to use the C word).

Text 3 for "I'm not sure….Let's chat about it over coffee or a drink."

(Now write a short paragraph or 2 about you. If you need some examples, check out the Chapters on Fun, Job, First Date, etc. as well as the APPENDICES.)

Pretty slick! Use your imagination to come up with your own Secret Ingredient Word. Good Profiles always have at least one "Secret Ingredient". In Pizza language, what would a cheese pizza be without the cheese? What would a Pepperoni Pizza be without the Pepperoni?

Cookie-cutter and cliché Profiles don't have a secret ingredient. Cookie-cutter Profiles all sound and taste the same. They all sound alike because they do not focus on the one or more ingredients which make the man special. Don't make that mistake. Stand out from the crowd by focusing on one or more key aspects of you.

Everyone has secret ingredients. These are your **WOW factors.** Your wow factors may be: *your humor; your job; your hobby; your intelligence; your kindness. It may be your athleticism; it may be you have the time and resources to travel; it may be the fact you're new to the city; it may be you know your city inside out. It may be you're a great gardener; it may be you're an activist; it may be you're a really nice person.*

You have lots of secret ingredients once you start to think about it. Ask yourself... What about you appeals to women the most? Most men will have a number of things on their list.

If you can't think of anything, you've got some work to do. Find a way to make yourself more appealing to women. How do you do that? Take an interesting class, volunteer, go back to school, get a job, get a better job, take up a new hobby. All those things make you more datable.

Lots of men are very datable but try to list everything that makes them datable. Don't do that. Do the opposite. Pick 1 or 2 or 3 things that make you datable. And be specific!

HUMONGOUS SECRET: BE SPECIFIC and use details so she can visualize what you're talking about. Specifics tell "stories". Stories are interesting and memorable. <u>People remember STORIES. People don't remember a list of words.</u>

For example, "athletic" is forgettable. A story of you swimming with porpoises is memorable. A story of you skiing last winter in Vail is memorable. A story of you snorkeling in Maui or running the Boston Marathon is memorable.

"Success in business" is very commendable but boring. A story of your latest success at work is memorable. A story of you starting your own company is memorable. A story of you doing a business deal in NYC or Japan is memorable.

"Good dancer" is boring. A story of you trying to win a salsa dancing contest is memorable. A story of you doing the moonwalk or a triple, Michael Jackson spin is memorable.

Many men make the mistake of trying to fit their whole life story into their Profile. Your goal in your Profile is NOT to tell every single thing about you. Your goal is to tell the woman enough so she wants to get to know more about you. Like good pizza, good Profiles make you want another slice.

If you want to make a Pizza from scratch, it's worth doing. This isn't as fast as the Frozen Pizza. It takes about as long as it takes to order a Pizza, and have them deliver it… and eat it and watch the Super Bowl Game.

Like most good things in life, you get out of it what you put into it. If you're not having the success online that you'd like, the woman of your dreams is probably worth the time of one football game and a pizza delivery.

A real pizza is made up of 3 groups of ingredients: the crust, the sauce, the toppings. Your *Pizza Profile* has the same 3 groups of ingredients in the Secret Formula. They are all Free, and you don't have to go to the grocery store at midnight to find them.

INGREDIENT GROUP 1: THE CRUST

Choose the TOP 5 to 10 POSITIVE words or short phrases you would use to describe YOU. Consider this first group as your Pizza Crust. Here are some suggestions: **funny, intelligent, athletic, affectionate, successful, hardworking, well-traveled, golfer, good skier, easy-going, energetic, calm, outgoing, friendly, creative, nice, sensitive, fun, Type A, not Type A, financially responsible, adventurous, looking for long-term, independent, introspective, conversationalist, inquisitive, healthy, financially secure, generous, nurturing, unconventional, kind, a Mr. Fix-It guy, doctor, lawyer, Indian chief, giving, thoughtful, not a geek, is a geek, accomplished, romantic, strong hands, multi-cultural, witty, etc.**

INGREDIENT GROUP 2: THE SAUCE

Choose the TOP 5 to 10 POSITIVE words you would use to describe HER (the woman you want to date). Here are some suggestions: **friendly, caring, romantic, smart, fit, gentle, good listener, outgoing, affectionate, good sense of humor, organized, likes to dance, likes to travel, feminine, tomboy, zest for life, compassionate, professional, retired, good conversationalist, best friend, lover, life partner, patient, enjoys her work, loving, sensitive, confident, looking for long-term, insightful, playful, active, health conscious, family-oriented, giving, considerate, compassionate, empathetic, enjoys intimacy, etc.**

We've got the ingredients for the pizza crust and the sauce. Now comes the most important part... that's the toppings or the WOW ingredients.

INGREDIENT GROUP 3: THE TOPPINGS

Your toppings should be the TOP 3 THINGS that make you unique and special and interesting. Ask yourself what 3 things are the MOST interesting and attractive about you?

Ideally one should be about work or retirement (or school if you're still in school). Women want to know you're responsible and managing for the future.

The second should be about one of your favorite activities or hobbies. A good 3rd topping would be something about who you are "emotionally". A good way to convey that is to describe your idea of a romantic dinner or evening.

Some of the 3 things that make you unique and special and *interesting* might include: **You started your own business, you just got a promotion at work, you are a skier and know all the best places to ski in Colorado, you're a newbie skier, you can sing on key, you're taking art lessons, you work on Main Street as a teacher, administrator, salesperson for high-tech gadgets, you are a fabulous cook, you're taking lessons to learn to cook, you follow the stock market, you're a soccer coach, you grow organic vegetables, you have a gentle quarter horse named Horse, you're an engineer, you're a CPA, you're a school counselor, you're going for an advanced degree, you do your own taxes and usually get a refund, you still work on Wall Street, you work for the government in D.C., you finish the crossword puzzle most days, you're looking for someone to help finish the darn crossword puzzle, you experiment with recipes like pizza with portabella mushrooms and pepperoni......**

Now it's time to combine all your secret ingredients. The keyword is combine. You're going to combine your ingredients and tell her an interesting story or two about you. You made a list of words so you could convey the *ESSENCE* of those words and concepts in your story.

Let's say the following words are in your list of words about you: *humorous, athletic, financially sound, giving, nice.* Do not list those words. Instead, tell a STORY that illustrates those words. If you need some help, channel your inner child, ask your kid for help, or keep reading. Here's an example how to do it using the underlined words above:

> **Last winter I took a week off and rented a condo in Vail and went skiing and snowboarding. I've skied for years, but this was my first time on a snowboard.** (NOTE: This sentence shows you're athletic and have financial resources.)
>
> **If you've never been there, I know you'd love it. And if you don't ski, I'm a great teacher.** (NOTE: These sentences show you're giving.)
>
> **If it's your first time, I promise not to laugh. Well...maybe with you, but not at you.** (NOTE: These show you have a sense of humor and are genuinely nice.)

Humor, athleticism, giving, nice, financially sound were all conveyed _without_ listing those words! Amazing! If you like, you can elaborate on each of the sentences above to let her see where you went on those skis or snowboard, what you saw, if it was snowing and blowing or was the sun shining? Where did you stay? What did you do?

HUMONGOUS SECRET: Remember these 3 words, and you'll be GOLDEN: **_Paint the picture!_** Use your words to let her see you. Women are visual, too. *Getting all the senses involved is a winner.* Let her see the picture, smell the mountain air, taste the pizza!

BIG SECRET: **Giant, long paragraphs and a Wall-Of-Words are hard to read.** Many men forget to put paragraphs in their Profile. Their Profile looks like a gigantic, difficult essay. Women avoid giant essays and walls-of-words especially when it's late at night and they've been working all day. The Enter Key is your friend. Use it to put blank lines between your paragraphs.

Women also avoid reading Profiles which are difficult to read. If your dating site allows you to set the colors of the text and the background, choose readable and cheery colors.

Let's choose another group of words which might be in your list: *spontaneous, likes to share, likes to travel, financially secure, wine tasting, organized, family-oriented, independent.*

Here's how to put them in a story:

> **It's winter now, but I'm looking forward to summer. Last year I took my kids hiking in the Grand Canyon. It was exhilarating. This year I plan to travel to wine country in Napa Valley.** (NOTE: This sentence shows family-oriented, financial resources, wine tasting, likes to travel.)
>
> **I've done this in years past by myself, but it would be so much more fun to do it with you.** (NOTE: This sentence shows likes to share, independent.)
>
> **We can be spontaneous and wing it, or get together and start planning now.** (NOTE: This sentence shows spontaneity and organization.)

Starting to get the idea? Flesh out your story with more details, and she'll feel she was right there with you. You're creating a story she can remember rather than a list of forgettable, cookie-cutter words.

It's easy once you understand the trick: **The trick is to tell a visual story.** <u>Your stories</u> convey the words you chose. In other words, you don't tell her you're funny. You tell a funny story. Instead of saying you're successful or giving, you tell a story that shows your success or giving nature.

<u>HUMONGOUS SECRET:</u> If you spend time writing your Profile, she'll notice. You'll get lots of extra points. Be ready to suggest your favorite Pizzeria for the first date.

If you don't spend time on your Profile, she'll notice. You'll LOSE points. When women see you haven't made an effort with your photos or Profile, she thinks *"Hmm.....if this is the kind of effort he puts into trying to get a date, I can imagine what he'll be like on that date."*

The second part of the Pizza Profile works in the exact same way. The only difference is you use the words you chose for what kind of match/date/mate you are looking for. You create a story the same way you did when you used the words that described you.

You do the same thing with your 3 Secret Ingredients. Tell a story which illustrates your 3 unique qualities. Let's take 3 unique qualities and see what we can come up with: *teacher, loves to travel, financially secure.*

> **Do you like to travel and see wonderful buildings like the Empire State Building, the Tower of London, and the Leaning Tower of Pisa?**
>
> **I do, too, and every summer I take a trip to see unique buildings. I'm a teacher of history, and buildings are a great way to bring history to life.**

ZOWIE! It isn't hard once you've picked out the words and concepts you want to incorporate. Play with the recipe. Have fun with it. The Internet Dating Police won't issue you a ticket for being clever and innovative. You don't have to use all your words and all hers. You can use 7 and 5 and 1. Or 4 and 3 and 2. You can use them all at the same time instead of in 3 separate groups.

You are the mastermind and Head Chef. Your goal is to avoid creating a cookie-cutter Profile and create a memorable one. Create a pleasant and unique impression that lets her know who you are, what you have to offer, and what you're looking for in a match.

HUMONGOUS SECRET: Your story will get extra high marks if it tells what you are bringing to the relationship. Sound the SMOKE DETECTOR please! If you want to generate sparks, your Profile will tell her *what you bring to the relationship.*

- *GOOD PROFILES say more than "I want, I want."*
- **GOOD PROFILES say "I BRING, I BRING."**

Don't forget to spell check and proof your Profile. Add a great ending (which we'll cover in a little bit), and post it with confidence.

Profiles are not set in stone. Whatever you post at 9:00 p.m. you can change at 9:01. If you see a typo or you come up with a better way to phrase something, not to worry. The Internet is open 24 hours a day, including holidays.

SECRET RECIPE #5:

RIDDLE-ME-THIS PROFILE

How can you tell if a lawyer is well hung?

We'll answer that riddle in a minute. But first a question: Do you think the Riddle-Me-This Profile begins with a riddle? Of course it does.

We began this chapter by asking you a riddle. You want to know the answer to the riddle. You want to know if you got the answer right or wrong. That's human nature. People like riddles and mysteries. They like answers to them even more.

Create an interesting riddle or question **_for her_**. She'll want to read on to learn the answer. After your riddle/question, use the technique from the regular Pizza Profile.

The following Riddle-Me-This Profile was constructed by using the 3 groups of Ingredients from the Pizza Profile. The man used 5-10 words about himself, 5-10 about the woman he wants to meet, and 3 unique things about him. He wrote "stories" and preceded many of his stories with questions.

The riddles/questions are underlined so you can't miss them. The riddles/questions make this Profile "conversational". They pull the reader in and engage her attention.

His 5-10 words about himself were: *smart, skier, wine, hike, travel, active, wants long-term relationship, manager, humor.*

His 5-10 words about her were: *active, hike, ski, travel, interest in wine, companionship, good conversationalist.*

His 3 special and unique qualities were: *cooking, humor, likes to share.*

GOOD SAMPLE PROFILE (RIDDLE-ME-THIS):

<u>Can you guess where I went on vacation last year? Here's a hint... Do you like touring wine country? Traveling to foreign countries?</u> If that sounds good to you, let's go to Italy again this year!

I'm been active all my life, and have done the proverbial work hard and play hard, trying to have good balance. I wish I could say I were an Olympic skier, but all I can brag on is that I can make it down the Blue Slopes without wiping out or hugging the trees.

I'm better at being a halfway decent wine aficionado and choosing what wine goes with what food. I know the difference between Chardonnay and Cabernet (<u>Chardonnay is the white one, right? :D).</u>

Quirky humor appeals to me (think Dilbert and Far Side and Pearls Before Swine). I got hooked on Dilbert at work. I work for a large corporation that specializes in Information Technology. I get to be the manager of some really brainy people. Sometimes it's like herding cats.

I'm lucky I enjoy what I do, and I'm lucky I've got 2 great kids who are doing well and almost ready to fly the nest. I am proud of them! Now I'm looking for someone to share the rest of my life with.

> **Do you like walking, traveling, skiing?** If so, we'd make a great team. I enjoy nights on the town, going to dinner and a movie, and I also like to cook. Some of my "specialties" are Beef Stroganoff and Cinnamon French Toast. It's more fun cooking for 2 because good conversation and sharing are the most important. I like being active and doing fun things, but the activity is never as important as who I'm with.
>
> We spend more time in the grocery aisles than the Greek Isles, so I'm looking for someone who is comfortable in both places. I'm looking for that special long-term relationship that lasts a lifetime, not just someone new to date for a few weeks.
>
> However, it all starts with that first date! RSVP to me, and let's get acquainted! **So how do you like your coffee, and do you like Cinnamon French Toast?**

As in the regular Pizza Profile, the writer makes sure to "ask for the sale". Even confident women sometimes like a nudge. Do you have to "ask for the sale" and invite her to contact you? Try it both ways. You'll soon know what works the best. A humorous invite is usually very appealing.

Women often hesitate to go first. She might like you and be interested in you, but she wonders if she's tall enough for you, good-looking enough for you, career-oriented enough for you, too career-oriented for you. If your site has "winks", she wonders if she should wink or email. She doesn't want to be rejected.

Women wonder if you'll think she's being "too forward". By inviting her to contact you, she knows it's okay if she goes first and contacts you.

HUMONGOUS SECRET: Issue the invitation politely or humorously.   Both work.   A little nudge goes a long way into getting her to go first, but coming across over-eager and desperate is a no-no.   That said, remember women EXPECT you to go first!

Here's the answer to the well hung lawyer question that was posed at the beginning of the chapter: *He's well hung when you can't get your finger between the noose and his neck.*   Here are a few more lawyer jokes... uh, we mean questions... to prove the point that riddles and questions are an effective way to keep the reader interested and anxious to read more.

- How can you tell when a lawyer is lying? *His lips move.*
- What did the lawyer use for a contraceptive? *His personality.*
- What do you say when you see a lawyer buried up to his neck in sand? *Not enough sand.*

WARNING: Lots of lawyers are online. Some love lawyer jokes. Others can't stand them. Be cautious using them in your Profile unless you are a lawyer. Then you can get away with it *and* defend yourself. The ones used here were intended for professional use only and are protected by an amendment or two. You know, that Free Speech thing.

You have the right to express yourself online, but aim for appropriate humor. Before you send a potential date a lawyer joke, make sure the woman has a well-developed sense of humor. A good way to find out is to email her. Ask her if she thinks lawyer jokes should be made illegal except on Wall Street, Washington D.C., or shark-infested waters.

SECRET RECIPE #6:

USE HUMOR PROFILE

Boycott shampoo!   Demand the REAL poo!

The secret of the universe is @!!*^^^ ~~Sorry, No carrier~~

Experience is something you don't get until just after you need it.

Humorous Profiles are some of the most fun to write and the most effective. That's the good news. The bad news is that they're also some of the most difficult to write.

One of the best ways to start writing a funny Profile is to read funny Profiles. You'll find yourself trying to emulate or outdo them.

Even if you're not into writing humor, not to worry. Enjoy these and maybe they'll tickle your funny bone enough to try one yourself or incorporate some humor into your Profile.

HUMONGOUS SECRET: ALL Profiles benefit greatly by a funny line or story or joke. Getting the woman to smile or laugh earns extra points. If your Profile grade is a "B", humor brings it up one FULL GRADE to an "A".

Humor in your Profile shows the woman you're not an overly serious, serious man. But ya say ya don't know any jokes? Not to worry.

The Internet is your friend. Use Google or your favorite search engine to look up "jokes" or "blonde jokes" or "lawyer jokes" or "programmer jokes". Pick a few short jokes.

Don't be surprised if reading jokes gets you smiling and laughing and feeling happy. Use the energy to write your own humorous Profile.

Use the humor in the following Profile as a template to write a humorous one of your own. A good way to start is to make a non-humorous list of your Top 10 Deal Makers and Deal Breakers (aka Turn-Ons and Turn-Offs). Once you have a good Turn-Ons and Turn-Offs List, put a slight twist on them to make them humorous and put them in a narrative form.

Confused? Don't be. Here's an easy example. Let's say one of your Deal Makers is *fiscally responsible but not cheap"*.

Here's how to do the Twist:

- **If your friends come to you for bankruptcy advice due to your vast personal experience, we're probably not a good match.**

- **If your idea of roughing it is a hotel without room service, you're my kind of match.**

- **If your idea of a romantic dinner is splitting a Big Mac and Super-Size fries, we're not going to match.**

- If your idea of a romantic gift is matching electric sanders, we're not going to match. I already have a sander. But I could use a new cordless drill.

Take your sarcasm gene and put it to work. Then tone down your sarcasm to witty. If you're stuck, ask your kids or a friend's kids to help. Kids are great at being silly and sarcastic. Here are more examples of humorous twists:

TWIST ON ATTRACTIVENESS: **It would be great if you look like Angelina Jolie, but I don't look like Brad. I'm more a combination of Anderson Cooper and Bart Simpson. You know, brainy and cute. Who would have thought.**

TWIST ON ATTRACTIVENESS: **You don't have to be movie-star gorgeous, but if you look like Elvis (or Priscilla), please tell me ahead of time so I can dust off my blue suede shoes.**

TWIST ON INTELLIGENCE: **If you say you're intellagent and you say you're looking for your solemate (sic), it's probably not me.**

TWIST ON INTELLIGENCE: **I aced Speeling and Gramer!**

TWIST ON POLITICS: **Do you think Politics is corrupt but vote anyway just in case somebody honest wins and keeps their campaign promises? If so, we need to talk.**

TWIST ON PHYSICALLY FIT: **If you've climbed most of the 14ers and bike 20 miles on an easy Saturday, and do triathlons on your vacations, would it be okay if I was just there for you at the finish line?**

TWIST ON PHYSICALLY FIT: **I love to ski. If you think Black Diamond is a new type of jewelry, we're probably not the best of matches. On the other hand... I do like to give unexpected gifts!**

The next Profile uses humor well.   It wasn't written in 5 minutes. The User posted a good Profile while this one was being written and tweaked. First get something up and running. Then work on making it or the new one even better.

GOOD SAMPLE PROFILE (HUMOR):

Hi!   Glad you stopped by.   First things first....I'm not looking for an email relationship, I'm looking for a great relationship. Here are some things to help you decide if we'd click....

**If you're cuter than I am, ignore this list & email now.

**If you have something green and fuzzy and bigger than a cantaloupe growing in your frig, before you respond, please figure out what it is, and let me know.

**If you have more than 6 piercings in each ear, please also own a jewelry store if you respond.

**If you have more clothes under your bed than in your closet, please clean your room before responding.

**If you keep forgetting to take your Prozac, please do not respond.

**If you're still trying to find yourself, you need not respond.

**If you're still trying to decide which sex you prefer to date, you know the drill.

**If you're still wondering if that rash is contagious, you got it!

I'm looking for a co-conspirator to drive down the path of life. I'm a consultant by day, and a dad by night.

> I enjoy easy-listening music or books on tape (mostly NY Times bestsellers) when I drive. I like all shades of green which is why I drive a hybrid SUV. I enjoy traveling but am also a homebody and like to plop a steak or some fish on the grill and relax on the back deck.
>
> If you're looking for someone who shows up, who smiles at life's absurdities, and who loves good coffee, send an email my way. Let's find some great coffee and get acquainted.

§ § § § § § § § § § § §

Here's another humorous Profile that began by writing a list of Deal Makers and Deal Breakers. After the list was written, it was turned into narrative form.

GOOD SAMPLE PROFILE (HUMOR):

> **Is it all about asses???**
>
> You're laughing your ass off, you're working your ass off.
>
> You're covering your ass, you're kicking ass.
>
> You're kissing ass, you're up to your ass in alligators.
>
> You're trying not to act like an ass, you're chasing ass.
>
> You're assessing your assets, you're asking for directions (yes!!!).
>
> About me: Humor and learning are big turn-ons. My personality runs to the gentle, laid-back, and quiet side. What....you didn't guess that from my opening lines? Oops...guess I forgot to tell you I'm multi-faceted.

If you're assiduous and astute, you have my attention. Do you find it ironic that most of us joined this dating site so we can get off this dating site?

My 10 year old niece is into blonde jokes these days. Do you know why blonde jokes are so short? So brunettes can remember them.

I confess to having brown hair, and I confess to liking School-of-Life smarts and book learning smarts. Someone who likes to read bestsellers...I'm exhilarated!

Things that turn me on: real popcorn; intelligence; live theater (reality TV doesn't qualify); humor from Far Side to online profiles (hmm...sometimes that's not a big stretch is it?); blazing red sunsets; steaming hot coffee; feather pillows; cute bottoms (ok, no more stupid cracks about asses).

Thanks for sharing part of your day with me. I hope you smiled a time or two. Oh yes...if you think you're too good for me, you're probably right. And to be really sure, we should probably discuss it via email. Send ONE email for Yes or two for Definitely.

Hmm....sometimes sitting on your ass does yield unexpected surprises. :D

§ § § § § § § § § § §

SECRET RECIPE #7:

QUOTE SOMEBODY FAMOUS PROFILE

If the wind will not serve, take to the oars.
(Latin proverb)

Sometimes the wind is blowing favorably. Other times you need muscle power and need to use the oars. A good quote from a book, movie, or popular song can put muscle power into your Profile.

Some bright person said something witty which you can borrow. Pick one quote, and use it as your Opening Line to capture her attention. Do not go on to say, *"Tell me where the quote came from."* Do not say, *"You get extra points if you can tell me where the quote came from."* People don't like tests unless they're fun tests.

Watch how the writer of the next Profile cleverly handles the fact the woman may not be familiar with the quote. Watch how he conveys his "open-mindedness". He does this not by using the word "open-minded", but by demonstrating it when he talks about "winks".

HUMONGOUS SECRET: After reading what this man says about "winks", you might be well-advised to follow his example and invite your readers to WINK (if your site allows winks).

GOOD SAMPLE PROFILE (USING A QUOTE):

"Spread love everywhere you go, most of all in your own house....let no one ever come to you without leaving better and happier."

It's a wonderful quote, and while it might sound like a quote from a romance novel, it isn't. If you don't know the author, I won't keep you guessing. It was Mother Theresa. If you like it, email me, and I'll send you the whole quote.

Who knows....this might be the start of a beautiful friendship! Was that Humphrey Bogart in Casablanca who said that? No, it was me talking to you. :D

More about me: I have a great job in the Tech industry and am both left-brained and right-brained. I like analytical things and artistic things. I've always wished I could sing, but my repertoire is limited to Happy Birthday and Xmas songs.

I like sports but am not a sports nut. I do like to watch the big games whether it's the Super Bowl, the Masters and British Open or the Olympic Games.

I hesitate to say I believe in soul mates and chemistry because everyone says that. However, I do believe in romance and in showing it in big ways and little ways. My ideal match --- she laughs at my good jokes, laughs harder at my bad ones, goal-oriented, interesting career and/or a wonderful family. I know, I have high standards, and I'm guessing you do, too!

If that sounds like you, with a little luck or fate or karma, I think we'll find each other. Recently, I changed my opinion about "winks". I prefer emails, but I understand the reason for winks. People are busy, and winks are easier and faster. So wink away although I still prefer a first contact that tells me something about you.

I'm enjoying my journey through life and online dating, but ideally I'm looking for "the one". If you think we might click, I'd enjoy you clicking on Wink or Send Email.

P.S. – I've always wanted to go to the British Open. One of my dreams is to go when it's at St. Andrews. How about you?

§ § § § § § § § § § § §

BIG HINT: A clever P.S. at the end of a Profile can be powerfully smart. This man not only used a good quote, he used a good P.S.

If you don't know any good quotes, start looking (like maybe in the next few pages of this chapter). You can find good quotes everywhere (like in the next few pages of this chapter). You can find good quotes in literature, in movies, in songs, and in the next few pages of this chapter. Are there any good quotes in the Appendix? You get 2 guesses, and the 1st one doesn't count.

Quotes to Use (or to Inspire you):

- "Nothing shows a man's character more than what he laughs at." (Goethe)

- "Some people come into our lives and quickly go. Others stay awhile, make footprints on our hearts and we are never, ever the same." (anon)

- "Don't walk in front of me, I may not follow; Don't walk behind me, I may not lead; Walk beside me, and just be my friend." (Albert Camus)

- "The road to a friend's house is never long." (Danish Proverb)

- "All you need is love." (John Lennon)

- "To teach is to learn twice." (Joseph Joubert)

- "A person who never made a mistake never tried anything new." (Albert Einstein)

- "Every path has its puddle." (English proverb)

- "The journey is the reward." (Chinese proverb)

- "Take heed: you do not find what you do not seek." (English proverb)

- "Better a diamond with a flaw than a pebble without." (Confucius)

- "Man who stand on hill with mouth open will wait long time for roast duck to drop in." (Confucius)

- "Some cause happiness wherever they go; others whenever they go." (Oscar Wilde)

WARNING: Just because someone famous said it, just because it's hysterical or historical does not mean it's a good quote to use.

The following quotes are good for a laugh but probably not good for your Profile. If you can't figure out why, ask the next woman you date (but only if you don't want to see her again).

As one anonymous man put it: *"When a man talks dirty to a woman, it's sexual harassment. When a woman talks dirty to a man, it's $3.95 a minute."*

Here are quotes to amuse, but probably not to use:

- "You know that look women get when they want sex? Me neither." (Drew Carey)

- "Sex is hereditary. If your parents never had it, you probably won't either." (Anonymous)

- "During sex, my girlfriend always wanted to talk to me. Last time she called me from a hotel." (Rodney Dangerfield)

- "Golf and sex are the only things you can enjoy without being good at them." (Jimmy DeMaret)

- "I only take Viagra when I'm with more than one woman." (Jack Nicholson)

- "Sex is one of the nine reasons for reincarnation. The other eight are unimportant." (Henry Miller)

- "Women need a reason to have sex. Men just need a place." (Billy Crystal)

- "Pizza is a lot like sex. When it's good, it's really good. When it's bad, it's still pretty good." (Anonymous)

- "Sex is like snow, you never know how many inches you're going to get or how long it is going to last." (Anonymous)

- "The last time I was in a woman I was visiting the Statue of Liberty." (Woody Allen)

Whew....who knew?? As another famous quotation goes, *"Don't shoot the messenger."*

HUMONGOUS SECRET: What if you write the best, most spectacular Profile on the planet?   What if you channeled the eloquence of Shakespeare and the wit of Johnny Carson, and your Profile is worthy of a Pulitzer Prize for Best Darn Profile on the planet?

Sniffle, sniffle, shed a teardrop.   You may be too perfect. You may be scaring off some great women with your wit and copious vocabulary.   They may think they can't keep up with you. They don't know you slaved over your Profile for 2 weeks, 1 hour, and 6 minutes.

It's okay if your Profile isn't the best Profile on the planet. More than that, it's good it isn't.   If you wrote the best Profile the world has ever seen, mess it up!

Models do this.   They want their beauty to look natural, not staged.   They mess up their hair, pull out their shirttail, roll up their sleeves.   Too perfect isn't what you're after.

If you absolutely love your perfect Profile and don't want to mess it up, here are 3 ways to handle the situation:

__WAY ONE:__ CONFESS! Write something like this in your Profile: **In case you're wondering, I'm only half this witty in person. I make time for things that are important to me.   I spent 2 weeks, 5 hours, and 8 minutes thinking about what to write and trying to make my profile reflect my intelligence, wit, and humor.   Finding a special lady is important to me.   I hope it's you, but only you can tell me if I succeeded via wink or email.**

**WAY TWO:** CONFESS!....and tell her you probably are too good for her: **If you're wondering if I'm too good or too smart for you, you need to know I'm only 78% this smart in person. Just to prove it to you, we ought to compare notes over coffee. I need to warn you though. Coffee makes me at least 10% smarter. So where should we go for coffee?**

**WAY THREE:** CONFESS!....and tell her SHE'S probably too good for you: **If you're wondering if you're too good for me, you're probably right. In fact, I'm 98% sure you're even more fabulous in person than you are in your Profile. To make 100% sure, we ought to compare notes over coffee or dinner. Which would you prefer?**

I've never tried skydiving. That's because I hate jumping to conclusions.

The conclusion of your Profile is as important as the Opening Line. Now that she's come to the end of your Profile, what do you want her to do? Email you? Wink at you? She can't read your mind. She doesn't like jumping to conclusions any more than you do.

As with any marketing endeavor, it's smart to ask for the order in a classy way. Put an ***RSVP2ME*** at the end of your Profile. You can write: ***Email me, send up a flare, a smoke signal, skywrite it over the Empire State Building. Let me know you're interested.***

If your Profile is good, many women will make the first move. Even so, most women like the men to do the pursuing. You know, that "chivalry" thing. Many women aren't aware men are flattered when women contact them first. Women worry about appearing too forward. Telling her you welcome her email is often the nudge she needs to go first.

Here are examples of good Endings for your Profile. If you want more good Endings, look at THE END... that would be the Appendix.

- <u>GOOD ENDING</u>:   Just like you, I'm looking for my match. There are lots of good ways to make contact: wink, email, crystal ball, Ouija board, telepathy. I'd say try #1 or #2 for best success.

- <u>GOOD ENDING</u>: Hi, I've got a great lemon tree in my backyard here in Southern CA. It's loaded with ripe, yellow lemons. I've got lots to share. I'm good at turning lemons into lemonade (literally and figuratively). Email me and tell me if you want 1 dozen or 2 dozen, or if you want a gallon of the best-tasting lemonade on the planet.

- <u>GOOD ENDING</u>: I make a great apple pie... and as Eve said to Adam, "What harm could eating an apple do?" I also have an apple tree. How many would you like? :D

- <u>GOOD ENDING</u>: I'm looking for a best friend, a lover, a co-conspirator in this adventure we call life. If your interests and values correspond with mine, let me know by skywriting it over Colorado Springs or by sending an email. Your choice.

- <u>GOOD ENDING</u>: Hey, thanks for stopping by! If you think we have enough in common, let's have a conversation in my favorite restaurant. Let me know by RSVPing by email or phone. (Email if you don't know my phone number! :D).

- <u>GOOD ENDING</u>: The world is complex and exciting and waiting for us to dive in. Let's start by sharing a cup of coffee. Email once for yes, and twice for yes yes!

SECRETS COME WITH AGE

and with AGE comes WISDOM...

(if you're lucky)

How do you make right decisions?
Experience.

How do you get experience?
Making wrong decisions.

Along the journey of life, you get smarter. With a little luck, you also get wiser. Some travelers on life's path are fast learners. Others take more time, especially when it comes to learning about the opposite sex.

If you want to get wiser faster, many of the dating sites have all kinds of Forums. There are Forums on Writing a Profile, Single Parent Dating, Sex Questions, and many more. Forums are informative and entertaining. You can read or participate or both. Your choice. Reading is a good way to start. If you're going to post on the Forums, it's always a good idea to read the Forum rules and some of the threads before you start participating.

While you're online, there's another great place with great ideas. It's probably somewhere you haven't been before. Check out the Profiles of men who've had more life experience than you.

If you don't want these men to know you're reading their Profiles, go into Stealth Mode. Most sites let you HIDE your Profile so people don't know that you've viewed them.

Older men may or may not have a higher IQ than you do, but they've attended the School of Life longer. Experience is a great teacher. The older men often have found the words to express what younger men sometimes struggle to articulate.

That isn't to say the 20 and 30 and 40 year olds are clueless. Many young men are old souls. However, due to successes and failures, challenges and hard knocks, accomplishments and all-around life experiences, the older men have a point of view worth checking out.

While you're at it, check out guys your own age. See what your competition is like and what they're saying in their Profiles.

And hey... older guys! Check out what the "kids" have to say. What restaurants are new? What books are being read? What music is being played? Recharge the battery. The only thing constant is change, and you might enjoy exploring both the new and the old with your date.

Another good place to look is in the women's Profiles. *Emphasize what you have that she's looking for.* Last but not least, read the upcoming chapter on What Women Want. It won't give you X-ray vision, but your vision will improve dramatically.

SECRETS ABOUT FILLING OUT THE REST OF YOUR PROFILE...

You've got it made!

Some men drink at the fountain of knowledge and take it all in. Others just gargle.

You've been drinking hardy at the fountain, and most of the hard work is done! HURRAY! You can coast downhill from here... well almost. On some Dating Sites, there are a number of little "specialty" sections to fill out. Those 10 topics are a walk in the park compared to the gigantic Big-Box known as "the Profile". These 10 topics are easy because we give you plenty of examples.

Some Dating sites have *separate sections* OR *questions* which cover the following 10 Topics:

1. FOR FUN
2. MY JOB
3. MY ETHNICITY
4. MY RELIGION
5. MY EDUCATION
6. FAVORITE HOT SPOTS
7. FAVORITE THINGS
8. LAST READ
9. PETS
10. FIRST DATE

One of the most common mess-ups is leaving any of these sections blank. By not filling out these sections, you send a negative message to the women. If you can't take the time to answer what you do for fun, for a job, etc., women view you as someone who doesn't like to communicate and isn't interested in finding a match.

It's easy to come up with answers, especially after you read some of the many examples from the next chapters and Appendices.

HUMONGOUS SECRET: If your dating site includes these as separate sections, the *lack* of info is conspicuous. Fill out all sections. If you don't include info about your job or profession or education, it's a gigantic Red Flag.

BIG SECRET: If your particular dating site doesn't include these as separate sections, make sure you include information about your job, education, favorite places, etc. in your "freeform" Big-Box Profile. These are things she's interested in knowing.

HUMONGOUS SECRET: If you're having trouble filling up the big, intimidating white box on your Dating Site that is labeled Profile, divide it into your own sections. Pick 5 to 10 of the above Topics (for fun, my job, favorite things, etc.) and use those topics to write individual paragraphs inside the giant, blank Profile Box.

IF your site doesn't have these as separate sections, you can type the heading of each of the topics in all CAPS so it's easy to see where you change from one section to another.

Fill out the information in each section using the suggestions and examples in the upcoming chapters. You'll find it's an easy way to organize your ideas and make your Big-Box Profile more interesting and more readable.

Your Big-Box Profile format would look something like this:

MY JOB: xxx (**imitate something witty**) xxx

xxx (**from the APPENDIX**) xxx

FOR FUN: xxx (**imitate something witty**) xxx

xxx (**from the APPENDIX**) xxx

FAVORITE THINGS: xxx (**imitate something witty**) xxx

xxx (**from the APPENDIX**) xxx

1st DATE: xxx (**imitate something witty**) xxx

xxx (**from the APPENDIX**) xxx

---

§ § § § § § § § § § §

WHAT DO YOU DO

FOR FUN?

Give a man a fish and he will eat for a day. Teach him how to fish, and he will sit in a boat and drink beer all day.

If you don't want her to think you're sitting in your boat, or your brother's boat, or your friend's boat drinking beer all day, tell her what you do "for fun". *Be specific.*

If your Dating Site has FUN as a separate Section and you list good specifics, you'll hit a home run. What if your Dating Site has one Big Box for your Profile instead of separate sections? Easy solution: Incorporate specifics from this FUN section and some of the next 9 sections into your Big-Box Profile, and you'll hit a home run.

If you have 1001 things you do for fun, don't list them all. Narrow it down to several. Do not put, **"There isn't enough room to list everything I like to do."** List the top 3 or 4 things you do for fun. Women like when you share. Women like when you communicate. It won't hurt much!

Here are examples for you to imitate. Check out the APPENDIX for many more examples.

- <u>FOR FUN</u>: Like most people, I enjoy travel, but 90% of my fun time is spent at home. For fun in the evening, I'm a big fan of sitting on the back deck and enjoying the sunset with a nice glass of Riesling or a hot cup of cocoa or coffee. After that…a good DVD! Care to join me?

- <u>FOR FUN</u>: Swimming, hiking, biking, skiing, anything outdoors. I especially like going to ski resorts where I've never skied. It's not just the adrenaline rush, it's the beauty of the outdoors and sharing it with someone special.

- <u>FOR FUN</u>: I like sailing when the weather is nice and the fog lifts. Also strong coffee and making dinner for someone special. My Cashew Chicken and peapods is mouthwatering. My 5-cheese lasagna… even better! Email now to make a reservation.

- <u>FOR FUN</u>: I'm lucky I like my job and most days it is fun. I also love to travel travel travel. I've been to many countries in Europe, once to Japan. Hmm… is your Passport current? I like theater, art shows, flea markets, and good bookstores.

- <u>FOR FUN</u>: I like movies, DVD's, music and most of the "normal" stuff. Here are things I don't enjoy very much: 1) Broccoli 2) Cleaning house (but I do it for the results) 3) Getting up on cold winter mornings (I'd much rather curl up with you).

Don't make the mistakes the next men did. When women read things like these, they go, *"UH-OH"* and pass you by.

- <u>UH-OH FOR FUN</u>: **I'll fill this out later.** (Do it now. If you write you'll do it later, it shows you don't care much about finding a real relationship. "Not doing it" signifies how truly low on the list she and a future relationship are.)

- <u>UH-OH FOR FUN</u>: **I'll tell you later.** (If you don't want to share information about you, that's bad. Women like men who share. Show her what she gets if she catches you, and show her you're worth catching.)

- <u>UH-OH FOR FUN</u>: **I like to do whatever you like to do.** (This shouts that you have no interests of your own and are clingy. Not good qualities to most women.)

- <u>UH-OH FOR FUN</u>: **I like to do a lot of things.** (If you want to catch the right woman, you have to show her you're worth catching. The comment of "**doing a lot of things**" tells her nothing except you don't communicate well. This is not attractive.)

MY JOB

or PROFESSION

Santa Claus has a great job! Do you know why Santa Claus is always jolly? He knows where all the naughty and nice girls live.

She knows what Santa Claus does for a living. Now she'd like to know what you do. What you do for a living tells a lot about who you are, what you enjoy, and what drives and motivates you. If you list specifics, you'll hit a home run.

If you don't list anything under "My Job" or "Profession", you probably won't be spending next Christmas at her house. Women like men who have achieved success in their life be it through career or family or personal growth. Not many women are looking for financially or emotionally needy men.

No matter what age you are, if you've had success in your career or schooling or raising a family, this is the place to shine. Do so humbly and with grace.

If you just graduated school and are looking for a job, focus on your profession and skill. If you're in school, put "Student" instead of "flipping burgers" as your profession. Working your way through school is admirable, but don't give her the impression that burgers are the pinnacle of your career.

If you're a student, include something about your goals, your ambitions, and your future profession. Are you studying to be a teacher or an accountant? Are you working on your Bachelor's degree in Business, or on your Master's in IT? Brag on yourself (modestly of course). Give the woman an idea when you'll be through with school and what career path you plan to choose. Women like men with education and goals.

If you're in the work force, share what you do *and why you like it.* Women like men who like their jobs. It means they come home from work in a good mood. If you don't like your job, focus on what you do that helps people or makes a positive difference in people's lives.

But what if you are between jobs or were just laid off in the latest economic disaster? Whether you have a job, are between jobs, are retired, or are looking for your first "real" job, write about your *profession*. Be factual, but don't go overboard. Do not start with the first "Employee of the Month" award you got when you were 18 and keep bragging and bragging.

If you have kids, trying to list every award and great thing about your kids is egotistical. If you try and list everything, you'll ooze hubris and arrogance rather than confidence and humility.

What if your child is only 8 or 18 and isn't a CEO yet? What if you have a good job but don't have a six or seven figure salary? What if you don't have a gigantic title? What if you have a normal job with a normal salary?

She isn't expecting you to be the next Bill Gates or have a daughter named Hannah Montana. Those people are one in a *hundred million or billion.* She is hoping to see you have a good job. If you have kids, she is hoping to see your kids are well-launched or you're raising or have raised good kids.

Shine the light on the positives. There are many ways to shine. How does your company help people? Does your company make something people use? If so, what? How do you make a difference?

Women are searching for all kinds of men. Many women who have had success in the business world are looking for the successful businessman to complement them. Other women are looking for a less career-occupied man who has substantial time to devote to her and family.

Focus on the positives. Specifics are good. If you're a manager or parent or programmer or lawyer or retiree, or whatever, don't simply list manager, parent, programmer, lawyer, retiree. That's boring. Give details.

Here are some examples to get you started. Dozens more can be found in the APPENDIX:

- <u>MY JOB:</u> **Do you need a computer wizard? I work in IT (information technology). That means I am on a first-name basis with the magic elves who run your computer. If that nasty blue screen of death takes over your system, I do computer magic!**

- <u>MY JOB:</u> **I'm a manager for a Fortune 10000 company. No, that isn't a typo...our company is much smaller than a Fortune 1000 company. It's growing rapidly and may become one of the 1000 in a few years. I love my work, but there are those days!**

- <u>MY JOB:</u> **My most important job is raising my kids to have strong self-images and do well in school. In addition to being a dad, I work for a not-for-profit corporation that represents the interests of teachers.**

- <u>MY JOB:</u> **Yeah! Retirement! I worked 31 years and now love being retired. A typical day is reading the paper, making time to get together with family and friends. In the life before this, I worked for a magazine and helped people market their products. Let me know how well I've done marketing myself.**

Paint a visual picture of your job. Let her see what you do. If you like what you do, express how you feel about it. Being proud of what you do is fine, but aim for informational rather than braggadocio. Don't go overboard with the bragging, or you'll come off as arrogant and unapproachable.

If you skip filling out the MY JOB section or don't divulge in your Profile what you do, the message is you're embarrassed about your job or lack thereof. Another message is that you aren't good at sharing or communicating.

If you only say **"I like my job, and I'm good at what I do"** or **"I have one"** or **"Chief"** or **"Just ask"** or **"Ask Me"** or **"Yes"** or **"Big Cheese"** or **"I'll tell you later"** or **"Head Ninja"**, that tells her nothing. **<u>NIX all those</u>**.

You might think you're being mysterious and clever, but you come across as closed and non-communicative. Not many women are looking for secretive, non-communicative men. Not many women are looking for men without jobs. She wants to know you can afford to buy her a cup of coffee *and* a Danish on the first date.

Read the following Job entries. Women figure you won't be able to afford the coffee let alone the sweet roll:

- <u>UH-OH JOB</u>: **I have a job.**
- <u>UH-OH JOB</u>: **I'm in business for myself.**
- <u>UH-OH JOB</u>: **I work.**

Pretty lame. Women don't like being kept in the dark when it comes to a man's job. The first place loser for bad job description is one many men have tied for. The loser is: The man who leaves his job description blank.

Blank is the worst job description you can have. But what if you hate your job? Instead of saying "**I hate my job**," talk about what you like about your job. Talk about the people you've been able to help or the good results you get. Negativity will not win you any dates.

Ditto being out of a job. Don't say you're out of a job. Instead talk about successes you've had and the type of work you did (accounting, mortgage broker). Rather than talk about the lack of a job, talk about your profession. What are you skilled at?

Layoffs are a fact of life in any industry especially during recessions. Saying you're out of a job or on unemployment is a sure fire way to end your dating career before it even starts. Hopefully by the time you find the right lady to write, your job prospects will have turned around.

BIG SECRET: If unemployment is high in your field and you've managed to weather the storm, humbly spill the beans your job is secure. Otherwise, she'll think you're unemployed. Here are some examples of how to handle it:

- **I've been in banking for 10 years and being in a Midwest town surrounded by a productive farming community helped us weather this economic mess.**

- **I'm a mortgage broker and fortunately work for a large company which didn't need government assistance.**

- **I'm a stock broker, and while I didn't call the bottom of the market, I got my clients out quickly. Doing what's good for your clients is always good and translates into appreciation as well as success.**

MY

ETHNICITY

ETHNICITY: *I enjoy being intimate in the morning, or during the day, or in the evening. Oh wait, did you say Ethnicity? I thought you said INTIMACY! :D*

Ethnicity is a place for you to shine. If Ethnicity is one of the section boxes on your dating site, don't skip it. Ethnicity can be very interesting. Even if it isn't interesting to you, it's often interesting to a prospective date. You don't need a family tree to be able to fill this out. An overview and a few countries of origin will do.

Ethnicity comes from the Greek word "ethnos" which is translated as "people" or "tribe". Did your ancestors come from England or Egypt? Russia or Rome? Asia or Australia? Ethnicity is your heritage, your roots.

If you have traced your family tree back and have some famous or infamous folks to mention, go for it. Every little bit helps in setting you apart from the average John Doe (providing your relatives weren't Count Dracula or terrorists).

Check out the samples below to see how you can turn middle class, middle age, Midwestern roots into much more than mildly interesting. Use these for inspiration, and check out the APPENDIX for more examples of Ethnicity.

- ETHNICITY: **I am the 4 F's: fortyish, from the middle class, from French ancestors, from Florida. I am tolerant about most things but have little tolerance for discrimination against age, sex, race, or religion.**

- ETHNICITY: **Born American to Austrian parents. Austria isn't where Koala bears are from, it's where Arnold Schwarzenegger (the Governator) is from. Considering the state of California's economy, maybe a koala bear would have been a better choice.**

- ETHNICITY: **One of my ancestors came over on the Mayflower, and I think that's where I got the gene for traveling. I've been to Chicago, NYC, L.A., D.C., Italy, and London. Japan and China are on my list of places to see. Care to join me?**

- ETHNICITY: **The blonde hair is Swedish, the blue eyes Danish, and the stubbornness from some darn Scotsman (that was probably adopted, I'm sure). Me... American born with a yen for Chinese food. Go figure!**

- ETHNICITY: **If you like romantic war stories, be sure to ask me how my Mom and Dad met. My Mom was a Vietnamese war bride, my Dad an American serving overseas. Two of my great-grandparents came through Ellis Island in 1919 from Russia.**

MY

RELIGION

God grant me the serenity to accept the things I cannot change; courage to change the things I can; and wisdom to know the difference. ...Serenity Prayer

"I think the very motion of our life is towards happiness..." ...Dalai Lama

Religion can be a tricky subject, but it doesn't have to be. Some people skip answering the Religion question for fear of eliminating potential matches.

Sooner or later any date who is serious about you is going to want to know your views on religion. Since religion is often a Deal Maker or Deal Breaker in a relationship, think about including a sentence or two about your religious views if it's important that your date matches you in that area.

Putting "happy to discuss religion when we meet" is a good way to make sure she won't meet you. Most women think there isn't much sense starting to date someone only to discover you're polar opposites on religion.

Here are sample entries for the My Religion section. They show ways to address different aspects of religious and spiritual beliefs. Many more excellent examples are in the APPENDIX.

MY RELIGION:

- MY RELIGION: **I am open to any faith that accepts and tolerates the beliefs of others. My house of worship has as many pews as the mountains have streams and trees.**

- MY RELIGION: **I don't belong to a specific faith, but I am open to all. I do believe there is a higher power and am open to exploring other spiritual paths including Buddhism. I also believe....what goes around, comes around.**

- MY RELIGION: **I believe in the moral teachings of my faith (Christian). I go to Church regularly, and I do believe in an Almighty Being...not the one in the long beard and robe, more like the Almighty Spirit or Life Force.**

- MY RELIGION: **I believe in the goodness of people. I'm not naïve, and I do know that sometimes evil does win out. The good folks have to work harder when that happens. I believe in the beauty of nature, and I believe that we can make heaven here on earth.**

- MY RELIGION: **I have enough trouble figuring out the Sunday Crossword Puzzle that I think I'm going to pass on figuring out the Supreme Deity. I live my life by the Golden Rule, and when my time comes, if there is a God, I will not have regrets or worry about being judged.**

- MY RELIGION: **My religion is based in Christ, and I believe Love is the most powerful force there is. I believe Love and Fear drive us and that the greatest gift to give and receive is Love.**

MY

EDUCATION

Are you smarter than her last date who refused to eat the M&M's because they were too difficult to peel?

Inquiring women want to know. Yes, it's déjà vu all over again. Specifics! If you have an advanced degree in the School of Life, brag modestly on your accomplishments. If you went to college or beyond, say so.

Women like educated men be it formal or informal education. Don't brag to the point she wonders if your head is going to explode.

If you have a degree in social work or psychology and are divorced, take note of the first example below. Women figure if anyone should have avoided divorce, it was you. Watch how the social worker competently handles his divorced situation in the example below. Many more examples of Education can be found in the Appendix.

- <u>MY EDUCATION:</u> **I have a master's in social work from U of I. If anyone should have succeeded at marriage, it was me, but even therapists get divorced. In my case, we learned that getting married and** starting a family at 21 usually isn't a good idea. We were "kids raising kids". If we knew then what we know now......but that's the beauty of life. We get wiser.

- MY EDUCATION: I worked in construction when the kids were young. I went back to school and became a construction investigator for a legal firm that specializes in construction defects.

- MY EDUCATION: Good education at UCLA, and I'm grateful for all it's given me. That said, life is the greatest teacher.

- MY EDUCATION: I am a licensed barber and have 2 years of college. I love what I do. I'm not sure what job I would like more than I like this one.

- MY EDUCATION: I was the first in my family to go to college. I worked part time thru school and my folks helped, too. A good education is worth every penny you pay for it! I have a degree in Business from Columbia.

- MY EDUCATION: I started at Concordia (in Canada) and did an exchange program at Univ. of Queensland in Australia. I teach computer science. I learn everything twice...once when I learn it and even better when I teach it.

BAD entries for "MY EDUCATION":

- UH-OH EDUCATION: I am smarter than I look.

- UH-OH EDUCATION: Ask me about it when we meet.

- UH-OH EDUCATION: I went to college but didn't finish. (Don't focus on the negative. Focus on the field you studied, what you learned, how it enabled you to get your job, etc.)

FAVORITE

HOT SPOTS

I just got lost in thought. It was unfamiliar territory.

If you haven't been on a date in a while and your favorite place to be is lost in thought, check out the examples in this chapter for suggestions of good Hot Spots.

Hot Spots are usually specific places. However, it's a common mistake for men to mention the name of the place and leave the woman in the dark as to what kind of Hot Spot it is.

If you live in a megacity like Chicago or London or Toronto, the name of your "Hot Spot" may be familiar to you, but the women reading your Profile may not know if it's a restaurant, a coffee house, a dance club, or a strip club.

Here's how to handle the identification:

- **Seasons 52 is the best! It's a great restaurant downtown that specializes in seasonal cuisine.**

- **Ricardo's for salsa dancing on Friday night. Great exercise and great music.**

- **The Summit steak house is always good and has live music.**

- Timbuktu is a cozy coffee house in the mountains that makes you think you're in Timbuktu.

Here are more examples of Hot Spots, and many more are in the Appendix. Imitate these or use them as inspiration to write your own.

- FAVORITE HOT SPOTS: My favorite spot is a small piano bar called Café Mozart not too far from here. It's on the water with easy-listening music. The food is CA cuisine…light and fresh with lots of seafood choices.

- FAVORITE HOT SPOTS: My back deck… made even better with a good steak on the grill. Racine's (great coconut shrimp and Turtle pie) is one my favorite places. Art Museums, coffee shops, and big bookstores are at the top of my list.

- FAVORITE HOT SPOTS: Locally I like: the Blue Dog Café and the Comet Theatre for live comedy. On my list of things to see someday are: the Great Wall of China and the Louvre in Paris. Went with friends from America to the Tower of London last year and saw a performance at the Globe Theater. I'd go back in a heartbeat.

- FAVORITE HOT SPOTS: Fourth Story, the Grizzly Rose, and Toadstool are some of my favorite restaurants. I live downtown and know all the good eateries. I've traveled extensively, but it seems like every time I check off a city or country, I add at least one more.

FAVORITE

THINGS

Chocolate: The OTHER major food group.

Beer: It's not just for breakfast anymore.

Chocolate is specific. Beer is specific. If you want to sizzle with your Favorite things, be specific. Describing them *and* how you feel about them adds even more impact. Here are several good examples, and more pages can be found in the Appendix.

- FAVORITE THINGS: **Interacting with friends; all shades of green (including hybrids); the latest bestseller; vanilla ice cream with hot fudge. Delish!**

- FAVORITE THINGS: **18 inches of new snow at Steamboat, and they close Rabbit Ears Pass. After a full day of skiing, sitting in front of a fireplace sipping champagne or watching the latest DVD is great.**

- FAVORITE THINGS: **Helping others achieve their goals. On a lighter note, I love thin-crust pizza and homemade chicken burritos so it's a good thing I got the skinny genes.**

- FAVORITE THINGS: **Watching a baseball game at Yankee Stadium; a hockey game; a basketball game. Watching the Olympics and Wimbledon on TV. Yes, I like sports and play tennis. If you don't play, I'm a good teacher and assistant coach at the High School.**

Here are some terrible entries for Favorite Things. They are weak or wimpy or overtly sexual. Don't make the same mistake these men did:

- <u>UH-OH FAVES:</u> Blue is my most favorite color.

- <u>UH-OH FAVES:</u> Answering this question will take too long.

- <u>UH-OH FAVES:</u> I'll share mine later and hope you share yours.

- <u>UH-OH FAVES:</u> Lots of things.

- <u>UH-OH FAVES:</u> I hope my favorite things will be... Your face, your smell, your touch. The essence of you. Warm, passionate kisses and strong hugs. Your face against mine, your body.

- <u>UH-OH FAVES:</u> My kids. I have 2: ages 5 and 9. (Putting this as the only thing in your Favorite Things sends up a Red Flag you only have time for kids and little time for anything else.)

- <u>UH-OH FAVES:</u> To many to list! (He's too lazy to list anything. He spelled the first "too" wrong. 2 strikes, and he's already out of this game.)

LAST

READ

Who is General Failure, and why is he reading my hard disk?

If the last thing you read was the error message on your computer, you might want to choose to imitate one of the examples below when you fill out the Last Read section. If your site doesn't have a Last Read section, consider putting something in your Big-Box Profile about your reading interests. Many women like to read and often send an email based on your reading preferences.

If you like to read, add "reading" or specific authors to your Keywords or Interests. On many sites, women can search on Keywords and Interests. Details like these give the woman a "conversation hook" for a 1st email.

If your site has a Last Read Section, do NOT put **"Your Profile"** as the last thing you read. So many men do this, we're going to repeat the above warning twice. Do NOT put **"Your Profile"** as the last thing you read. Do NOT put **"Your Profile"** as the last thing you read. We're going to repeat it again so you can see how annoying it is: Do NOT put **"Your Profile"** as the last thing you read.

The first or second time she reads **"Your Profile was the last thing I read,"** it sounds cute. After she's been online for a week or two, it becomes annoying and unoriginal the 3rd, and 4th, and 150th time.

Another mistake people make in this section is saying, **"I don't read anything."** Don't crash and burn and let General Failure take over now. If you don't read anything, start reading something. Buy a newspaper or a magazine. Ask the librarian to suggest something. You never know, she might be cute and single.

Intelligence never has a bad hair day. It's a scientific fact that bigger brains make you more handsome and attractive.

WARNING: It's best not to list titles of sex books (i.e., *Passion and Intimacy, How to Make Love to a Woman, Loving for a Lifetime*).

WARNING: It's best not to list titles of self-help books (*Alcoholism and the Family, Getting Kids to Listen to You, Finding Yourself, Conflict Resolution*).

The books may be outstanding and the definitive word on the subject, but avoid listing any books which might easily be "controversial" or "misunderstood" by the person reading your Profile. If you're reading a book about *passion and intimacy,* she may wonder if you are cold and unfeeling and you need to learn about being touchy-feely. Alternatively, she may wonder if you're a sex fiend and all you think about is sex.

If you're reading a book about alcoholism, she won't know if it's for you, your kids, or to help a family friend. If you're reading a book entitled "Space Aliens and other Conspiracy Theories" you invite all kinds of questions and doubts into inquiring minds. Avoid book titles that cause an eyebrow to be raised. Avoid "TMI" and stay off Too-Much-Information Highway until you get to know her better.

Some men make the mistake of thinking what you read doesn't say much about you. Some make the even bigger mistake of admitting it in their Profiles or their Last Read Section.

What you choose to read says a lot about you. If the last book you read was *"1984"* or *"To Kill a Mockingbird"*, it often sends the message you rarely read. These are great books, but most people read them in high school or college and never pick them up again. If you last read *"The Da Vinci Code"*, it sends the message you like bestsellers, but you don't read them when they are first released. The Code was popular years ago. You'll score more points if you include something more recent.

If you don't think what you read makes a difference, ask yourself this question: Would you prefer to date someone who read the latest bestseller or someone who last read Soap Opera Digest? Nuff said.

Here are some samples of Last Read. Many go far beyond listing books and magazines. They give recommendations and thumbs up or down. This makes your Profile or your Last Read section more interesting and makes it come alive.

Choose Thumbs-Up reading material over ones that are Thumbs-Down. "Glowing" about a book is more attractive than "glaring" unless you do it with a light hand. Glaring will make her wonder if you're critical about everything.

Use these Last Read examples for inspiration to write your own, and make the APPENDIX your latest 'Last Read' if you need more examples:

- <u>LAST READ:</u> **Really enjoyed Geography of Bliss... bestseller about an NPR reporter who travels to Iceland and Switzerland and India and about 6 other places trying to figure out what makes people happy. Fascinating book and fascinating glimpse of various countries and cultures.**

- <u>LAST READ:</u> **I only read on days that end in "Y". Eclectic reading tastes from sci-fi to biographies. NY Times bestsellers are on my "Have Read" or "Want to" list. Grisham is one of my favorite authors.**

- <u>LAST READ:</u> **Orange County Register (great local paper). Read Kite Runner a while ago and highly recommend it. Just starting Time Traveler's Wife, bestseller by Niffenegger, engrossing. I like "time-travel" books (Time Machine, Wrinkle in Time).**

- <u>LAST READ:</u> **I like non-fiction and how-to books. The travel section and I are on a first name basis. I especially like Rick Steve's off-the-beaten-path travel books. You get the mainstream, but don't miss the hidden gems.**

- <u>LAST READ:</u> **Love to read, new or old. Some of my older all time favorites: Lost Horizon, Atlas Shrugged, Brave New World. Newer: Harry Potter series, The Summons, The Alchemist, Tipping Point.**

Some people who say they are avid readers do not list any books in their Profiles. If you say you like to read and list nothing, that is a Red Flag. Most readers enjoy sharing what they've read.

Here are some terrible entries for Last Read. Make sure your entry doesn't resemble these.

- UH-OH LAST READ: **Confession: I do not read novels.** (Put something positive here even if it means you need to go out and buy a magazine, or make a trip to the library, or surf the Internet for something interesting/informative. It never hurts to have some current topics of conversation in your repertoire so you can talk about more than sports and the weather when you take her out on a date.)

- UH-OH LAST READ: **The last book I read was on conflict resolution. Trying to build a business has rather limited my reading selection.** (This will make her wonder if you're full of trauma-drama. Confessing that your business is filling up your time will make her wonder if you have time for her.)

- UH-OH LAST READ: **I don't remember the last book I read, but I do read and watch the news a lot. I love discussing the world's events and politics.** (Many educated people believe what's on TV is a highly edited spin as to what's really going on. Start reading.)

- UH-OH LAST READ: **Are you pulling my leg? Who cares! The important thing is that I do read!** (And he does do rude very well, too, don't you think?)

MY

PETS

The blonde poured Spot Remover on her muddy dog. Now he's gone. Her boyfriend suggested she put an ad in the paper, but she said it was no use – her dog can't read.

How can you make a mistake talking about your loveable and adorable pet? Some people are really good at being negative, giving out too much information, or being clumsy.

Here are good examples which show how to write about your pets (or lack thereof):

- PETS: I have a cute orange cat, Sweenie, who looks like Garfield but never eats lasagna. He is big on Fancy Feast and catnip.

- PETS: I have a smart cat (Cruiser) and a smarter dog (Rusty Rex von Teucereaux). He has a long pedigree (per the shelter where I adopted him), but don't tell Rusty. I don't want to inflate his ego.

- PETS: I like animals but my only pets now are the butterflies and hummingbirds in my garden.

- PETS: I like pets, but my only pets now are my outdoor plants. Only need to feed them once or twice a year, and my dogwood doesn't bark at the mailman.

- PETS: I live next to the state park. Lots of deer, coyotes, more deer, a few red foxes, pheasants. Nice!

- PETS: I have a pet chicken, a pet cat, and a pet dog. Oh yes, I also live in the country. They're more than just pets, they're contributors: organic eggs, organic mouser, eco-friendly alarm system.

What not to do:

- UH-OH PETS: My 10 year old dog Jennie is so sweet. I will miss her when she's gone.

- UH-OH PETS: I have always loved animals. I have 5 cats and 2 dogs.

- UH-OH PETS: My dog died last year.

- UH-OH PETS: I have a dog named Spotty, and yes, that's where she got her name.

- UH-OH PETS: My black German Shepherd is a great guard dog, and he isn't as mean as he looks in the photo.

- UH-OH PETS: My dog is the best! But he does have a gum problem so I brush my dog's teeth every day. It really does help with his bad breath.

If you go on and on about your pets in the Pet Section, it doesn't take a pet detective to start wondering, *"Gee, I wonder if he gets along with pets, but not people?"*

Don't assume a person with pets is looking for someone who has pets. Many people are looking to date someone who likes pets but is pet-free. Pets make it more difficult to travel. Many women are glad you don't have pets because she doesn't have to worry if your pet will get along with her pet.

If you have no pets and you like pets, include something along those lines in your Profile or your Pet section. You expand your dating pool.

Keep your Pet section short and sweet. Personalize it by including the pet's name if it isn't something like BUGGER or DINGBAT. Yes, people name their pets all kinds of things.

While we can go on and on about pets, we're not going to. We've kept pets short and sweet. Please remember to do the same.

FIRST DATES

Where to go? What to do?

FIRST DATE: I'm not sure I believe in online dating, but I've heard it works. So either help make me a believer... or...

```
------|||||------- Put this on your
------|||||------- profile if you
----|||||||||||----- know someone who
------|||||------- died of old age
------|||||------- looking for their
------|||||------- perfect match
------|||||------- on a dating site.
```

Many dating sites have a separate section called First Date. Your first date should sound appealing. It's an enticement for her to meet you.

Even if your dating site doesn't have a separate section for first date, it's good to include a first date suggestion somewhere in your Big-Box Profile. ANTICIPATION works.

Many men put the cliché coffee date as a first date. That's not horrible, but you can do better. Use the First Date section to WOO the woman and get her thinking how great it would be to go out with you.

202

You can take the First Date section literally, or use it to describe an ideal first date. Either way, the more appealing it is to the woman, the more likely it is she'll accept a date.

Too many men make the fatal mistake of saying what they would *not* like to do. Negativity is not the way to get the date. Many men say, "Let's not go to a movie; we can't talk there" or "Let's not go for a hike in the mountains. I want you to feel safe."

Instead of saying what you do not want to do, say what you want to do. Keep it safe. A walk in the moonlight on a secluded beach isn't appealing to a woman who just met you. Neither is the man who says, "Let me surprise you." She doesn't know you yet. It's not very likely she'll trust you enough to let you surprise her.

Another fatal mistake many men make is saying, "Let's go out for a few drinks." Whenever you say "drink<u>S</u>", a Red Flag is being waved. How much you drink? A drink (singular) is better to suggest than drink<u>S</u>. That doesn't mean you can't have a 2nd drink when you go out. It means what you have in your Profile won't get her wondering if your middle name is Jack and your other middle name is Daniel.

Here's what TO DO in the First Date section:

1) Be ORIGINAL and INTERESTING.

2) If you use something "cliché" like coffee, make sure you describe an original and unique place to sip the coffee.

3) BE SPECIFIC and DESCRIPTIVE. Use your words to paint a place she can see, a beverage she can taste, yummy cooking she can smell, the warm sunshine on her face, the taste of salt water in the air. Get the idea? Involving MULTIPLE senses always helps set the scene.

4) Pick a SAFE place. That means a place where there are other people around.

5) Pick a place where you can have a "conversation". Women want to get to know you and vice versa.

6) Make your 1st Date FUN and something she will look forward to. Women don't like to feel they are being interviewed or interrogated. Even though that's what you're probably doing, you can't let it sound like that! You want her to look forward to the experience of meeting you, not dread it.

Adding comments about the date is also good. For example, one smart man who was looking for a Long-Term relationship said in his Profile, *"Let's go on a First Date that we'll be able to tell our grandchildren about."*

Your First Date doesn't have to be earth-shaking and "grandchildren" memorable, but it does need to be fun and safe and enjoyable. If you include a suggestion of a good first date in your Profile, your chances of going out on the date go up exponentially.

Here are some examples of First Dates that are bland. After those are BARNSTORMING rewrites of the same thing. Many more examples of good 1st Dates can be found in the Appendix.

- <u>BLAND 1st DATE</u>: Let's go for coffee.

- <u>BARNSTORMING:</u> Let's go for coffee down at Dana Point Pier. They've got great coffee and hot chocolate, and they've got the best Apple Danish on the coast.

- <u>BLAND 1st DATE</u>: Let's go for a drink.

- <u>BARNSTORMING:</u> If you like good Mexican food and margaritas, the best place in town with great food and margaritas to die for is Emilio's. It's a mom and pop restaurant just off Welton and 14th (almost in the heart of downtown).

- <u>BLAND 1st DATE</u>: We could go for a walk somewhere.

- <u>BARNSTORMING:</u> We could take a walk along River Park. The tulips are usually blooming this time of year. Or is it iris that bloom now? We should go and see! From there we can walk up the street and get ice cream at Stone Cold.

- <u>BLAND 1st DATE</u>: Let's decide later.

- <u>BARNSTORMING:</u> Let's search for BIG FOOT! There's usually a sighting at least once a year here, and last year a man claimed the way you attract BIG FOOT is with Hershey Bars. I'll protect you and bring the Hershey Bars. Alternatively, we can have hot chocolate or coffee at the mall and go ooh and ahh at the Xmas decorations.

- <u>BLAND 1st DATE</u>: I like anything.

- <u>BARNSTORMING:</u> **I like active dates... hiking in the Rockies, biking in the State Park, skiing at Vail, whitewater rafting. If it moves and is outdoors, I like it and hope you do, too.**

- <u>BLAND 1st DATE (and a turn off):</u> Something short in case we don't like each other.

- <u>BARNSTORMING:</u> **You choose: A delicious coffee concoction downtown at Carrido's, appetizers/tapas for lunch at Tapeo, a drink or dinner at Corridor 44.**

- <u>BLAND 1st DATE (and sounds like an interrogation):</u> Coffee and talking so I can find out more about you.

- <u>BARNSTORMING:</u> **Hmm... Let's meet at Pete's Place for coffee and biscotti. If you like great food, my favorite is mouthwatering Spanish appetizers and dinner at Baca Baca with a glass of wine. Just thinking about it makes me hungry. Quick, email me so we can go there soon!**

- <u>BLAND 1st DATE:</u> A glass of wine and good conversation is a good place to start.

- <u>BARNSTORMING:</u> **A glass of wine at Fourth Story and the best crab cakes in town? If that doesn't appeal to you, how about browsing through the big, used bookstore on the mall? There's a great coffee shop across the street. That's heaven... good books, good coffee, and great company.**

The First Date is a place to WOO and WOW the woman. It's not mandatory that you go to the place you suggest. The First Date suggestion is just that...a suggestion. It gives her an idea of the kind of places you like to go on a first date. Even if you ultimately decide to do the typical "coffee date" or "a drink" for your First Date, she has an idea of what the future may hold.

The 1st date suggestion is an opportunity to be creative or funny or down-to-earth or romantic. It's a place to be awesome, not awful like these are:

- UH-OH 1st DATE: **You tell me.**

- UH-OH 1st DATE: **A nice night in front of the TV!**

- UH-OH 1st DATE: **I prefer to have a 1st date on the phone.**

- UH-OH 1st DATE: **Take me to the nearest stripper bar, and I'll be yours for life.**

- UH-OH 1st DATE: **Movies suck for a first date. Let's not go there.** (It's amazing how many men say this. Don't be one of those men.)

- UH-OH 1st DATE: **Txt n c k**

- UH-OH 1st DATE: **Let me surprise you.**

SEARCH ME??

KEYWORD SEARCH, MUTUAL

SEARCH, REVERSE SEARCH

If you find a path with no obstacles... it probably leads nowhere.

There are many paths leading to the woman you'd like to date. Some dating sites send you matches. Many let you search for your own matches and have a boat load of criteria to search by: age, location, height, body type, education, income, and dozens more.

If you live in a large city and the dating site you're on has a lot of members, you can be very selective in your ideal criteria and your searches. If you live in a less densely populated area, you soon learn ways to ease up on your perfect criteria.

Easing up doesn't mean "settling". Expanding your mileage range is the easiest way to expand your dating pool without sacrificing your "perfect" criteria. Expanding the age criteria slightly and the height criteria work well, too.

Besides the "normal search" most sites offer, some sites offer specialized searches. On many dating sites you can search by Interests or Keyword. Don't forget to enter KEYWORDS (aka INTERESTS) on your own Profile, and don't forget to search for them on others if it's mandatory you find a woman with similar interests.

For example, if you are looking for a bilingual woman, you can perform a Keyword Search on the word "bilingual". If you are looking for an "affectionate" woman, you can perform a Keyword Search on the word "affectionate". Search on "golf", or "Italy", on the author "Grisham", or whatever word you like.

If she has listed the word in her Keywords or Interests, her Profile will come up. She can do the same thing and search on your keywords and interests to find you.

Enter 10 to 20 KEYWORDS or INTERESTS in your Profile if your site has this feature. More than 20 spells desperate, or egocentric, or A.D.D. (Attention Deficit Disorder). Your Keywords and/or Interests are displayed when she reads your Profile. These Keywords give her more information about you. Your 10 to 20 Keywords count. They are a short summary of who you are and what interests you.

Think of these words as FREE advertising space. What's not to like about FREE advertising? Use them, and use them wisely. Spell check them. Even bright men accidentally misspell Australia.

Some sites let you do a MUTUAL SEARCH. Mutual Searches look at your criteria and at her criteria and match you up. If your parameters mutually match, the woman is selected. This is an excellent way to see who meshes with you. It's also a good

209

reality check. You may find you've been so selective in your age, income, location, height, and other criteria that you've severely reduced your matches.

Another search you can use on some sites is the Reverse Search. This is a good reality check to see who is looking for you.

Last but not least, many Internet Dating sites will do searches and email them to you. On many of the services, you can select if you want to receive them daily, several times a week, once a week, etc.

REMEMBER: Women expect you to search for them! They are doing their own searching, but they like confident men who contact them first.

BIG HINT: Many dating sites have a **WHO'S VIEWED ME** and a **FAVORITES** section. Check yours regularly. Women often look and don't contact you EVEN if they're interested. They sometimes mark you as a FAVORITE and leave it up to you to make the first move. Read her Profile and see if you mesh. Many times she's waiting for you to go first.

WHAT

WOMEN WANT

"My girlfriend doesn't know what she wants."

"You're lucky. My girlfriend does."

Regardless if you select your own matches or if matches are sent to you, BEFORE you start emailing women, you need to know..... What Women Want!

We know Men are from Mars... and Women are out of this world. True fact. If you're in doubt, ask any woman. Men and women think differently and are turned on by different things.

We know you know that. But you gotta do more than know it. You gotta put it into practice. Millions of articles and books have been written on the subject.

Before we reveal the Road Map to the lady's heart, one caveat: This is a great road map, but it's a map of the Country not of every side street and brain cell.

If you want a map that shows every stone along the roadway, read Freud or Skinner or Dr. Drew or Dr. Phil or chat with a smart therapist for a few days or a few decades. You'll probably need to bring the woman with you for accurate results.

You can also check out Amazon or your favorite local bookstore. Make sure you've got a high limit on your credit card, and bring lots of recyclable shopping bags.

If you're in a hurry to immediately know ALL the answers to What Women Want, let the Internet come to the rescue. Here's what we found:

- "What Women Want In Relationships": 37,500 articles
- "What Women Find Attractive": 232,000 articles
- "What Women Want": 255,000 articles
- "What Women Want In A Man": 3,230,000 articles

You can spend this lifetime and the next 1000 lifetimes reading about relationships and what she wants. There are plenty of good books, and we recommend you read a few on relationships, on sex, on being a good spouse, effective parent, mentoring grandparent, etc.

There's also a lot to be learned in the real world. You quickly learn what the books did *not* tell you. You quickly figure out what the books told you, but you didn't quite learn.

HUMONGOUS SECRET: Here's the definitive TREASURE MAP to finding out What Women Want:

1) **READ HER PROFILE.** **It's in there.** Reread her Profile. Many women specifically say: *I want- I want- I want.*

2) <u>START WITH HER USER NAME, HEADLINE, AND WHAT SHE LISTS FIRST</u>.

What does her user name tell you? Is she friendly, funny, clever, touchy-feely, matter-of-fact, lonely, harsh, obscure?

What does her Headline tell you? Is she telling you what she *offers* you, or is she an I WANT woman? Is her headline too syrupy or too desperate or too overly sexual? Is it a "nice" headline, a witty one, a classy one, or a crude one?

What does she list FIRST in her Profile? A Profile is like a <u>**grocery list**</u>... the important things are usually at the top or listed first. Sometimes they're in the Profile 2 or 3 or 4 times but in different words. If it's in there a lot, she WANTS it a lot!

Look between the Lines. Is she a GIVER or a TAKER or BOTH? It's there.

If you're so inclined, print out her Profile and underline and highlight the key passages; or use a word processing program to do the same thing. If you're looking for a life partner, her Profile "story" is far more important than most of the ones you read in school. Spend time on it if you're interested in dating the woman for a long-term relationship.

3) <u>LOOK AT WHAT SHE DOES NOT SAY</u>. **What's MISSING from her Profile is just as telling as what's there. Sometimes more so.**

If she doesn't say a word about her job or career, often it's because it's low on her lifestyle totem pole. Or, she may be out of a job or retired. Occasionally it's because she's concerned about Gold Diggers.

If there's nothing in her Profile about physical activities, those things usually aren't very important to her. If there's nothing touchy-feely in her Profile or it reads like a resume, emotional and physical bonding may be low on her want list, or she may have trouble expressing emotions.

Is her Profile "*too short*"? Is she a woman who doesn't tell you much about herself? This may spell a very uncommunicative or uncaring woman, or a woman who is hiding something, or she may be a woman who isn't ready for a relationship. "Too short" leaves you in the dark, and you're going to have to do some emailing and chatting to shed some light.

Is her Profile "*too smooth*"? *Are the emails she sends you just too perfect?* She may be "the One", and she knows it's important to write a good Profile and send good email. Or, she may be a serial dater who knows what you want to hear. Is she a pretty wolf in sheep's clothing? Is she looking for male Nurse or a Purse? Watch her actions for clues.

The more Profiles you read and the more First Flirts you send and respond to, the better you'll get at figuring out the woman behind the Profile. You'll be able to better define if the Profile is the woman or a figment of her imagination.

4) **LISTEN TO WHAT SHE SAYS**. *She'll tell you what she's looking for and what attracts her.* This is common sense, but many people get nervous on a date and do more talking than listening. You have 2 ears and 1 mouth for a reason. Listen at least as much as you talk if you want good information.

5) **HISTORY OFTEN REPEATS ITSELF**. A good way to find out how she arrived in Internet Dating Land is through emails and conversations. Women who are looking for relationships usually welcome a man who talks about more than the weather and football games.

Email the woman or ask, **"What adventures in life brought you here?"** That's a whole lot more tactful than asking, *"What worked for you and didn't in your last relationships?"* The latter will work, but only after you've established an openness and comfort level with the other individual. Women who are seriously interested in a new relationship will be asking the same questions of you. Be prepared to answer them.

6) **WATCH! HER ACTIONS WILL SHOW MORE ABOUT HER THAN ANYTHING SHE SAYS.** It's not just what she says, it's what she *does*. It's also what she does *not* say and what she does *not* do. Actions always speak louder than words. ACTIONS SHOUT! Make sure you're listening and watching.

Watch her "body language". Body language is harder to interpret than words, but it's often more honest and accurate.

If her words are warm and fuzzy and genuine, her body language should be relaxed. She'll touch your arm, run her hand through her hair. If she tousles your hair, she's definitely relaxed and comfortable with you.

If she's sitting across from you with arms folded tightly across her chest in a closed posture, things aren't going so well.

Here are other examples of actions:

- Does it take her days to respond to emails? **BAD sign.**

- Does she often call you at the last minute to reschedule a date? **BAD sign.**

- Does it take her days to return your phone calls? **BAD sign.**

- Does she sometimes take you out and pay for the date? **GOOD sign.**

- Are you always the one initiating the dates? **BAD sign.**

- Does she appreciate being taken out to dinner and being "courted" months after you started dating? **GOOD sign.**

- Does she offer to help you with things (cooking dinner, washing dishes, grocery shopping, picking out new curtains, planting flowers, weeding the garden, staining the deck)? **GOOD sign.**

- Does she follow through on what she promised? **GOOD sign.**

- Does she forget your birthday? **BAD sign.**

- Does she remember your birthday with a card *and* something personal like a new shirt or a cool electronic gadget? **GOOD Sign!**

- Does she remember your birthday with a mushy card, a romantic candlelight dinner, lots of "cuddling", a new shirt, and a new car? **WHOA! Wake up! You're dreaming.** If not… this woman is probably a keeper.

7) <u>MAKE A PIZZA FOR YOUR IDEAL WOMAN</u>.

Here's a clue about that ideal woman thing… Cinderella isn't real, Barbie is in a box on the shelf, and Princess Leia still lives in a galaxy far, far away. If you like psychology and analyzing people, you'll like this section. If you're more like George, skip this section, and go on to the next.

Who's George? George is the guy whose girlfriend just ran off with his best friend. When George heard that he said, *"That's just great! That's 2 less people to buy Christmas presents for."*

If you have the sensitivity of George and think planning for the future is buying 2 cases of beer instead of one, skip ahead to the next section. Fuggedabout making a pizza, and order a Pepperoni or Veggie one because this section takes some dexterity and introspection.

This section tells you how to make a Relationship Pizza. Life coaches do this with their clients all the time. There are various recipes. Relationship Pizzas aren't constant, but they usually change slowly over time.

Forget the flour and getting the kitchen dirty. Get a pencil, an eraser, and 1 piece of notebook paper. On the paper, draw 2 large circles. Section each so each has 10 pizza-pie pieces.

Now comes the hard part. In the top pizza, write down the 10 most important things you want in your life and in a relationship. Put one item in each of the 10 pizza sections.

Be brutally honest. Nobody's peeking over your shoulder. Here are some suggestions you might want to put in the 10 sections: *Sex, Money, Adventure, Career, Security, Family, Companionship, Fun, Romance, Travel, Respect, Power, Status, Success, Similar Interests, Fitness/Health, Travel, Spiritual Growth, Activity Partner, Friendship.*

You aren't allowed to use the words Love and Happiness and Soul Mate and Chemistry. Those aren't specific enough. You need to define what you mean by those words. Is it Sex and Romance/Intimacy? Is it Money and Security? Is it someone being there for you? Is it having a lot of together time? Is it having a balance of companionship and alone time? Be specific in your pizza toppings.

Now for the hardest part. What is the most important? Are they equally important? If so, all the slices of your pizza are exactly the same size. That's rare. Most people's Relationship Pizzas have slices of all different sizes.

Is Sex more important than Companionship to you? Are Money and Career more important than anything? Is Family at the top of your list? Is Career at the top? Are Career and Family equal?

Your 10 pie slices need to have a number value assigned to them based on how important each item is. The higher the number, the more important. *The total of the 10 numbers must add up to exactly 100.* Here's how a mythical pizza might look with the numbers assigned:

1) FAMILY 30%
2) SEX (and Romance) 30%
3) MONEY 30%
4) FRIENDSHIP 30%
5) FUN 30%
6) FITNESS, HEALTH 30%
7) CAREER 30%
8) SAME HOBBIES/INTERESTS 20%
9) ADVENTURE 20%
10) TRAVEL 20%

Oops…it adds up to well over 200%. No wonder finding the road to Happily-Ever-After is so difficult. There are more priorities and things to do and achieve than hours in the day.

Adjust your numbers to add up to 100. Resize your Pizza slices accordingly. If you know yourself well, your pizza will be a reflection of your written Profile. If it isn't, guess who's got some rewriting to do?

Now for the fun part! Read the Profile of the woman you'd like to date. Does this woman look like she has what you are looking for? Be still my thumping heart!

Before you start ordering wedding invitations, make *her* Relationship Pizza. How do you know what's important to her? Read her Profile. Check out her photos. What she places importance on will be in her photos and in her Profile.

Are all her photos "work-related", or do her photos show her in work clothes and casual clothes? What do her home photos reveal? Where does she like to go on vacation? Are all her photos indoors? Do her photos reveal a love of nature? A love of adventure? Security? Her photos are more than a picture of her. They represent her life.

Pay attention to her User Name and her Headline. Pay attention to the order in which she says things in her Profile. It's worth repeating…<u>Profiles are often like **grocery lists**. What you want or need the most is often at the top.</u>

You're out of milk. It goes at the top of your grocery list so you don't forget it. You're out of bread. You write it in capital letters. You're out of Peanut M&M's. You may hide them from yourself when you get them home, but they are on your grocery list with a star next to them so you don't forget them. **Her Profile is her Grocery List.**

What does her Profile tell you about what she needs and wants? Is she a fun-loving woman (i.e., she loves fun fun fun)? Or is she a fun, loving woman (i.e., she's into fun and into loving).

Gee, the little itty-bitty comma between the words Fun and Loving makes a lot of difference. So do all the little things in real life.

Is she looking for a soul mate? Or a play mate? Is she into chemistry? If so, she'll want to meet sooner rather than later. Is she a family woman? A career woman? A giver or a me-me-me woman?

Pick 10 descriptions of what she's looking for and what's important to her and write them in her Pizza circle. Assign number values to each of the 10, and make sure they add up to exactly 100. Draw her slices bigger or smaller so you can visualize her better.

COMPARE YOUR 2 PIZZAS. Does she have what you're looking for? Do you have what she says she wants? If you've got most of what she's looking for and vice-versa, you're ready to start flirting!

Knowing what she likes and what she doesn't like will help you flirt more effectively whether via email or in person. You'll also soon learn if her emails match her Profile.

Some women are nothing like their written Profiles. These are usually the women who write exactly what men want to hear. They read men's Profiles and mimic what the men want in their Profile. Did you really think all those women who say they like motorcycles really do? Wake up and smell the gasoline fumes!

But ya say you don't like to play games and analyze her and appeal to what she wants? Ya say you want her to like you for who you are?

Who are you? You are the man who rolls out of bed in the morning with bedhead hair, a beard that needs shaving, and the *"just give me five more minutes to sleep"* expression on his face.

The *real* you is also the man who took a shower, shaved, combed his hair, had his first cup of coffee, and is dashing off to conquer the day. That's you, too.

Before she gets to know the bedhead, sometimes-grumpy-in-the-morning you, find out if she likes the rest of you. Making your Relationship Pizza and her Relationship Pizza will give you a good idea if cooking together is in your future.

If you absolutely, positively can't figure out from her Profile what she wants, check out the next chapter. Men and women attract each other in different ways, but there are many more similarities than differences in what they want in a relationship. If that wasn't true, no one would ever date or live together or get married.

Knowing what turns women on will help you appeal to the woman you're looking to attract. That's covered in the next chapter. The following benchmarks of What Turns Women On may not be national monuments carved in stone like Mt. Rushmore, but they are gigantic roadside markers that abound on the highways.

WHAT TURNS WOMEN ON

& KEEPS THEM TURNED ON?

Eve to Adam: Do you love me?

Adam: Who else?

If you remember the above joke, you will remember one of the most important ways to keep your woman turned on. She likes you to tell her how much you care about her.

Words are wonderful, but ear candy alone won't do it. She has other needs and wants. What are her specific needs and wants? Look in her Profile. Her Profile and her photos tell you what she values.

TIME OUT! What happens if she has few photos and wrote a super-short Profile? What if you can't figure out what the woman wants? Not to worry. This chapter will help you understand (gulp....yes, understand) the female psyche. As one smart man said, *"You can't understand women, they're all crazy."* As another smart woman said, *"Yeah, but guess who made us that way."*

The following info isn't carved in stone, but it's more solid and more fun than a bathtub full of jello. It will open your eyes into the wacky and wonderful world of WOMEN.

Women usually like to move slower than you do:

Emailing a woman *" **Wanna F ?** "* is a good way to get her to block you. When you walk her to her car and zoom in for that French kiss on the 1st date, that's too fast for most women.

If you're not doing either, that's not smart. Not the French kiss, silly, the car thing. If you're not walking her to the car and making sure it starts, it's often why you're NOT getting a kiss goodnight or a 2nd date.

Most women need to have more than 1 email before she agrees to date you let alone sleep with you. **Instead of asking for a date on your 1st email, be considerate of her need to know more about you.**

You need to show her you're worth meeting and that she will be safe. Women don't want to email for eternity, but they need to feel safe and secure before they meet you.

Do not offer your phone number or your personal email address in your first email. That spells desperation, and it's too forward and too soon for most women. That's like saying, "I'm really horny" or "Call me at 1-800-LONELY1."

Smart men will not ask the woman for her phone number in a first or second email. **That's space invasion.** Don't ask her where she lives. Don't ask where she works. Respect her privacy until she gets more comfortable knowing you. If you want to chat with her, offer your phone number after a few emails. Don't ask for hers.

Some women like to chat with a man and hear his voice and how he "talks" before she'll consider dating him. Do not be dismayed if she wants to talk to you but wants to block her phone number. If you know her phone number, you can often find out where she lives.

It's possible she might be blocking her number because she lives in a crummy house or because she lives with her parents and doesn't have a place of her own, or she's married and she's fooling around. However, the most likely reason is because she's concerned about her safety.

Don't ask her for her full name until she's ready to give it. She knows you can easily find out where she lives by checking the public records.

Public records work both ways. Don't boast about your wonderful half-million dollar house when the County records show it doesn't exist.

If you contact a woman who moves really, really slowly, she's either not that into you, or she's inexperienced. If she's inexperienced in dating, take the lead. Women like confident men and expect the man to lead and ask for the date. If you're inexperienced, fake it till you make it! Put out your hand and hold hers. There's something to be said for going down the new road of experience together.

Women like security: Women want good providers. A good provider has been valued since caveman days. Survival back then meant the man had to be smart, resourceful, a hard worker, strong, and sharing. Those qualities are still valued by women. They spell SECURITY. Women like security.

Today a good provider is a man with a good job and who's protective and supportive. A good education is also valued by women. The more you show her in your Profile that you are a secure man, the more appealing you will be to most women.

Women like TIME with you: Women like that you have a job and interests of your own, but making TIME for her is at the top of her want list. TIME means sharing activities. It also means "talking". "Talking" is less excruciating if you combine it with an activity you like.

Women like healthy and strong men: Health and strength fall under her need for Security. If she wants children, she's looking for a healthy man to father them and raise a family.

If she has children, she's looking for a man who can assist her in raising her family and possibly start a new family. Older women appreciate healthy and strong. They have little desire to be the "nurse" or the "purse".

One of the best ways to show you're fit is to post a full body photo. Athletic and in shape mean different things to different people. Full body photos do more than all the words you write about being fit and in shape; but keep the shirt on and don't do the naked torso thing.

Women like adventure, but not as much as you do:

Many men and women love the adrenaline rush of activities like whitewater rafting and skydiving as well as from tamer activities like skiing and surfing. As a general rule, men are more daring and adventurous than women.

The flip side of adventure is stability and dependability. Both appeal to most women. Most women are done with wild parties and wild adventures before men are. Most want to settle down and have the cozy house and maybe a child or two. If your Profile is coming across as wild guy, adventurous guy, party guy, go-out-every-night-on-the-town guy, guy who never wants to grow up, or fun-fun-fun guy... that may be why you're not having the dating and relationship success you did a few years earlier.

Women like attractive men:
Duh! Here's the great news for millions of men on the planet who don't look like Brad Pitt or Usher or the latest James Bond actor... women put much less emphasis on looks than men do. Aren't you lucky!

Women find a wide range of men "attractive". If you have any doubt, check out the dates and mates of supermodels and top actresses. The men range in looks from handsome to homely.

Women are more apt to value intelligence and personality and security over looks. Intelligent men are attractive. Men with good jobs and good personalities are attractive. Men with similar interests and goals are attractive. Women value your sense of humor and your kindness and sensitivity.

On the physical front, women find many kinds of men attractive. They like men with short hair, long hair, no hair (yes, it can be verrry sexy), thin men, husky men, tall men, rugged men. Women have physical and age preferences, but the good news is the range of what they find physically attractive is extensive.

Many women are looking for "chemistry", but "chemistry" is almost impossible to define. On the other hand, "attractive" is easy to define. Figure out what "attractive" means to the woman you are thinking of dating. Attractive to her may mean taller than she is by a few inches. Attractive to her may mean you have a good job. Attractive to her may mean you have a good education. Attractive to her may mean you're physically fit and healthy.

Read the female Profiles and pay attention. After reading enough Profiles, you'll get better at seeing what the woman finds "attractive". You'll know if it's your sexy bod, your sexy personality, your sexy mind, or your sexy wallet.

Women like masculine men: This goes back to the "Security" thing. Masculine equates with being a strong man, a good provider, a man to father her children, a confident man. Women like all those things. That's not to say women don't appreciate sensitive and caring men. They do. But they enjoy the "protector" factor. They want to be feminine and cuddly around you and have you comfort them. Sensitivity in your Profile is good, but it's not smart to say you cry at the movies. Stay off of Too-Much-Information Highway until you know her better.

Women are visual: If you didn't know that, it's time you did. That's why it's important to post the right kind of photos. Visual isn't just what you look like and what you wear. It's also the place you pick for your first date, what your car looks like (did you wash it and clean the inside, too), what your house looks like, the cleanliness of the kitchen, the towels in the bathroom, the inside of the refrigerator, the pictures on the wall, the furniture, the pillows and sheets on the bed. Women take it all in.

Women like sex: You did know that, right? Some women are looking for *fun* sex. Many more are looking to *make love*. If you don't know the difference between "sex" and "making love", you are going to get hurt. Or you're going to hurt someone. Women don't like being hurt any more than you do, and considerate men practice consideration.

There are women who have sex with you to *"try you on for size"*. How do you fit physically and mentally and emotionally? Do the sparks fly? Is the chemistry there?

Sometimes women are *"trying you on for the future"*. What will it be like to live with or to be married to this man? She's looking for a man who has similar sexual desires and likes and dislikes. Most women are looking for a man who believes in monogamy.

Men and women use sex to say many things. It may be *"WOW, I'm horny"* or *"WOW, I like you"* or *"WOW, I care about you"* or *"WOW, I love you."*

It's easy to be confused and misinterpret sex. She's going to be asking herself: How considerate is he in the bedroom? How considerate is he out of the bedroom? You should ask yourself the same thing about yourself and about her. The bedroom is important, but you spend most of your day out of the bedroom.

Be informed about women, toys, and the joys of sex. There is plenty of good info out there. Need we say... Be Safe.

Lots of unfun and communicable stuff is out there. The latest statistics are that 1 out of 4 people have herpes. The "old" and wrong medical advice was you couldn't catch herpes if the person didn't have an active outbreak.

Read up about herpes and chlamydia and all the other STDs. Talk to your doctor about staying safe and keeping your partner safe if you have an STD.

Many men and women talk about getting mutually tested for STDs before they jump into bed with a new partner. Women appreciate men who care enough to be concerned about her health and his own. *"Thanks for sharing"* is a lovely sentiment, but not when it comes to sexually-transmitted diseases.

Women like to be appreciated: Women like to be complimented with sincere praise. Women like to hear that you like how they look, how they smell, how they dress, how they make love, how they live their life, that they're good at their job, a good mother, a good person. The fact that you noticed *and told her you noticed* goes a long way towards pleasing the woman.

Women have the same kind of insecurities men have. Praise her and tell her how delicious the meal was that she cooked for you; tell her she's got a flair for decorating her house; tell her how great she looks in those new jeans or the new dress; tell her you're proud she got the promotion at work.

Tell her she's raised great kids; tell her she's really progressed at her golf game; tell her you like the way she kisses, that she gives the best hugs.

Tell her that you like her nose (that may be a little crooked), her ears (that may stick out a little), her hips (she's curvy and huggable). She likes to hear it from you just as much as you like to hear those things from her.

Women like to know you want her and respect her:

Women like to be courted and wooed. There's an old saying....Men pursue, women select. She likes that you want to date her. She likes that you want to kiss her goodnight. She also likes that you respect her boundaries and don't go too fast too soon.

She'll often give you a clue she wants the goodnight kiss. Ditto with the foreplay. Pay attention to her body language. She likes that you initiate foreplay and will often clue you into her receptiveness.

You can always set the stage with a special candlelight dinner that you cooked just for her. If she shows up with her overnight bag, you can probably assume she likes you.

231

Women like emotional bonding: Women like men who have time for them and who are willing to listen to them. Women like to share their day and their ups and downs and be heard. That doesn't mean they want to be "fixed" and have all their problems solved. Often they just like to be heard, and valued, and respected.

Women often want and need the emotional bonding *before* the physical bonding. Connecting emotionally first works better than trying to jump into bed with her on the first or second date.

Women like men who are willing to wait or work for her affection. If you don't get a goodnight kiss on the first date, it doesn't mean she doesn't like you. She might like you very much. It's important to her that you know what her standards are. The guys she loses are the ones she knows she's better off losing.

How do you know if she likes you? Ask her if she had a good time. Ask her if she'd like to go out again. ***If she accepts a 2nd date, she liked you, dude!***

When you're in a relationship for a while, women still like bonding. She likes to feel cherished and valued and appreciated. She likes to tell you about her day and hear about yours. She likes to be teased and surprised and courted. You like to be flirted with, and so does she, whether it's 2 weeks into a relationship, or 2 months, or 2 years.

Talking and communicating are high on the list of her wants. If you've ever heard a woman say, *"I love cuddling",* it doesn't mean she didn't like the sex. It means that the "cuddle" was the icing on the cake. It gave her the tenderness and bonding that were high on her list.

Women like action, but they need more than action:

Men like to do things, especially active things: golfing, hiking, skiing, biking, horseback riding, surfing, rafting, making stuff, making love. They also like to watch active things: football, basketball, soccer, baseball, NASCAR races, hockey, action movies including sexy action movies.

Women like to do active things, too, but if you're a smart man, you'll include talking in the activity. You look at most activities and experiences as bonding. For her, the bonding often needs to include talking and communication as part of the activity.

Women like status, but not as much as men:

Women like that you drive a nice, clean car and have a nice, tastefully decorated home. If you have a job, she likes that you have a good job. If you have young kids, she likes that they're good kids and doing well.

If you have grown kids, she likes that they're successful and independent. If you're retired, she likes that you were successful and achieved financial independence that allowed a comfortable retirement.

However, for many women, it's not the status that's important in and of itself. It's the security that comes with having the status.

Women like power, but not as much as men: Career is important to many women, but many times women forego or cut back on careers to concentrate on family. One of the biggest complaints men hear from women is *"You don't spend enough time with me."*

Many women resent that the man spends too much time at work. Many men are put off that the woman is not supportive and doesn't understand the demands of his career.

If you have a challenging and time-consuming career, finding time for the two of you may be challenging but not impossible.

Realize that most women like the security your job offers. She also likes a man who can find time to share the fruits of his labor. Smart couples figure this out early and find a way to balance work and play.

Women like their alone time: Remember the "caveman" concept? It's the concept that men need to head to their cave and do their own thing and have alone time.

He wants to think or decompress or have his space. Women are the same way, but usually less so. She needs time to recharge her batteries. She also needs her alone time to get ready for her date with you.

If you think she woke up with her hair combed, her lip gloss on, and her mascara in place, you've obviously never been married.

Women like toys, but not the kind of toys men like: What did you give your last girlfriend for her birthday? If it was an electric sander and she never used it to sand your deck, this section is for you.

Most men like things such as electric sanders, cordless drills, fast cars, old cars, cameras, computers, bikes, motorcycles, things with motors, skis, golf clubs, pool tables, fishing gear, camping gear, boats, jet skis.

Women like toys, but they really like sentimental things from their man. She likes getting a gift from you which she can wear *and think of you.* Clothes, lingerie, perfume, and of course, the ultimate gift for women... Jewelry! We're not talking an engagement ring, we're talking other jewelry such as a pair of earrings, a bracelet, a necklace. All are wonderful gifts to most women.

Jewelry is high on the gift list because jewelry is sentimental. It's also "practical". Any women will verify that statement. Jewelry lasts for decades. Getting something special for your woman is not that complicated. *Think feminine and sentimental.* Sentiment will do it every time!

HERE'S WHAT MOST WOMEN DO NOT LIKE

Women do not like critical men: Your date is cooking dinner for you for the first time. You look down at your dinner plate and say, "Uhh...is this weird stuff supposed to be chicken or is it some kind of awful-looking meatloaf?"

No hugs and kisses for you tonight. You don't like critical women. She doesn't like critical men. When she messes up, she wants you ON her side and laughing with her not at her.

No one likes a person who constantly says or implies, "You're not good enough" or "You could be better." Women like supportive men. Women like men who are on her side, who watch her back, who are there for her in the good times and the bad.

Do not say in your Profile..."I like a woman who will stand up to me" or "I like a woman who will call me on my B.S" or "I'm good at calling you on YOUR B.S."

She's not looking for a sparring partner; she's not looking to be your mom; she's not looking for you to be her dad. Most women are looking for an equal, a best friend, and more.

Women do not like needy or controlling or angry men:

Women like confident and strong men. Angry men with tempers are shunned by most women. Women want men who show good self-control over themselves and their resources. She isn't there "to make you happy" or "to complete you" or "to make you laugh" or to be your court jester. It takes two to make a relationship. Most women want to be a mate, not a mat.

The man who says "I'm looking for someone who will love me for me" doesn't come across as sensitive and caring, he comes across as shallow and needy. The man who says, "I'm looking for a woman who will make me happy all the rest of my life" isn't going to get a chance to date her because he comes across as needy. Women are looking for men who fill their buckets, not ones who take and take.

Women do not like it when you won't express your emotions:
Women do not like it when you won't talk about the relationship. That should come as no surprise. Women like to talk more than men, and talking about "the relationship" is high on her list. She likes hearing how much she means to you. *(Remember the Adam and Eve joke at the beginning of this chapter!)*

When you talk to her about "the relationship", she feels a sense of bonding. She feels you care about her. Talking about the relationship and hearing how much she means to you gives her... yes... Security.

Most men hate to talk about the relationship. That's near or at the TOP of the list of things men would rather not do. Instead, men want to be *"actively relating"* rather than talking about relating. Most men do not like to gab on the phone or lay in bed for minutes or hours talking about *"the relationship"*. They'd rather be doing fun and active things.

Women like to be active, but they also like the bonding that talking brings to their lives. Women like to hear that their man missed them, that their man thinks she's cute, that their man appreciated the dinner she cooked.

Most men are NOT good at expressing their emotions. Most men will devour the dinner and ask for seconds, but he won't say, *"WOW, thanks honey."* He'll work out with her at the health club, but he won't say, *"WOW, you look fantastic."* He'll nibble on her neck, but he won't tell her, *"WOW, am I ever lucky!"*

She's not a mind reader. If you open your mouth and let some sentiment find its way from your brain to your vocal cords, you might be surprised at the appreciation she shows you in return.

It is not enough to do your emotional bonding via activities: sharing breakfast together, watching a DVD, working out, walking, taking in an art museum, having fun in the bedroom. She wants *talking about emotions, too.* Yes, it may be boring to you, but one of her biggest sex organs is the one between her ears. If you think of it that way, maybe talking will be less boring in the future.

Women don't like it when you don't share or give:

Sharing means sharing your day, your thoughts, your emotions, your time, your resources. She doesn't want a workaholic who she never gets to see. She wants to share activities and conversations with you. She wants to hear how your day went, how your job is going, what your plans are for the future. She likes to share in return. Men who listen are very smart men.

Sharing goes hand in hand with giving. She wants a demonstrative man whose middle name isn't "Cheapskate". If you can't afford to woo her now with your attention and affection and gifts, she'll most likely write you off as a long-term prospect.

Women do not like it when men don't respect their time:

Waiting until Saturday afternoon to ask her for a date on Saturday night is usually not smart. If you're in bed with her, you could probably get away with it.

If you want to go out on Saturday, ask her early in the week. Anticipation is foreplay.

If you don't respect a woman's time, you may find out sooner rather than later she's not willing to be your "beck and call" girl. Women like men who respect them and that means respecting their time.

Women do not like it when you skimp on foreplay:

Women need more romancing than most men. There's a reason women buy most of the scented candles, the mushy cards, the cookbooks to cook a romantic dinner, etc.

Emotionally and mentally and physically, women like more foreplay than men do. Many men still haven't figured out that foreplay is much more than massages and kissing and cuddling before and after.

MEN... you need to fulfill her romantic and sensitive and emotional side. You may have to ask her to give you some tips on her wants and desires. Women are usually very happy that you asked and sometimes offer a guided tour. If she's new to the world of foreplay, it's fun to learn together.

Women don't like fireworks... except in sex: Most women don't like trauma/drama. She gets enough trauma/drama at work or with the kids. She might like fireworks at the beginning of your relationship, but trauma/drama gets old in a hurry.

If you have kids, she likes that your kids are well-behaved and that you're not shouting at them every other minute. A woman's home is her castle, and she'd just as soon come home to a comfortable castle than one that's on fire.

Women don't like competing for your affection: She doesn't want to compete with your mom or sister or ex or children or friends or job. This is a biggie. Women like to feel they are the joy of your life, the one. She loves that you like your job, but she wants you to make time for her, too.

She doesn't mind that you spend time with your mom or sister or friends or kids or talk with your ex about raising the kids. However, she doesn't want to feel like she's competing for your affection. If you don't make her feel like she's the queen of your castle, she won't treat you like the king of the castle. The word is commitment. She wants to know you're committed to her.

Let's summarize: MOST WOMEN like... security, safety, going slower, praise, attractive men (which means much more than looks), masculine men, confident men, visual things, no fireworks except in the bedroom, sex, talking, bonding.

She likes to share and converse; she likes a man who respects and appreciates her and who shows his appreciation with gifts and sentimental tokens of affection and with his words.

She does not like trauma/drama, or needy men, or whiny men, or angry men, or controlling men. She likes it when you show your emotions and talk about "the relationship". She likes it when you make time for her and give her space for her alone time.

What do you do with all the information? Key in on what she likes when you email her, when you talk to her, when you date her. PLAY the tunes she likes. You'd like it if she did that for you.

A wise sage once said a good relationship isn't 50/50. It's 100/100. You give 100%, and the other person gives 100%. That's smart. There's no keeping score on who gave more. Those are the relationships that last.

FIRST FLIRTS

(1ˢᵗ Emails)

Man to cute woman: *Do you hear the ambulance siren? I think it's coming to pick me up because when I saw you, my heart stopped.*

You found her! She's kissable! Attractive, great smile, beautiful eyes, and more. Her written Profile is a winner! WOW! Your heart is thumping! Physical and mental chemistry look promising.

You think about making a Relationship Pizza to chart her Profile, but you're in a hurry. You'll do it later. You know she is heads above the rest. What should you do?

There's only one correct answer: **EMAIL HER.**

Do not Wink. If you don't have the confidence to write, many women think you're not worth dating. She wants a confident man, and she wants to hear what you have to say.

Some women get so many winks, they can't keep up. Ask yourself when's the last time you picked up a woman in the real world by winking at her? It's not much different in the online world.

Do not mark her as a Favorite. Some sites call Favorites "Preferred Date" or "Bookmark". Whatever it's called, don't put her in the Favorite box (yet).

Send her an email. Many women don't check their Favorites section regularly. Lots of "players" and "serial daters" mark women as Favorites and sit back and wait for the cuties to reply. If you want to date her, EMAIL her. You can mark her as a Fave AFTER you email her.

If you're not comfortable sending the First Flirt email, too bad, so sad. You aren't going to change evolution by wishing it were different. Women expect you to take the initiative. Don't wait too long. *Another man may start dating her while you're thinking it over. If that happens, she might hide her Profile, and you won't be able to find her.*

Women expect you to be confident. *Even if she saw you first, it's the solemn duty of the man to make first contact.* That's how the online world spins. Don't get into a <u>stalemate</u>. A stalemate is when you are waiting for her to contact you while she's waiting for you to make the first move. Nobody wins.

But you say you hate to send emails only to get a written rejection or no answer? Boo Hoo! Get over it! Sexy, good-looking women often get inundated with email when they first join a dating site. They're "fresh meat" to the hungry wolves. That's why it's critical you send a great First Flirt and stand out from the salivating howlers.

Write your First Flirts and all email in a word processing file. Spell check what you write. Copy the email into the online dating program to send it. Reread all your emails before sending them. It's easy to mess up and say you're looking forward to meeting a new *"fiend"* when you meant to say *"friend"*.

Shorter First Flirt emails are better than longer ones. Don't pour out your whole history. Pouring it out all at once is like hitting her with a tidal wave. Don't make her think you're carrying a whole shipload of baggage with you on that wave.

Focus on the present. Focus on the positive. Talk about what you have in common and what you liked about her Profile.

Remember: Women like approval and praise. So do you. The emails you like the best are ones that appreciate something about your Photos and Profile. Those are the kind of emails she likes best, too.

Be genuine with your praise. Be succinct. Don't lay it on so thick that she'll need hip-high boots to wade through it. ***Asking one question in your email is a good way to get a conversation going.*** Read her Profile carefully and ask something that is based on her Profile. Faking that you like her hot buttons works, but not for the long term. Facades get heavy to carry after awhile.

Be interested in her. If she likes movies, ask if she's seen the latest Oscar winner. If she's a skier, ask if she's gotten up to the slopes this year. If she's a reader, ask what she's read recently. If she's posted a photo of herself in Rome or Egypt, ask what she thought of the city or country. If she says she's new to online dating, ask her how she likes it. If she's been online for awhile, ask her how she likes it.

Most women like to talk about their jobs. They like to talk about their families. Even if they don't like their families, they'll be happy to vent about them. Check out her Profile. You'll usually have dozens of easy questions you can ask to get the conversation started.

A GOOD FIRST FLIRT is made up of 2 parts:

> 1) The **SUBJECT LINE**
> 2) The **FLIRT**

Many men mess up on both. Some forget to put a subject line or put in a wimpy one like "Hi". Other lame ones are "Hey" and "Hello" and "I liked your Profile."

First Flirt emails need catchy subject lines. "Oooh sexy!" grabs her attention but not in a good way. The subject line needs to grab her attention in a good way. **"Wow!"** and **"Amazing!!"** and **"I can't believe it!"** and **"You Win!"** are examples of good Subject Lines. You've got her curiosity aroused. She wants to read more. Check out the good subject lines below. More examples are waiting to grab your attention in the Appendix.

GOOD SUBJECT LINES for 1st FLIRTS:

- **This is a test, this is only a test...**

- **What a coincidence...**

- **I can't believe you said that!**

- **That was TERRIFIC!**

- **Maple Salmon or Prime Rib??**

- **Did I pass the interview...**

- **Your mom told me to call you...**

- **Your boss said...**

- **Is it too soon to tell you...**

- **I don't believe in horoscopes, but ...**

Do not use "Hi Honey" or "Hi Sweetie" or "Yummy". Hot fire or sloppy sentimentality is too much too soon. That's like the man who said, "My idea of a perfect first date is to have sex in a public place and then go have coffee and get to know each other."

HUMONGOUS SECRET: Subject lines that leave her wondering *"What the heck does he mean by that"* or *"What the heck is he going to say next"* are usually good Subject Lines as long as they're not crude or rude. You have her on the edge of her seat waiting for you to say more.

HUMONGOUS SECRET: After the Subject line is the short and sweet First Flirt. <u>Short and sweet means 3 to 5 sentences.</u> That's plenty for a first email. Slightly flirtatious and slightly flattering is good. Too much of either will cause you to crash and burn.

HUMONGOUS SECRET: Mention something SPECIFIC from her Profile. Show her you read the Profile and paid attention. Show her you didn't cut and paste your email from the last one you sent. Or if you did cut and paste, you took the time to insert a sentence that pertained to her. Don't focus solely on her looks. Focus on her Profile. She wants to know it was more than her pretty face that attracted you.

Your whole Profile is "foreplay", but now you've stepped it up a notch to *INTERACTIVE FOREPLAY*. Asking for a date for tomorrow night is too fast. If you're moving too fast, that may be why you aren't getting dates. Women like to feel safe and secure before accepting a date. It's usually best to flirt for a few emails before you ask for the date. Don't email for weeks on end. She'll lose interest. *She wants you to ask for the date before she turns 65.* If she's already 65, she's often thinking, "Time's a wastin." Ask sooner rather than later.

HUMONGOUS SECRET: All good First Flirts end with you including your *real first name* at the bottom of your flirt. It sounds obvious, but many men leave off their name or sign their screen names at the end of their flirt. Women like to flirt with men who have REAL names.

There are no examples of bad First Flirts because you probably already know how to compose those. What? You don't know how to be boring or crude and rude? Insensitive and callous?

Okay, since you twisted our arm, here are examples to never, ever use. Then again, if your emails sound like these and they're working for you, the number one rule is *"Don't mess with success."*

Different men are looking for different things. Some men send emails like these because they're looking for sex and only sex. As one man expressed quite candidly, *"There are a lot of sl*ts online. I usually have to send 10 to 100 emails, but I can finally find one."*

<u>DO NOT USE THESE HORRIBLE FIRST FLIRTS:</u>

- Hi Sweetie-Pie, BIG WET KISS. Imagine my arms wrapped tightly around you. Email me. I think I'm the one! Your sweet lovin, and Xxxtralovin ME!

- I think you're HOT! Wanna chat?

- I bet I can make you holler, "Don't stop!"

- I have a lot of stamina!

- My nickname is Big Mike! Guess why!

- You know ya wanna... wink wink!

If your First Flirts look more like erupting volcanoes than flickering candlelight, check out the soft glow of the good First Flirts below.

As you'll see from the sample First Flirts, ending your flirt with a question is a good way to keep the conversation going.

Don't think one good question deserves another. It doesn't. This isn't the Spanish Inquisition. One or 2 questions are plenty. If you want pages and pages of original First Flirts, the APPENDIX can't wait to flirt with you!

GOOD FIRST FLIRTS: (many more are in the APPENDIX!)

- FIRST FLIRT: **Hey! Not fair! Foul! This was a clever setup! You purposely used intelligent banter to lure innocent men into your web, I mean profile. There is not one mention of candlelight or sunsets. No fine wine by the crackling fireplace? If these things are unacceptable, please release me back into the wild. Zack**

- FIRST FLIRT: **Houston we need a solution. A highly intelligent woman with an advanced sense of humor and wearing a denim jacket has been located. GPS tracking must be implemented immediately. She is an endangered species and must be handled with extreme care. Aaron**

- FIRST FLIRT: **You made my day! A cute woman who is intelligent and can spell those long multi-syllabic words. I'm intoxicated! Seriously, I liked your profile a lot.**

And your photos, too, especially the one in the mountains. Please check out my profile and see what you think. Pete

- FIRST FLIRT: **Hi! I found your profile witty and humorous (loved the story about Maui) and liked your pictures. Was wanting to strike up a conversation. I'd be pleased if you read my profile. Are we potentially matchificent? Will**

- FIRST FLIRT: **You and I are probably not enough of a match because....A) you're heavy duty athletics, I'm lite to moderate; B) you have nicer looking hats than I do; and C) you're a darn liberal and so am I so we'd have nothing to fight about. So, what say you?? Mark** (Based on her Profile, pick 2 or 3 things and state tongue-in-cheek that you're "not enough of a match". Women are intrigued by a challenge and saying she's NOT a match for you makes her want to be one. Can you say *"reverse psychology"*?)

- FIRST FLIRT: **You have a charming and creative profile. I especially like that you volunteer for "green" causes. Too bad I don't get into Boston a lot. How's this online dating thing working for you? Any good pointers for the new kid on the block? Daniel** (This is a good way to see if the mileage is a deal breaker. If she finds your Profile attractive, often she's flexible on the miles. She may have family or friends in your city. She may travel to your city on business. This gives her the opening to tell you.)

- FIRST FLIRT: **You can't be better in person because you're already cute, articulate, and your dogs put you over the top. My dog thinks I'm cute and smart and**

250

funny, and he has high standards. Any ideas how I can bribe him into vouching for me? Would enjoy hearing from you. **Brad**

- FIRST FLIRT: While I'm one inch from your height qualifications, you'd swear I was 2 inches taller in person. I'm devastatingly cute (if you squint) and a good cook, though from your profile, I bet you're better! Tonight I'm trying a new shrimp and veggie recipe. What's on your menu? Marcelo

- FIRST FLIRT: I enjoyed your profile a lot and since you say you're addicted to good coffee, I wish I was closer to invite you to share a cup of coffee with me. I'm hoping you'll think (like I do) that the distance presents an interesting "challenge" vs. an obstacle. Looking forward to hearing from you. John (This is a good way to see if the mileage is a deal breaker. If she finds your Profile attractive, often she's flexible on the miles.)

Internet Dating is like going on a fishing trip. You have to make a lot of casts (First Flirts) and put a lot of hooks in the water. If you go fishing and expect the fish to jump in the boat, you're going to be disappointed.

The same thing is true with dating. Women aren't going to be chasing you or any man only from your photo (well... maybe Brad Pitt, but he's probably taken.)

But you say you don't like to be rejected? You say your modus operandi to attract women is to wink and send "canned emails" because you don't like to be rejected? How's that working for ya?

You say you're waiting for her to contact you because you don't want to send the first email and not have her answer? How's that working for ya?

Even a broken clock is right twice a day. Your technique will work sometimes. You can continue doing what you've been doing, or you can find a better way. No one likes rejection, but guess what? Rejection happens to the best of us.

Super - attractive - super - rich - super - talented - super-successful - super - duper movie stars and rock stars and doctors and lawyers and Indian Chiefs get rejected every day of the week. Nobody is immune. You can mope and throw yourself a big, pity party. Or you can throw yourself an itty-bitty, pity party and get over it. It's better finding out sooner rather than later she wasn't a good fit.

The bad news is if your Photos or Profile or First Flirts don't represent the real you, she may have turned you down for the wrong reasons. That's why it's critical your Photos, your Profile, and your First Flirts put your best foot forward rather than show you with your foot stuck in your mouth.

How do you start flirting? That's easy. Based on the information in her Profile, wing it by writing 2 or 3 practice First Flirts for her. If you haven't had good success at winging it, do a

Relationship Pizza for her. See what her hot buttons are, and focus in on what you have that pushes those buttons.

Pick one flirt and send it to one woman. You may want to pick your Favorite woman, or practice with a second or third choice so you don't risk blowing it with your Fave.

Many men flirt with several women at the same time. If you're new to Internet dating, that can get complicated in a hurry. If you thought juggling 3 balls in the air was hard, try juggling 3 women. They're not as easy to catch.

BIG SECRET: **DO NOT email the woman for weeks or months on end without meeting her.** Why? Because you may not like the way the woman looks in person. She may have posted photos from 5 or 10 years ago. She may have a squeaky voice which is more irritating than attractive. She may have said she's a non-smoker but smells like tobacco.

On the other hand, you may have been the one who "fudged" a bit too much. If that's the case, it's best for both of you to meet in the real world sooner rather than later.

P.S. – A POST SCRIPT

is Powerfully Smart

Post scripts are powerful and smart to use. They are effective and make your email stand out from the crowd. People often read the P.S. before they read the email. The P.S. gives you an extra chance to WOW her.

- <u>FIRST FLIRT with P.S.:</u> **Your photos and Profile were matchificent! Please RSVP if you find my profile as interesting as I find yours. Loved the story about your vacation. Jason**

  <u>P.S.</u> – Why did I find you "matchificent"??   We share many of the same interests, and wow… you've got gorgeous eyes and a great smile.

- <u>FIRST FLIRT with P.S.:</u> **Your dad must have been a thief… he took the stars from the heaven and put them in your eyes!   Let me know if you bought that line! Seriously, you have beautiful eyes, and anyone who can teach high school kids must be a genius with a big heart. Dave**

  <u>P.S.</u> – if you didn't laugh at the "thief" line, I dare you to send me your YOUR corniest pick-up line.

- <u>FIRST FLIRT with P.S.:</u> **You can cook, and I would love to learn! I have tons of FF miles so meeting you for dates would not be a problem at all. The only problem is since we're only 25 miles apart, it might be faster by car. Jim**

  <u>P.S.</u>- So, should I fly or drive? What do you think?

- <u>FIRST FLIRT with P.S.:</u> **I don't know if we'll click, but if we do, I'm willing to lie and tell everyone we met in the Greek Isles rather than the grocery aisles. I see Whole Foods is one of your favorite places. Mine, too. Nicholas**

  <u>P.S.</u> - I'm headed there now... I'll be the one by the Greek olives. I hope today is one of your shopping days.

SHOULD YOU FLIRT WITH

NO PHOTO WOMEN?

She has a face like a flower. A cauliflower. But at least she goes to the dentist twice a year. Once for each tooth. She looks like a million... every year of it.

What do you do about No Photo Women? Do you ignore them or take a chance and flirt with them? The first thing you do is read her Profile. Often her Profile explains why she doesn't post a photo (safety concerns; too much mail from horny guys half her age, etc.).

Some women have valid reasons for not posting a photo. Others do not. Some women are older or not as attractive as their Profile implies. Some are married women who pose as single.

Many no photo women have a line in their Profile that tells you to ask for a photo if you're interested. If you are interested and she seems above board, send a First Flirt. You can ask for the photo immediately or wait. If she sends it with her reply, you're on a roll. If she doesn't send it or offer it, ask for the photo sooner rather than later in a classy way:

- **P.S. I'm looking forward to your photo. I'm sure your smile is as lovely as your Profile.**

- **P.S. I'm looking forward to seeing the photo of the woman who matches this great Profile.**

- **P.S. And you promised a photo... I'm looking forward to seeing your smiling face.**

- **P.S. Send me a pic of your dog, too. Not for me, for my dog, silly!**

If she doesn't offer a photo after 1 or 2 emails, *ask for the photo pronto*, or run for the exits.

Good-looking women can get away with <u>not</u> posting a photo. You can't. Even so, women who post photos are more likely to find their match. Women know there are fakers of both sexes online, and she doesn't want to look like that. Women and men fudge about their age, weight, body type, and sometimes their marital status. Fudgers purposely avoid posting photos.

Proceed with caution when the woman doesn't have a photo gallery. She may be fine... or she may be a fraud. Be cautious when the woman comes up with a zillion excuses as to why she can't send a photo.

As one man put it rather bluntly, ***"She may be a looker, or she may be a hooker."*** Obviously the man was delusional. Hookers know men are visual. Smart hookers post photos.

Ah yes...Welcome to the World of Internet Dating. It's just like the Real World... only faster!

Don't be a JUNK MALE

who sends JUNK MAIL

"Yummilicious! Woman...you're a hottie! Check out my Profile, okay?"

Crude and rude mail is *obvious* JUNK MAIL. There are other kinds of Junk Mail that will get you Read/Deleted as quickly as crude and rude email.

Email that looks like it was cut and pasted from the last woman you sent it to is junk mail. She figures you're either trolling for sex or are so desperate you have to send tons of mail to get one date.

If you are cutting and pasting, and it looks like a cut and paste job, your emails are going to be shredded by all but the online novices. No amount of glue will help.

If you're going to cut and paste your emails, make sure you include at least one or two sentences in your email to PERSONALIZE it to the woman.

Here is some typical Junk Mail:

- JUNK MAIL from a JUNK MALE: Your profile really impressed me. No, that's not a line, I've never said that before. You seem like you are the proverbial "entire package"- beauty, brains, morals, and tenderness. I'm looking for a woman with the potential and desire to become my "best friend" because I believe that friendship is the foundation for a lasting relationship. I would be honored if you checked out my profile. I've tried to give you an accurate snapshot of who I am. If you have any questions, I'll be happy to answer them for you. Frank

- <u>JUNK MAIL from a JUNK MALE:</u> You have a great smile, and there was so much in your profile that I read through it several times. You obviously put a lot of time into expressing who you are and what you're looking for. Your profile really made me think, and you have a great way of expressing yourself. I think we have a lot in common, and I'd like to know what you think. Jake

- <u>JUNK MAIL from a JUNK MALE:</u> Hi! Your profile touched me, and I had to write and say hi. I don't know if we're a good match, but I really liked what you had to say and how you said it. It seems you are that rare woman who has just as much (or more) going for herself on the inside as the outside. I would consider it an honor to get to know you. Les

HUMONGOUS SECRET: An exceptionally long email is often a telltale sign it's cut-and-paste Junk Mail. If you're sending mail like that, STOP! If you receive a super-long, first email from a woman – BEWARE!

The Junk Male who wrote the email below was smarter than most. He camouflaged his cut-and-paste email by putting in a few sentences that were specific to the woman he was writing. Those sentences are underlined in the example below.

One or two personal lines in a Junk Mail are often enough to fool the woman into thinking the email is genuine and from the guy's tender heart. However, experienced daters know better. Alarm bells go off when a super-long mail like the one below lands in the mailbox.

- <u>CAMOUFLAGED JUNK MAIL from a JUNK MALE</u>: Hi...we have a lot in common. <u>I like playing golf, too</u>, <u>and I like doing anything around water</u>, swimming, canoeing, boating. People who know me say I am smart, funny, considerate and dependable. Few know that I am romantic and affectionate. I get along with almost everyone, but I can't stand people who are pushy or inconsiderate of others.

  I am an easy-going person with a keen sense of humor, an eye for adventure and a hopeless romantic. I am financially secure, have achieved success in my life.

  <u>I'm glad to know you like to garden and travel.</u> My house and garden are my sanctuary. <u>I love to travel, too,</u> and would love to know where you want to travel to on your (maybe our?) next vacation. How about a week in the Paris countryside, staying in small inns, enjoying old villages, great dinners?

  I'm looking for someone special to share life with, and you seem to have many special qualities. It shouldn't take long because we will know if it is right. I'm looking for someone real for a lifetime relationship. Looking forward to getting to know you.

  Yours fondly, JUNK MALE

OMG...

SHE EMAILED ME FIRST!

"Hi MysteryMan001, Your Profile made my day! And your smile made me smile..."

It's ALL GOOD when the woman emails you first! It's all good when she winks at you or marks you as a Favorite.

Women are more likely to go first if you give them a little encouragement in your Profile. A woman may be confident, but she worries you'll think she's too forward if she goes first. A little nudge in your Profile can help overcome those concerns.

When she goes first, jump and shout and do a woo-hoo victory dance. Pat yourself on the back! Celebrate a while!

Wow, that was fun! Next, go read her Profile. Did you attract the kind of woman you were looking to attract? If you posted the right kind of photos and followed the formulas for a good Profile, you will have. You might get a few weirdos emailing and winking, but that's dating life on the Internet. Be glad you don't get the amount of junk mail women get.

If she winked at you, don't respond with a wink. That's lame. Email her. She can get away with winking and marking people as Favorites, you cannot.

Don't answer her 2 seconds after you got her email or wink. Desperate isn't a good color on any man. Just right is somewhere between 2 hours and 24 hours.

If you're serious about dating, check your email daily. You appreciate timely responses, and she does, too.

Begin your Come Back Flirt with a THANK YOU:

- **Hi, what a nice compliment to mark me as a favorite…**

- **Hi, glad you winked!**

- **I must have missed you standing in line at the grocery! Thanks for writing!**

- **Great timing! I was going to write to you this weekend!**

- **I see you beat me to marking you as a Favorite…Wow! Kismet!**

- **What a wonderful surprise… an email from you…**

- **You must have been reading my mind….**

- **Glad you stumbled across my profile….**

After you thank her, add a First Flirt the same way you would if you initiated the contact. If she asked you a question in her email, make sure you answer it.

See the First Flirt chapter and Appendix for more examples of First Flirts.

BIG SECRET: Women who initiate and email you or wink first found your Profile and photos "safe". That's good! You can usually ask her for a date sooner rather than later.

Examples of the "Thank You" with the First Flirt:

- COME BACK FLIRT: **Hi and thanks for the email. I read your profile and really enjoyed it. The story about your vacation and your winter skiing photos were terrific... as is your smile! Have you gotten up to the slopes this year? Richard** (Focus on one or two things you particularly liked from her Profile. Don't make it all physical.)

- COME BACK FLIRT: **Hi and thanks for the wink. I see we have a lot of common interests. I'm a big believer in chemistry, and your profile and smile spell Chemistry to me. Do you like to meet sooner rather than later? If you'd like to meet, maybe we can meet for coffee or lunch next week? Shaun** (Depending on her Profile, this might be a bit "fast". Tone it down by substituting a question such as *"Have you finished your Christmas shopping yet?"*)

- COME BACK FLIRT: **Hi and thanks for the email. I see we're both readers and hikers. I just joined a few months ago, and it's been quite a learning experience. What adventures brought you to Online Dating Land and how do you like it? Rick** (Note: You may wish to wait before asking about "adventures" and ask how she likes the site.)

HUMONGOUS SECRET: Think very carefully before you state in your Profile you don't answer winks (if your site allows winks, that is). Many fine women who are not comfortable sending you an email are comfortable sending a WINK your way.

Do you want to eliminate the "winkers" when they read your Profile? If so, do it with class. If you say, "*I don't answer winks, so don't wink*", you sound like a jerk. That will turn off many women, even those who planned on emailing you. Instead, try:

- **Please send an email if you're interested.**

- **Winks are flattering, but emails make me smile more!**

- **Winks are good, but I'd much prefer to hear more about you.**

- **Wink only if it's after 2 a.m. and you're too bleary-eyed to type.**

- **We can start with a wink-a-thon, but I'd rather hear more about you.**

- **Wink if you're interested. Email if you're interesting AND interested.**

BIG SECRET: **Pay special attention to the last one above.** You can substitute any flattering adjective for interesting... smart, funny, etc. If the woman winks, she admits she's not interesting. What woman is going to admit she's not interesting or smart or funny? You've tricked her into emailing you instead of winking, you smart man, you!

SHE SAW ME...

but she didn't Email or Wink

She saw your Profile before you saw hers, but she did nothing. ~sniffle~sniffle~

She didn't wink. ~Sniffle~ Boo-Hoo~ She didn't email. She didn't call. So what if she didn't have your phone number? That's no excuse.

Does she like you? Does she find you attractive? Only one person knows, and that person is her. Don't sit around trying to read her mind. Don't waste your money on a crystal ball or an astrology reading. Save that for a wild and crazy, future date. Right now, she's one click away.

If she did wink or mark you as a Favorite, that's your immediate cue to contact her. If you see a woman has looked at you and not marked you as a Favorite, don't despair. Even women who are interested in you often don't like to go first. If you're interested in her, send her a First Flirt like the ones in the First Flirt Chapter or one like this:

- FIRST FLIRT when she sees you FIRST: **Since we've looked at each other's profiles, shall I wink first or should you? My wink would mean I like the fact that** you said _____. **Seth** (Put 1 thing from her Profile you particularly liked and found winkable.)

- FIRST FLIRT when she sees you FIRST: **Somehow you stumbled onto my profile. How could anyone not respond after reading yours and seeing you said _____. (Put 1 thing from her Profile). Finding a way to meet might be tough, but maybe it could be? Care to trade emails and discuss it? Ryan** (Location can be flexible if the Profiles mesh. If you don't find romance in your backyard, expand your mind and your mileage.)

- FIRST FLIRT when she sees you FIRST: **Hi... I saw you took a look at my profile and.... I liked what I read in yours... especially that we share common interests in music and hobbies. If there's some mutual interest, please give me an electronic jingle. Have a wonderful Saturday. Ethan**

- FIRST FLIRT when she sees you FIRST: **Hi ....I noticed you viewed my profile. I'm flattered by being viewed by someone so far away and so attractive. It appears we have similar careers and like to do the same things for fun. Interested in getting acquainted? James**

Many times saying *"thanks for looking"* is all it takes. Many times lamenting the distance between you is not a deal breaker. Sometimes the woman will come back with *"Do you ever vacation in CA"* or *"I get to your city a few times a year on business."*

Be the hero and go first. She looks, but she wants you to make the first move. Women figure you're big and strong and can handle rejection much easier than they can. She knows you're checking **"Who's Viewed Me"** and who marked you as a **"Favorite"**.

The only way to get better at flirting and contacting is by doing it. Read a dozen Profiles of women who looked at you. Read two or three dozen. Put on your suit of armor, pick out a woman who seems to be a good match, and send a great First Flirt.

COME BACK FLIRTS

IF SHE SAYS, "Thanks, but no"

"Sorry, I'm busy Saturday night. I have to get a head start on my 2050 tax return."

What if you send a First Flirt to her, and the response you get is *"Thanks, but no"*? What if her response looks like this:

- Thanks, but I'm dating someone and want to see where it goes.

- Thanks, but I'm already corresponding with 2 people, and that's already 1 too many.

- Thanks, but I'm taking a break from dating.

- Thanks, but we're not enough of a match.

- Thanks, but I don't think the chemistry is there.

- Thanks, but I don't think we have enough in common.

If she said *"Thanks, but we're not enough of a match"* or *"I don't think the chemistry is there,"* she knows herself better than you do. No sense beating a dead horse. On the other hand, many times the woman leaves the door open.

BIG SECRET and REALITY CHECK: If you **frequently** get told *"no thanks"*, it's time for a reality check. You may find your original search criteria of finding a woman who is 10-15 years younger than you, who makes over $100,000 a year, who looks like the gal on the cover of Cosmo, who has her own jet and small yacht, and has no baggage other than a small Gucci carry-on is a bit unrealistic. It might be time for a reality check.

Read her reply carefully. If she says "*I'm dating someone now, but it's too soon to know,*" reread her Profile and look at her photos. See if you're interested enough to send a Come Back Flirt.

"I'm dating someone and want to see where it's going" is not all bad news. The reality of Internet dating is that she may not be dating that person next week or next month. The other reality is that she may NOT be dating anyone. She's telling you that to spare your feelings.

"I'm dating someone, and it's too early to say where it's going" is the #1 most common excuse people give when they're not interested. It's right up there with *"I'm taking a break from dating right now."* They're trying to be tactful. It's a lot more ego-friendly than her saying, *"Hey, I'm just not interested"* or *"Sheesh…you didn't even read one word of my profile, did you?"*

Many women are truthful when they say they're dating someone and want to see if it works out. Decide if this is a woman you're serious about dating. If you are, send a Come Back flirt. Let her know the door is still open on your end. Do we have examples for you? That's why this book is so darn long… and check out the APPENDIX, too.

269

Come Back Flirts to KEEP THE DOOR OPEN when she says, "Thanks, but not right now":

- KEEPING THE DOOR OPEN FLIRT: **Thanks for your response. You have confirmed what I thought about you. You are attractive both inside and out! If things don't work out, please think of me. Joshua**

- KEEPING THE DOOR OPEN FLIRT: **As they say here in Vegas, "You are too cool for the room." I wish you the best, and if your new date doesn't work out, I'd enjoying hearing from you. Rick**

- KEEPING THE DOOR OPEN FLIRT: **Hi, and all I can say is, "Why don't they make women that way around here?" Knowing you exist gives me hope! If your new date doesn't work out, I'd enjoy hearing from you. Wishing you the best! Ron**

- KEEPING THE DOOR OPEN FLIRT: **You deserve the best, and I hope for you that he's the one. I hope for me that he's not! :D Best to you! I'm just a click away. Good luck! Andy**

- KEEPING THE DOOR OPEN FLIRT: **If the new pen pal doesn't live up to your expectations, send me an email. I'm much nicer than he is! :-) Billy**

Leave the door open for the woman to reconnect. Don't pressure her, or she'll pull back. If she's never ready, so be it. Do not automatically think you did something wrong. She knows herself better than you do. It's not always about you. Sometimes it's about her.

"I didn't say it was your fault. I said I was going to blame you."

Computers crash. Internet connections break down. Kids accidentally delete important email. That must be the reason she didn't respond. Or not.

It would be wonderful if women responded to all emails. It's no fun when they leave you in the dark. Unfortunately, men are somewhat to blame (just ask any woman).

Many women have been conditioned by men not to respond. Too many men have sent rude emails after the woman politely replies, *"Thanks, but no."* After getting a few nasty emails, many women choose not to respond if they're not interested.

If a woman doesn't respond, it's a pretty good bet she's not interested. She thinks she's not a good match for you or vice versa.

If you don't hear from her, you can try emailing again with a **DESPERATION FLIRT.** These 3 might work, but don't be surprised if she doesn't answer. Or, don't be surprised if she blocks, you. She figures you didn't get the message the first time.

DESPERATION FLIRTS:

- **Hi Ms_XYZ, I don't know if you didn't get my first email, but in case you didn't, just wanted to say...** (Now put a regular first flirt here).

- **Hi Ms_XYZ, I'm sure you get a ton of email, and hope mine didn't get overlooked. In the event it did, I just wanted to say...** (Now put a regular first flirt here).

- **Hi Ms_XYZ, I didn't hear back from you and on the chance that the Internet ate it (don't you just hate it when that happens), I thought I would say hi again.** (Now put a regular first flirt here).

It's good to acknowledge you sent a prior email. If you don't, it looks like you blanket the world with flirts, and you don't remember who you sent them to. That you remembered you flirted with her is a point in your favor.

"Your Profile says you're attractive and intelligent. It even has your body type wrong."

"Sorry, I don't date outside my species."

There are good ways and not so good ways to say *"No thanks"*. It never hurts to be polite. When you email a woman to say *"Thanks, but no,"* if you want to leave the door open for a possible connection later on, make sure you do so. If you want to close the door, make sure you do. Here are examples of both:

CLOSING THE DOOR:

- <u>CLOSING THE DOOR</u>: **Thanks for taking a chance on me, but I'm one of those "darn liberals". I get along best with someone who is politically liberal. Best of luck to you! Ray**

- <u>CLOSING THE DOOR</u>: **Thanks, I'm flattered, but I'm looking for someone who lives closer. Long distance relationships haven't worked well for me in the past. Good luck. Logan**

- <u>CLOSING THE DOOR</u>: **Thanks, but the good news is that I'm dating a woman who may just be 'the one". I**

273

found her here online. I hope you find your Mr. Right, too! Wishing you the best. Eli

- CLOSING THE DOOR: Thanks for choosing me, but I mesh better with someone who is _____ (Fill in the blank). Adam

LEAVING THE DOOR OPEN:

- LEAVING THE DOOR OPEN: Thanks for the email. While I multi-task well, I don't seem to be able to do that when I'm dating. However, you sound both smart and nice. It's too early to know where it's going with the lady I just met, but you never know. Wishing you the best! Jon

- LEAVING THE DOOR OPEN: Thanks for the compliment. I just started dating a woman whose profile is quite similar to the core values in yours. It's too early to say where it's going, but if it doesn't work out, I'll be sure to let you know. Best to you! Ian

- LEAVING THE DOOR OPEN: Thanks but I'm taking a break from dating since I was one of the casualties in the latest economic mess and need to concentrate on job searches. I was a mid-level bank manager. Wishing you the best. Chris (Note: She might know of an opening. It's a small world.)

Another smart reason to be polite is because people change. The woman you turn down today because she isn't athletic may join a gym tomorrow. The woman whose short, spiky hair you didn't like may grow it out longer this year. The woman you turn down today for not being a college grad may go back to school in the fall. The woman who's wearing unattractive glasses may get contacts or LASIK eye surgery. She might win the lottery. It happens.

Women (and men) "bloom" at all ages. If you think the bloom is off the rose, you may be pleasantly surprised to see a new and more appealing rose has taken its place.

HOW LONG

SHOULD YOU WAIT?

"I'm busy now. Can I ignore you later?"

After you send your First Flirt or reply flirt, how long should you wait? If you don't hear from her in 24 or 48 hours, should you write her off? Absolutely not.

Some women don't get online every day. Some are on vacation and don't take their computers. Computers and Internet connections break down more than we like. If you're expecting her to run to her computer to check her email every hour, your expectations might be a little high.

Many sites keep track of and display the last time each user was online. Some sites call it "Last time online" or "Last Login time". Many sites tell you this info for free. Some tell you if your email was read. Other sites charge extra for this extra info.

On many sites, <u>if you pull up the woman's Profile,</u> it may not tell you if she read her email, but it often tells you the last time she was online. If she was online, odds are she read her mail.

<u>WARNING:</u> You may not want to pull up her Profile to check to see if she was online. On many sites, if you pull up her Profile, she'll know you're checking up on her. It registers in her list of "Who's Viewed Me".

Great news! Here are some <u>HUMONGOUS SECRETS</u> to help you get around that. Many sites give you ways to find out when she was online without her knowing you're checking up on her.

1) **Many sites allow you to hide your Profile.** This is called <u>**Stealth Mode or Hidden Mode.**</u> When you are in Stealth Mode, you can check out her Profile without her knowing you looked.

2) **On many sites, the "Who's Viewed Me" section displays last time online.** If she recently looked at *your* Profile, check *your* "Who's Viewed Me" to see when she was last online.

3) **If you marked her as a Favorite, your Favorites list often shows the last time she was online.** Conversely, she'll also know you were online if she looks at who marked her as a Fave.

4) **On many sites, another way to see if she's been online** *without pulling up her Profile* **is to run a search**. Search for a woman who has her age, location, education, etc. The last time she was online often displays.

The info displayed and where you find it varies by your dating software. It's helpful to know where to find it *before you need it.* When you Search, most sites do not alert the other person they were selected in your Search. Most sites put you in the "Who's Viewed Me" list only *after* you click on the Profile.

    If you're checking up on her, be slick. Do not click on her Profile when she comes up in your search.

If she hasn't been online to get your First Flirt, give her some time to respond. If she has been online and doesn't respond in 48 to 72 hours, you can think about writing her off.

HUMONGOUS SECRET: If you get a lot of **UNRead/Deleted** messages, do not assume she didn't check you out. Many women use Stealth Mode when viewing your Profile.

If you get a lot of **Read/Deleted** OR **Unread/Deleted** Messages, it's a clear message your Profile, your Photos, and your First Flirts are not working.

BIG SECRET: Many women use STEALTH Mode to see if the man *they're dating* is as honest and exclusive as he says he is. Some women are surprised to find out the man they're dating is always online or is online many times a day. If you've told your date that you've *"stopped looking"*, she often wants to be sure you aren't playing her. If she sees you're online all the time, she's going to be drawing her own conclusions.

As more than one woman knows, *"Never try and teach the pig to sing. It wastes your time and annoys the pig."* Nuff said.

ASKING FOR

THE DATE!

Would you like to go out for brunch or coffee on Saturday?

I need to pick up my Nobel Peace Prize on Monday. Want to come along?

If I told you that you had a fantastic body, would you hold it against me?

Before you get the privilege of being nervous on the first date, you get to be nervous asking for the date. If you're nervous, here's a secret... many men are nervous when it comes to asking for the date. Be brave!

Bravery is when only *you* know that you're nervous. She's probably nervous, too, but she expects you to ask for the date. The only way you get better at asking is the same way you get better at most things... PRACTICE.

TIME OUT FOR A HUMONGOUS SECRET: When you ask for the date and you are *really interested* in the woman, it's smart to offer *2*, count 'em, *TWO* CHOICES.

For example:

- **1) Coffee**   **or**   **2) Lunch**
- **1) Drink**   **or**   **2) Dinner**
- **1) Coffee**   **or**   **2) Brunch**

Remember the last time you were at the eye doctor? The doc said to you, "Is 1 better, or is 2?" You choose whichever is better. The woman who chooses to spend more time with you is usually more interested in you.

BIG SECRET: Similarly, she knows the man who offers her brunch or lunch or dinner is usually much more interested in her than the man who offers coffee or a drink. She knows you're willing to put money on the table. Women are usually more receptive to men whose "actions shout".

Way to go! You've sent out your First Flirt and are waiting for a reply. One of 3 things will happen:

1) She won't reply.
2) She says, *"Thanks, but no."*
3) YES! SHE IS INTERESTED!

Let's start with the first one. If she doesn't reply, she's eliminated. Finito. She's not interested, and she's not polite either. Or, she might be inundated with mail and can't answer them all. It is possible (though not probable) your email didn't get through. You can send a 2nd First Flirt (aka Desperation Flirt), but most likely she isn't interested.

If she isn't interested, reread her Profile and your own Profile as well as your First Flirt. Are you sending the message you think you're sending?

If you send out a lot of First Flirts, and get a lot of non-responses, it's one of three things:

- **Your First Flirts need some work.**
- **Your Profile or Photos need some work.**
- **Or...it's time to get a reality check.**

Learn from it. You might have some rewriting to do. That's fairly easy. On the other hand, you may have to adjust your expectations. That's harder. Time and more First Flirts will tell you quickly if she has an attitude problem or if it's a perception problem on your end.

BIG SECRET: **Focus on her.** Extroverts love to be the center of attention. Introverts do, too, if the group is small enough. You're a group of one. She can handle that. Quiet women like honest praise. Extroverted women will eat it up.

BIG SECRET: **Start slowly.** You won't have to wait long. Slowly to most women usually is measured in hours or days, not seconds. Women usually don't move quite as fast as you do.

Reread the chapter on *What Turns Women On and Keeps Them Turned On.* Don't just read it, put the concepts to work. She likes to feel safe and secure. She likes romance, and she likes to feel valued and appreciated. She likes talking, and she likes men who are confident and giving and who share.

If she wants to move it along faster, she'll often give a clue as to how fast is too fast and how slow is too slow. If you want to move it along faster, you can, but don't do it on the first day.

Smart men will be aware of her need to be safe and will not ask for her phone number. Remember, you're not at a party or club where she can see you in person. She doesn't know if you're fine or a flake. For all she knows, you're 69 years old, and you still live with your mom and her 5 cats. After a few emails, you can offer her your phone number with the caveat that when she's ready to chat, you'd enjoy it.

BIG SECRET you should already know: Rather than using your regular email address, think seriously about using a 2nd address which you only use for your "dating emails". That way if 3 weeks later you wish you had never met this woman, you don't have the hassle of her knowing your real email address.

If she asks if your photos are current, don't be offended. She's been burned before, or she's heard the horror stories of online men who post photos from decades earlier. An easy thing to do is take a new photo or use one of your recent ones which you haven't shared with the rest of the world. Post it online or send it to her personal email. A new photo is a way to prove you are who you say you are, and women like getting photos you didn't post for everyone else.

FREE DATES!

And More Ways To Ask Her Out

Picture this: She shows up at your front door, naked with a case of beer and 2 candles. Okay, forget the candles.

Naked with beer as a first date might be ideal for you, but don't sit by your front door waiting for her to ring the doorbell. That's probably at least the 2nd or the 3rd date.

Good First Dates don't have to cost an arm and a leg. There are lots of <u>FREE</u> and fun places to go and things to see. If you live in or close to a big city, the choices are huge.

Your quickest place to find <u>free</u> places for dates is the Internet. Search the Internet with the words "Free Entertainment" and the name of your city or the closest large city. You'll find free festivals, free art shows, free concerts, free wine tastings, free classes, free family fun, and much more.

Many community and non-profit groups offer events throughout the year. Cities offer free classes in all kinds of things from Xeriscape and Green Living to Art and Architectural Tours. Check your local library, City Hall, colleges and junior colleges, and neighborhood newspapers.

If you don't have time to run a search, a new old-fashioned, almost-free date is a picnic. Picnics are romantic, and this may turn out to be your Best-First-Date-Ever.

It goes without saying, choose a safe park with lots of people around not some secluded place. You bring half the goodies, and she brings the other half. You'll learn a lot about her by what she brings (and vice versa).

Does she bring a real picnic basket overflowing with goodies? Does she bring a Whole Foods, recyclable, green bag with a few choice selections? Does she bring 1 Coke and the smallest bag of Ruffles that they make? Does she come empty-handed because she "forgot" or "didn't know what to bring"? If that's the case, you know she won't be your Last-First-Date-Ever.

Picnics can tell you a lot. Besides picnics, there are hundreds of other free date venues. When you ask your date to one of these free events such as an Art Fair or a Concert in the Park, it's not usually necessary to announce that it's free.

There is ONE exception to this rule. Most Museums and Botanic Gardens and Zoos and State Parks have free days. If you're taking your date on a free day to a place that normally charges admission, let your date know it's a free day when you issue your invitation.

Preempt your invitation by saying something like, **"I saw in the paper that next Saturday is a free day at the zoo. I haven't been in ages. Would you like to go?"**

If you don't tell her it's a free day when you issue the invitation, she'll find out when you get there. That's not good. She'll think the only reason you asked her was because you were too cheap to pay.

The opposite of being a cheapskate is the man who spends a ton of money on the first date. That can be uncomfortable for many women. Some men purposely put out a lot of cash on the first date in hopes the woman will "put out" in return. Spending a ton of cash on a first date may lose you more points than it gains.

BIG SECRET: If you invite your new lady to a free event, spend some money on her. If you don't spend some money on her, you're going to look like a loser.

Offer to buy her a latte or an iced tea at the Botanic Gardens, a bratwurst or veggie wrap at the free concert, the beverages and peanuts at the zoo. It doesn't have to be a fortune, but it should be something.

What if she offers to pay her share? Should you let her? Great question! Check out the chapter on WHO PAYS! Find out what she's really thinking when the bill comes.

Here are classy ways to ask for the first date to FREE places. Check out the *APPENDIX* for more free date ideas.

FREE PLACES:

- The outdoor Art Fair is next weekend in San Clemente. Would you like to go?

- There's an Architectural walk downtown on Saturday morning. Would you like to go?

- The Taste of Chicago is next week. Lots of free music and dancing. Care to go?

- They're having a free Xeriscape class at City Hall next week. Does that appeal to you?

- Fidelity is giving a free investment seminar tomorrow night. Would you like to go?

- Do you want to join me for a walk in Wash Park for exercise on Saturday morning?

- I'm taking my dog to the dog park on Sunday. Would you like to go with us?

- Would you like to go for a hike with my mountain club?

- There's a book reading downtown I'd like to go to. Would you accompany me?

- I need to buy my sister a birthday gift. Care to help and go shopping with me?

HOLD THE PHONE! The above "buy a gift for your sister" is a great 1st date or 2nd date or 3rd date. If you don't have a sister, you can substitute the word niece or sister-in-law or co-worker or any female person.

Asking for her help is dynamite. You'll learn a lot about the woman. You'll learn what stores she likes; you'll see how she relates to store clerks. She'll reveal how she looks at finances, clothes, electronics, giving, etc.

Plus, you're not spending a penny on something you hadn't planned to buy. You don't have to actually buy the gift for your sister, but it's smart if you do. Why? Because the woman feels successful. Feeling successful feels good.

One other smart thing about gift buying. Ask the clerk if the gift can be returned if your sister doesn't like it. This does 2 things:

- It shows the woman if you get her a gift in the future, she can return it if she doesn't like it. That's the kind of "open-mindedness" women like.

- If you blow your budget, you can return the gift and get your money back. Hopefully you won't let your date talk you into spending more than you planned, but those things happen.

IMPORTANT SAFETY NOTE: Meeting at a big mall or downtown is smart. The woman feels safe. She doesn't advertise the kind of car she's driving or her license plate.

Once you've met the woman, you should always offer to walk her back to her car. If she feels safe with you, she'll say yes. Her car reveals a lot about her. Is it new or old, expensive or cheap, clean or needs a wash, trashed out or tidy as a pin?

If you want to know how the woman thinks about her mother (or father) you can do "shopping for Mother's Day". You can always be creative and invent a new holiday such as *My sister had her gallbladder out, and I want to get her a get well gift*". There are many scenarios for the 'gift' date: buying a gift for your daughter's soccer coach, for your neighbor's birthday, for the Christmas grab-bag at your office.

Here are more ways to ask for the date. These won't cost you a fortune, but they aren't 100% free.

ALMOST-FREE DATES:

- **The flea market is this weekend. I haven't been in years. Want to check it out? Lunch is on me!**

- **The Farmer's Market is downtown on Saturday morning. Care to go, and I'll buy us breakfast?**

- **I'm going to be in your area on vacation next month. Care to join me sightseeing? I'll buy dinner.**

- **I'm going to be in your area on business next month. Care to play tour guide, and I'll buy lunch?**

- **Our subdivision has a garage sale next week. Want to shop for bargains?**

Short, simple, polite, direct. The first part is figuring out where to go. The second part is working up the courage to ask. Or is the courage the first part? Either way, the more asking you do, the easier both get.

When you go on your date, pay attention. Pay attention to her because women like attentive men. Pay attention because you'll learn a lot about her. Pay attention to everything: her clothes, her shoes, her manicure (or lack thereof), her car, her manners. Does she offer to pay for her share of the date even though you invited her? Does she pick the most expensive thing on the menu? She's going to be looking at you, too. Little things can tell you a lot.

Don't be bashful in asking for the date. She's expecting you to ask! Most women like the man to be the pursuer. Smart men know that even independent women like confident men who ask for the date.

Remember to offer a 2nd choice such as coffee or a drink just in case your picnic idea or free concert is too much too soon for her. If you've asked politely, the woman will accept or usually give an idea of when or if she will be ready to accept.

WHO

PAYS?

Before letting her pay for the date, decide which you want more.

If you invited her, you should expect to pay. The man who offers to pay always gets high marks. A typical scenario goes like this:

YOU: **Ms. Fine, can I get you something to drink?**

HER: *Yes, but let me pay for my own drink.*

YOU: **That's very nice, but it's not necessary...**

HER: *I insist.*

YOU: **A gentleman ALWAYS pays for the 1st date.**

HER: *That's very nice. Thank you.*

If you invited her, **offer to pay 2 or 3 times.** If she insists 3 times, it's usually smart to let her win.

The woman who insists 3 times isn't comfortable "owing" you anything. Often she does this because she has no intention of seeing you for a 2nd date.

The woman who lets you win is comfortable with you. That doesn't mean she'll go out on a 2nd date, but it's a much better sign than the woman who won't let you buy a cup of coffee.

BIG SECRET: <u>If she was the one who suggested the 1st date,</u> <u>you should still offer to pay.</u> **Women like men who are gentlemen.**

As one lady put it, *"I always offer to pay my share. If the man lets me, I don't date him again."* Gotta watch those women all the time! The fact is... many women think like she does. Most women like it when the man pays for the 1st date.

If you find yourself going out on a lot of 1st dates and very few 2nd dates, go back and reread the woman's Profile. Was she who she said she was? Were you who you said you were?

Usually one or the other person "fudged" too much either on their Photos or their Profile. If that person was you, go buy a Snickers bar to satisfy your sweet tooth, and take the FUDGE out of your Profile. Make sure your photos look like you. If she couldn't recognize you from your photos, that's likely the reason you struck out.

On the other hand, if you couldn't recognize her from her photos, you've learned a valuable lesson. Not everyone is who they say they are. Emailing back and forth a few times can help you discern the real women from the fudgers, but there's no substitute for meeting in person.

If you email a few times and can't get a sense of who she is, check out the Chapter on free First Dates. Pick an activity you'd like to do. If she turns out to be full of fudge, you'll at least have enjoyed the activity without it breaking the bank.

HOW WELL

CAN YOU JUGGLE?

There are two theories to arguing with women. Neither one works.

Juggling 6 bowling balls is almost as difficult as arguing with 1 woman.

HUMONGOUS SECRET: Regardless if you flirt with 1 or 2 or 3 women at a time, keep track of your flirts and correspondence.

Dating is fun, but juggling lots of women can get complicated in a hurry. It gets even more complicated when you email the woman and call her Trisha, and her name is Theresa. Practice keeping track of who's who or practice your diplomacy (aka arguing) skills. You're going to need one or the other.

There are lots of ways to keep track of your correspondence. You can print them out. You can store them electronically using 1 file name for each contact.

The name of your file could be DenverSky 4_20XX. A naming convention that lists the User Name and month/year of contact is an easy way to keep track of correspondence. If DenverSky turns out to be a winner, you can easily rename the file to MatchDenverSky 4_20XX.

Cut and paste her entire Profile into your word processing file. Don't make the mistake of thinking you'll be able to get online and reread her Profile later. It may be hidden because she's dating you!

Emailing 2 or 3 or 4 women at the same time maximizes your chances of finding someone. It also increases your chances of messing up. What are you going to do if all 2 or 3 or 4 women respond at the same time to your flirts?

You'll be kicking yourself in the backside if you're overly successful with your flirts and lose the woman you're most interested in because you can't keep up.

What if you're in a huge hurry to find a date? What if your office Xmas party is weeks away, and you want to make sure you have a date? Send a flirt and say exactly that:

- FIRST FLIRT, NEED A DATE SOON: **Your profile caught my eye, and I liked what you had to say about _____. If you like Xmas parties, my office is having one in 2 weeks, and Santa is going to be there handing out gifts! So what are you asking Santa for Xmas this year? Andrew**

- FIRST FLIRT, NEED A DATE SOON: **Hi... you're extremely attractive, and I need an attractive woman to go with me to my high school reunion so I can be the envy of all my guy friends. Not really, but it seems to work in the movies. I'd be pleased if you checked out my profile and see what you think. Sam**

ABBREVIATIONS are LOL FUN...

but Don't Outsmart Yourself! :D

The blonde heard her friend had her appendix out and sent her a Get-Well-Soon email. The blonde ended her email with LOL.

Ooops! The blonde thought LOL meant Lots of Love. If you use abbreviations and text talk, wait until you know the woman speaks the same language you do before you bombard her with it.

If you know the latest and greatest net lingo, you probably text a lot or have kids. Many parents have visited websites such as Abbreviations.com and Netlingo.com to help them translate the abbreviations PAW (Parents are Watching) and BOHICA and DILLIGAS and WIIFM.

Be sure you don't make the recipient feel dumb if she's not as fluent as you in text talk. If you can't help yourself, teach her your language by putting a translation in parentheses after the abbreviation.

FYI (for your information), here are some GR8 (great) abbreviations including the ones used above.

ASAP...As soon as possible

BF...Best friend

BFF...Best friends forever

BI5 ...Back in five minutes

BOC...But of course

BOHICA...Bend over here it comes again

BTW...By the way

CID...Consider it done

CYA...Cover your ass/ See ya

DD...Due diligence

DEGT...Don't even go there

DILLIGAS...Do I look like I give a sh*t?

FWIW...For what it's worth

FYEO...For your eyes only

FYI...For your information

GMTA...Great minds think alike

GR8...Great

HAND...Have a nice day

IAT...I am tired

IMAO...In my arrogant opinion

IMHO...In my humble opinion

IMO...In my opinion

ISO...In search of

KISS...Keep it simple stupid

LMIRL...Let's meet in real life

LOL...Laughing out loud

NP...No problem

OIC...Oh I see

OMG...Oh My God

PITA...Pain in the ass

PCM...Please call me

QQ... Quick question

RBTL...Read between the lines

ROFL...Rolling on the floor laughing

RTFM...Read the f*cking manual

SOL...Sh*t out of luck

SSDD...Same sh*t different day

SWAK...Sealed with a kiss

SWDYT...So what do you think?

TIA...Thanks in advance

TLC...Tender loving care

TOY...Thinking of you

TTYL...Talk to you later

TYI...Tag you're It

UG2BK...You got to be kidding

WDYM...What do you mean?

WIIFM...What's in it for me?

WTG...Way to go

XOXO...Kisses and Hugs

YMMV...Your mileage may vary

4COL...For crying out loud

^5...High five

DECIPHERING

EMOTICONS

Emoticons are fine to use provided your whole Profile isn't sprinkled with them. One is plenty. If your Profile is writhing with moving "stuff" or looks like a piece of genius modern artwork, you've overused them.

```
(\_/)
(='.'=)
(")_(")        .·´¯`·.¸>÷+(((°>   `·.¸¸.·´¯`·.¸.·´¯`·.¸>÷+(((°>
```

Some of the more common emoticons are:

:-) Smiley Face	:D Smiley Face or Laughing Smiley
;-) Winking Smiley	:-)) Really happy Smiley Face
:-(Frowning Face	*<:-) Birthday Smiley
0:-) Angel Smiley	:-p Tongue out Smiley
:-# My Lips are Sealed	8-O Ohmigod Smiley
:-* Kiss Smiley	:-/ Undecided smiley

You may have seen emails using dozens and dozens of keyboard characters depicting Christmas trees and Valentines. Most men aren't into cutesy, emoticon artwork. On the other hand, some women enjoy a clever picture in an email.

Answering "WHAT HAPPENED TO YOUR LAST RELATIONSHIP?"

"Wow, I'm glad you're a brunette. They say Brunettes have sweeter dispositions than blondes or redheads. I married one of each, and I'm ready for a brunette this time."

Sooner or later you're going to discuss PRIOR relationships. When that happens, don't spill your guts. That's always messy. Sometimes she brings up prior relationships, and sometimes you're the one who wants to know *"What adventures brought you to Internet Dating Land?"*

HUMONGOUS SECRET: The **"adventure" question** is a great way to gently broach the subject of her previous relationships including any previous marriages.

Another way to say the same thing is: *"Please tell me a bit more about you."*

A third way to ask the same thing is: *"I'd be interested in knowing more. I'm willing to share what I'm willing to ask, and here's a bit more about me."*

If you give her your 3 sentence summary of your past relationships/marriages, she'll usually respond in kind. Her response will tell you a lot… often more than her Profile told you. If you're discussing this in an email, here's how to do it:

RELATIONSHIP INQUIRY: **I joined a few months ago. It's been quite a learning experience. What adventures brought you to Online Dating Land, and how do you like the site? Mark**

Some women may ask you point blank in the first few days, *"What brought you to Online Dating Land"* or *"How long have you been on this Internet Dating site"* or *"How do you like online dating?"* She might be very interested and say, *"Tell me more about yourself."* She might go even further and ask, *"What worked and didn't work in past relationships?"*

You are on a roll! If she asks you questions like that, don't panic. Get up, cheer, and do your best, touchdown dance. Women who ask questions like that are interested in you. If she wants to know what worked and didn't work in past relationships, she's looking at you as potential dating or relationship material.

Do not avoid the question. Don't say, ***"Let's meet, and I'll tell you."*** She's asking because she's trying to figure out IF you're worth meeting.

She is interviewing you. Here's how to pass the interview. Answer her question. Give a short and sweet answer in *__3 to 5 sentences__*. A good reply is: *"I'll be happy to answer your question."* Then go on to give her the TV Guide summary. If TV

Guide can summarize Lord of the Rings in 3 sentences, you can summarize your relationship life. Here are some good examples:

- RESPONSE to the PAST RELATIONSHIP QUESTION: **I'll be happy to answer any questions you have, and the short answer to your question is that I married very young and stayed to help raise the kids. They've turned out great, and that is gratifying. How about you? What adventures brought you here? P.S. It would also be gratifying if I could take you to coffee or brunch next Saturday...what say you?** (NOTE: To slow things down, leave out the last sentence.)

- RESPONSE to the PAST RELATIONSHIP QUESTION: **My last serious relationship lasted about 2 years. We had different career and life goals. She decided she didn't want to have kids, and I still wanted to have a family. So, what worked and didn't for you in your last relationship?**

- RESPONSE to the PAST RELATIONSHIP QUESTION: **I was married for almost 5 years, and we parted amicably. We were the classic "opposites attract" which works well for short term but not for a marriage. I'll be happy to tell you more. Usually I like to email a bit, but if you'd like to meet sooner rather than later, I would be happy to discuss it over coffee or lunch next week.** (NOTE: To slow things down, leave out the last sentence.)

- RESPONSE to the PAST RELATIONSHIP QUESTION: **I was married for 11 years and for the most part it worked well. We both had our own careers, and hers eventually became more important than spending time together. How about you? What romantic adventures brought you to online dating land? Care to discuss it over a drink or dinner?** (NOTE: To slow things down, leave out the last sentence.)

BIG SECRET: If you need to vent about prior relationships, do **NOT vent to her.** You aren't going to win any extra points for saying these things about the last woman you dated or married:

- **She was a real b*tch. She never helped around the house, and all she did was spend money. She could spend it twice as fast as I could make it.**

- **We parted because we grew apart.** (Tell 1 or 2 of the reasons you grew apart or she's going to wonder if she left you because you were an alcoholic, abusive, etc.)

- **We were married for 20 years, and she unexpectedly wanted a divorce.** (She'll either not believe it was "unexpected", or she'll think you're the clueless one.)

- **The Diva never appreciated me.**

- **She turned out to be just like my last ex. I should have seen that coming.**

- **She got fat and lazy.**

- **She didn't take care of herself.**

- **All she did was read her romance novels and ignore me.**

- **She became depressed and wouldn't take her medication. It was hell.**

All those things might be true, but there's a time and place for saying it. The time and place is NOT when you're brand new to a relationship. If you show you're carrying too much baggage, she'll go on to the next man. She doesn't want a man who's crying in his beer or toting around a lot of old, worthless junk. She's looking for a man who's ready to have new adventures and make new memories.

PREDICTING THE FUTURE

OF ONLINE DATING

We apologize for the inconvenience, but the Psychic's predictions are delayed due to unforeseen circumstances.

The only constant is change. That's true in the real world and in the electronic world. While it's impossible to predict what features will be added to your particular Internet Dating Site, some things are certain. The *SECRETS* you learned in this book about Photos, Profiles, First Flirts, Come Back Flirts, What Women Want and much more worked yesterday, and today, and they will work tomorrow.

HUMONGOUS SECRET: **Before** your first date, do 2 easy things. One is fun. The other isn't as fun, but it will make your first date more fun. First, if you haven't been out on a date in a while, take yourself out. Find a nice coffee place and a good place for brunch or lunch. Find a place to have dinner or a comfortable, quiet place for a drink.

It's handy having a repertoire of date suggestions as long as you don't rattle them off like you're a serial dater. Plus, you don't want to meet at a restaurant with your date and find out it's a dump, or worse yet, the place has moved. That happened to one man we know!

The second thing to do is practice interviewing yourself. The more interested she is in you, the more questions she's going to ask. Practice your answers. It will reduce your first date jitters.

Your date might ask:

- **What do you think of the dating site?**
- **Have you dated a lot of online women?**
- **What attracted you to my Profile?**
- **Tell me about your job...**
- **Tell me about your kids...**
- **Where do you see yourself in 5 years?**
- **Why didn't your last relationship work out?**
- **What kind of relationship are you looking for?**
- **Where should we go on our 2nd date?**

She probably won't ask the last question, but she'll be thinking it. Be prepared to ask for the 2nd date if the 1st date went well. Have a few suggestions in mind. Ask her what she'd like to do. At the very least if you're interested in her, ask for her phone number if you don't already have it.

If you're uneasy about asking for the 2nd date because you're not sure if she'd accept, there are clever ways to ask for the date *without* exactly asking for it. It's pretty easy to do this, and the examples below step you through the technique.

For example, let's say there's a great wine tasting coming up a week from today. You could ask, *"Have you ever been to a wine tasting?"* You haven't exactly asked for the date, but if she responds favorably, you can go further and ask for the date.

Let's try another one: *"Have you seen Avatar yet?"* If she says, *"No, but I've heard it's great, and I'd love to see it"*.... it's your cue to ask for the 2nd date.

Let's try another: *"My mountain club goes hiking every month. Have you ever hiked the XYZ trail?"*

Basically it starts by asking a QUESTION about an activity. If you get a favorable nod from her, you can ask for the date. Do some pre-planning so you can suggest activities which dovetail with her interests and your own. Don't tell her you spent 2 hours on the Internet scoping out the wine tastings, hiking paths, art festivals, movie theaters, etc.

After the 1st date, walk her to her car. Make sure it starts. If you don't know why, reread the chapter on What Women Want. You can ruin a perfectly good evening by forgetting to be a gentleman at the end of the date.

There's another good reason to walk her to her car. She's much more likely to kiss you goodnight if you walk her to the car.

THAT'S ALL

MEN!

Awesome! Now it's your turn to put the *Awesome Secrets* into action! You know what to do and how to do it. The more secrets you implement, the better your online success will be. It's your turn to shine!

1) POST 8 to 10 good photos.

2) WRITE your Profile using the examples in this book.

3) PROOF and SPELL CHECK your Profile.

4) POST your Profile.

5) SEARCH for matches who meet your Dating Criteria, or review those who were sent to you.

6) CHECK OUT WHO'S VIEWED YOU and who has marked you as a FAVORITE.

7) SEND a classy First Flirt.

8) Revisit the chapters of this book to help you when necessary.

Finally (DRUM ROLL PLEASE) an important reminder:

- ALL Profiles and Photos get old and stale.
- UPDATE your Profile and Photos every 6-12 months.

Things will have changed. You will have traveled to new places, read new books, listened to new music, and learned a lot about yourself and the person you're looking to date.

Bring that knowledge to your Profile and Photos. The better you bring "YOU" to the online page, the better your chances are of finding "HER".

Remember...
it's not just about the destination, it's also about the JOURNEY!

ENJOY!

BEST APPENDIX EVER!

Your Awesome Buffet of Examples

TABLE OF CONTENTS

APPENDIX: CLICHÉS to AVOID like the PLAGUE

There are HUNDREDS of clichés. New ones come and go all the time. If you see the same expression in many other Profiles AND you have it in yours....NIX it. Come up with something better and original.

Uh-oh Cliché: **I like to laugh...** (NOTE: So does everyone else. Don't waste words saying the obvious.)

Uh-oh Cliché: **I'm a man who lives life to the fullest in search of a woman who does as well...** (NOTE: So does most everyone else. Don't waste words saying the obvious.)

Uh-oh Cliché: **I'm looking for someone who can take my breath away...** (NOTE: Aren't we all. See above note.)

Uh-oh Cliché: **I'm looking for my soul mate...** (NOTE: So are many people. What is a soul mate to you? Use words to describe some of the specific qualities that equal soul mate to you.)

Uh-oh Cliché: **I'm looking for a woman who can make me happy...** (NOTE: Most women think it takes 2 to make a relationship. This makes you sound like you think it's all up to her to please you. Good luck with that.)

Uh-oh Cliché: **I'm looking for chemistry and a good kisser...** (NOTE: So is most everyone else. Chemistry is different for everyone. What is chemistry to you? Use words to describe some of the specific qualities that equal chemistry to you.)

Uh-oh Cliché: **I'm picky and not any one will do...** (NOTE: This makes you sound like a snob and impossible to please.)

Uh-oh Cliché: **I'm looking for a woman with positive energy not negativity...** (NOTE: What man is looking for a negative woman or one who's an incurable whiner?)

Uh-oh Cliché: **I've seen things that other people don't notice like rainbows and sunsets...** (NOTE: Most people notice rainbows and sunsets. This comment makes you look like a snob and out of touch with other people.)

APPENDIX: HUMOR vs. SARCASM

<u>HUMOR:</u> I'm a man. I come with a road map so I don't have to ask for directions. Now where am I?

<u>HUMOR:</u> This is somewhat like filling out a job application. Just 200 words? We all know lawyers can't be brief, but here goes....

<u>HUMOR:</u> I'm willing to lie to our friends and tell them we met at Starbucks. It that's not acceptable to you... we can tell them we met at Whole Foods.

<u>HUMOR:</u> I'm open to just about anything except holding up banks and jumping out of airplanes. A lecture on global warming. A modern art show. A Bronco's game. An antique car show. A canoe trip.

<u>HUMOR:</u> I'm well-traveled and well-read. Five feet eight, but you'll think I'm taller. Especially when I wear my hiking boots.

<u>HUMOR:</u> Phun, Phinnish, Photographer, -- I'm Phunny, too – more Kelsey Grammer than Jerry Seinfeld with a dash of ventriloquist Jeff Dunham thrown in for good measure, but my lips move when I talk.

<u>HUMOR:</u> Yes, I am a Pulitzer Prize winner. Back in the 7th grade, Mrs. Pulitzer was my music teacher, and I got 2nd prize in the talent show. It's a great story! Ask me about it!

~~~~~~

<u>Uh-oh SARCASM:</u> I have only two PHOBIAS...big snakes and women with stinky, smelly, dragon breath. Tic Tac please.

<u>Uh-oh SARCASM:</u> If you can tie your shoes without the instruction manual, if you bathe once a month, if you brush your teeth at least once week, and if you don't spell intelligent with an "A", then you're the girl for me.

<u>Uh-oh SARCASM:</u> Are you the kind of woman who walks the road less traveled or are you one of the lemmings which follow the crowd off the cliff, have no opinion of your own, and are just plain boring and average? If so, then please stay in your closed, safe little world.

- Amateur cook available
- Let's give FATE a helping hand
- Is it really you?
- Were you looking for me?
- Alakazam…I turn strangers into friends….
- I have power tools and lend them to friends!
- I just knew you'd find me.
- What would you like for dinner?
- I promise to get off this dating site for you
- I was hoping you'd be here
- Dance with me?
- Whew…you found me!
- Direct from Paris….
- Can you come out and play?
- Lessons my kids taught me…
- Got niceness?
- I've got you cleared for landing
- Happiness is sharing
- I'm peanut butter looking for jelly
- Psst…hey you…This man seems nice
- Good at puzzles…want to join me?
- Are you good in science & chemistry? Me too!
- I bring smiles and laughter
- Blue eyes, good character
- May I have this dance?
- I am here, where are you?
- Sleepless in Centennial
- I'll wash, if you'll dry
- Life is good. Let's make it great!
- Let's double our joys! Care to share?
- We all look good on paper….
- Successful CEO looking for co-conspirator
- Let's tell our friends we met at _____

Do not use Excuses:

- Hey, it's the only picture I had
- I'll post some pics later

Do not use Desperate Headlines:

- Hate to travel alone
- Less of a jerk than most
- Looking for a fiend (NOTE: Spell check/proof.)
- Last shot at this!
- Empty but lookin
- Hardly the catch of a lifetime
- Once again, I'm on the used car lot –
- Lonely man looking for best friend

Do not use Sex Headlines: (If you only want to attract one type of woman, these might be appropriate headlines. If you're looking for more than sex, these will flop.)

- I give great back rubs
- Can I nibble on your neck?
- Sensuous mountain man seeks hottie
- Passionate man seeks passionate woman
- Bad girl wanted
- Lots of kisses for you
- Call me super-sexy and smart
- Can't wait to wrap my arms around you

Do not use Fun Fun Fun Headlines: (If you're looking for more than just fun in a relationship, these headlines will turn off a lot of potential matches.)

- It's time for fun

- Ready for fun and passion
- Fun loving guy seeks match
- Xtreme fun seeker wants wild woman
- Fun is the word!
- Let's have some fun
- For a good time....call

Do not use "Ready or Not" Headlines: (Most women view these men as not ready for a relationship.)

- **Ready to move on**
- **Ready to meet someone**
- **Ready for a commitment...** (NOTE: Sounds like you never were before. Red flag for women. The "C" word before you've met the woman can be a turn off to a lot of women. Many women are looking for Commitment, but not on the first date.)
- **Ready for a relationship**
- **Finally ready for someone special**

Do not use Shallow, Egotistical, Superficial, or Controlling Headlines:

- **A great man**
- **I'm awesome...no, I'm fabulous**
- **I want an attractive woman**

Do not use Mission Impossible Headlines:

- Looking for the perfect woman
- Looking for Barbie with a brain, no baggage, no kids, and lots of $$$. I want it all.

APPENDIX : G.O. (Good Opening Lines)

(G.O.): Hello... Thanks for stopping by....Kids are off at college, and I have a list of fun things to catch up on. Looking for someone to share quality time be it taking a cooking class together, working out, or clinking glasses over a nice meal.

(G.O.): Welcome to my little corner in this giant castle they call The Internet! So glad you made it across the moat and avoided that nasty dragon at the entrance. What am I doing here? Same as you, I guess. I believe in royalty, and I'm searching for a woman to treat like a queen, and in turn be treated like her king...okay, how about a prince...a duke....a knight.....uh...work with me here. I'm running out of options.

(G.O.): Maui coffee on my back porch on a crisp, autumn Saturday morning is always a treat. I also like Maui coffee in Maui watching the whales breach a mile off shore. Both are delightful in their own way. Is that how you think, too? If so, maybe it's you that I've been looking for? Maybe it's me that you've been searching for? I value the good things in life and the simple things.

(G.O.): Do you enjoy bookstores, libraries, and museums on a dreary New England day? How about discussing the latest bestseller or what's going on with the Stock Market?

(G.O.): A lawyer and a doctor walk into a bar...

(G.O): Intelligent women and origami are my 2 weaknesses. Maybe that's because a smart brunette with pigtails in 4th grade showed me how to make a paper crane.

(G.O): Mostly I'm here for the Forums. But if that special lady with her own desert isle rows by, I might have to reconsider. Oh wait....I have lots of Frequent Flyer miles....we can go 1st class and FIND that desert isle.

(G.O.): Do you like to travel? Are you looking for a man who you can spend the rest of your life with? Well, I'm looking for that woman. Maybe we should start a dialogue or maybe a travelogue.

(G.O.): Home is where the heart is for me. I've traveled a lot for work and pleasure, but coming home to the simple joys of living are the best. Put a good book in my hands, put on a good DVD like Avatar or a great comedy and curl up with me. That's living!

(G.O.): Being single has given me time to prioritize what's important to me…I've been successful in my career, and my 3 kids are well-launched. What's missing is a one-on-one relationship with that special "one".

(G.O.): Sniffles to snake bite….I'm your go-to-man! I'm good at taking care of people. I work in the E.R. in the health care field (nurse). I like most sports, and on rainy days you can find me playing "Find my Match". Okay, sometimes on sunny days, too. I don't know if I'm any good at it, but we can compare notes. I like working out and staying fit, and hope you do, too.

(G.O.): Top 10 Ways to know if the Guy is a REAL Catch: 1. If he's a REAL catch, HE always pays for the first date. 2. If he's a REAL catch, HE always pays for the second date. 3. Hmm…I sense a pattern here. (NOTE: Top 10 Lists can work well. Check out the chapter on how to create your own.)

(G.O.): About me…I come with a Honey-back guarantee. I'm domesticated and don't use a screwdriver for a hammer (even if I'm really desperate). I'm 5' 10" 170 pounds with lots of heart, and have a pegboard full of handyman tools (most of which I know how to use).

(G.O.): Hi! I'm the one who waters my neighbors' plants when my neighbors are on vacation. I'm the one my nephews call their "favorite uncle". I'm the one who volunteers at the Food Kitchen on Thanksgiving. I like to play, but I like to give back. I'm looking for someone who feels like that, too.

(G.O.): (It helps if you read this with an English accent since I'm from London. Really! I'll show you my passport.) Hi and thanks for stopping by. I'm new to the city. If you have an hour or two, I'd love to discover what your favourite places are. (NOTE: You can use this opening line if you have ANY accent that is different from where you currently live. If you just moved from Georgia to Chicago, you might have a lovely, smooth, southern accent. You don't have to be from London or Paris to use the above "technique". You just have to substitute driver's license or moving bill for "passport".)

(G.O.): Hey, Computer, is that woman looking at us? She looks nice, and her profile is interesting. Do you think she likes to golf? She looks pretty athletic. I wonder if she would like to take golfing lessons with me this summer?

(G.O.): Welcome! I used to say, "Gee....some day." Now I say, "Let's pack a lunch and go exploring." I love the desert in the early morning when it's cool, but my favorite exploration is driving the back roads in search of a quaint café or historic area that's off the beaten path.

(G.O.): Because I teach psychology, a men's group asked me to give a speech about how to find love after the age of 40 on the Internet. I told them this: 1) Be positive, NOT negative; 2) Take all the NO's and NOT's out of your online profiles; 3) Take this opportunity in your life to date all kinds of women, not just the ones you "think" you'd like. (NOTE: WOW! This psychologist gives good advice. Wonder if he read our book?)

(G.O.): We're all looking for our best friend and more. Someone to stand beside you, someone to watch your back. I'm looking for that special someone who can enjoy the everyday things and the on vacation things with me. Standing in a long line at the grocery can be a pain, but not if we sneak in a kiss and talk about what we should cook for dinner.

(G.O.): Brrrr...lots of snow and cold weather this year. While we're waiting for it to be Spring, let's get together and check out the bookstores and latest bestsellers. I can show you my favorite coffee shop, and you can show me yours. While we're at it, we can talk about what we'd like to do in the Spring!

(G.O.): Do you like living in the big city close to all the action? Are you turned on by good music and good conversation? Liberal to moderate? Home-oriented? Do you think it's bad luck to be superstitious? For a good time...call someone else. For a great time, wink or email.

(G.O.): I'm a marketing professional. Please read my profile carefully and send me an email with comments, questions, suggestions. Marketing is fun, but tricky, so let me know how I did at marketing myself.

(G.O.): I'm a good cook, and more importantly....I am willing to bring to the table all that I'm asking for ... and more.

(G.O.): What's ice cream without hot fudge? What's peanut butter without jelly? What's pizza without pepperoni? I believe in astronomy, but I'm not so sure about astrology. Oh wait, my horoscope says I'll meet someone online. Quick, email me, and make me a believer.

APPENDIX : B.O. (BAD OPENING LINES)

(B.O.): I am someone who doesn't look my age. I am pretty laid back have a great sense of humor and like to laugh.

(B.O.): Those who know me well would say I am optimistic and positive. I enjoy travel and movies.

(B.O.): I am looking to develop a relationship that has trust and honesty and mutual accountability.

(B.O.): I'm athletic and adventurous as well as laid back and introspective. I like meeting new people and going new places.

(B.O.): I like going places and doing things. I'm looking for someone who has similar interests to mine.

(B.O.): My friends would say I live life to the fullest. I am friendly, kind, smart, and hard-working.

(B.O.): I am good-looking, humorous, happy, and financially secure. I am looking for someone who shares my interests.

(B.O.): I enjoy many things – travel, kids, theater, fine wine, affection, working out, laughing, good conversation. I'm comfortable in jeans and equally comfortable in a suit and tie.

(B.O.): I am dependable and honest. I like being direct, and I don't like people who play games. I'm appreciative and fun with the right person.

(B.O.): My friends would say I am romantic and have a zest for life. Sometimes I'm sarcastic.

(B.O.): I DON"T NEED SOMEONE TO COMPLETE ME. I do not respond to emails that just say "hi how r u". Be intelligent and say something intelligent if you write to me. I do not respond to Conservatives. I do not respond to those without a college degree. (NOTE: This man starts with all negatives. Women who make it through his elimination process will not respond to his crass attitude.)

(B.O.): I've really never liked dating, and where I work I don't meet too many women.

(B.O.): Not looking to get married, not interested in being a Sugar-Daddy. If you have baggage, leave it at the door. Please have your own life, your own money, your own happiness. Don't contact me if you're not financially secure. I'm not deep pockets and your personal ATM. (NOTE: This man's personality could freeze water into ice cubes. His eliminators may be valid, but the way he comes across is bossy and vindictive and angry.)

(B.O.): After dating my last wife for several months... (NOTE: Do not start out your Profile with your ex-wives, or ex-girlfriends, or any other EXcuses.)

(B.O.): Ok, I find it uncomfortable to talk about myself. Not because I'm not great, but because I am really great! (NOTE: a gigantic Red Flag ego here. Yuck.)

(B.O.): I consider myself open-minded and kind. I am honest and generous to a fault. I'm usually successful at most things I do except maybe for my first and second marriages. Things just never worked out.

(B.O.): READ MY WHOLE PROFILE. I'm not interested in emailing. Only contact me if you think we'll be a good match. Don't waste my time otherwise! If you have no photo, I will not contact you. (NOTE: All these things are valid, but not as a 1st sentence and not expressed in this manner. The Deal Maker / Deal Breaker chapter addresses how to avoid crass, and say it with class.)

- You have an IQ over 120.
- You think IQ stands for I'm Cute.
- You love spontaneity and usually spell it correctly.
- You think it's bad luck to be superstitious.
- You think spontaneity is a character defect.
- You are a good cook.
- You like to kiss and you know…
- You like long conversations about everything .
- You are fiscally responsible.
- You own a desert island.
- You know someone who owns a desert island.
- You have lots of FF miles and want to find a desert island.
- You own your own house & no TARP funds were needed.
- You are affectionate.
- You love the "Bull Durham" kisses that last for days.
- You think PDA is a school organization.
- You enjoy going to sporting events.
- You actually watch the game between hot dogs and beer.
- U spel like this
- U like 2 txt
- Your idea of "roughing it" is a hotel without an ocean view.
- One of your favorite movies was _____.
- You can quote at least two lines from "Princess Bride" off the top of your head.
- You think "Groundhog Day" is one of the stupidest movies.
- You think "Groundhog Day" is one of the best movies.
- You liked "Groundhog Day" but admit it was a bit redundant. ;-)

- You think TV is watched only by morons.
- You know who Scott Brown is. (Substitute any person)
- You think Anderson Cooper rocks!
- You think Susan Boyle rocks!
- You enjoy reading.
- Brave New World is one of your Top 10 favorite books. (NOTE: Substitute to suit you.)
- Grisham is one of your Favorite Authors.
- You know who Nouriel Roubini is.
- You had 2 or more cars that qualified for Cash-for-Clunkers.
- You think Shakespeare was an event in the first Olympics.
- You have one or more pictures of Elvis hanging in your house.
- They're velvet.
- You sing opera in the shower (off key).
- You're so modest you shower with your clothes on.
- You are looking for a perfect man (here's a clue: he doesn't exist).
- You look more like Elvis than you look like Priscilla Presley.
- You'd like to live at Graceland.
- You have more hair on your back than I do on my head.
- You don't resemble Bride of Chucky.
- You like to dance (and are good).
- Your middle name is Ms. Fixit.
- You like when the man does the chair thing.
- You catch indoor spiders and put them outdoors.
- Politically you're Middle-of-the-Road but not chicken.

APPENDIX: DEAL MAKERS/BREAKERS by category

RELATIONSHIP:

I'm looking for my Last-First-Date and am hoping to start by finding my Best-First-Date. Or, we can start with coffee and make our 2nd date that best 1st one!

I am a widower who had a good marriage. I'm looking forward to being married again. It all starts with friendship.

Although I've never been married, I've been in long-term, committed relationships, and prefer that to dating.

Emailing is a great way to start, but going to a Monster Truck Rally or Tractor Pull is so much more fun. Kidding kidding. Theater and reading bestsellers are more my speed.

ATHLETICS:

I am into biking and golf, so bonus points if you enjoy one or both!

I'm looking for someone who likes to ski, bike, and hike. If you like to dance, I'm willing to learn, but my middle name isn't Grace, it's Ivan.

I usually go on long bike rides a few times a month, but I don't expect you to accompany me.

I'm an amateur but competitive athlete, and "No", I don't expect you to be one.

I've been athletic all my life and am attracted to athletic women.

COOKING:

If you don't cook, I do. I like trying new recipes.

I don't cook worth a darn, but I have a great wine collection and know what wines go best with what entrees and desserts.

GOLF:

I like to golf once or twice a day....well, not quite that much, but when the weather is nice, that's how I get my exercise and stay in shape.

You're welcome to join me or push me out of the house so you can have your own time. I'm easy.

DANCING and MUSIC:

I like most kinds of dancing. Salsa dancing is my current favorite.

I listen to music constantly so if you're not a music lover, I'm probably not the guy for you.

I think life needs a soundtrack...mine varies from light rock to R&B.

CHILDREN:

I'm looking for someone who understands that parenting and having a good relationship are equally important and not mutually exclusive. I'm a proud father to a daughter who's 12 and a son who's 14.

I have two children in grade school who stay with me often. If you have kids or like to be around kids, that would be a bonus.

I share custody of one wonderful daughter, age 12. You can read all the books about parenting, but doing it successfully says it all.

Spending time with my 2 boys is fun and a daily learning experience. I think I'm succeeding, because they're good kids and so far haven't taken the car without permission (they're 6 and 8). :D

Glad you checked me out...I am self-employed, self-sufficient, and share custody of two terrific sons 6 and 9. I'm not looking for a mom for the kids, I'm looking for a woman who enjoys kids.

I like kids...mine, and others. My kids live out-of-state with their mom, but they are an important part of my life. We talk a few times a week (webcams are great!) and see each other several times a year.

I love kids but I don't have any...unless you count the 45 children I visit almost every year. I volunteer for outreach programs that serve a Costa Rican orphanage.

I have 2 great daughters (13 and 15) who love the outdoors and soccer. If you have kids, I would be happy to integrate our 2 families, and the woman I'm looking for would want to do the same.

My kids are grown, and now it's time for us....we can fulfill our dreams and spend time acting like kids again!

My kids (8 and 10) live with their mom, and we share custody. I get them every other weekend. If you have kids, I welcome them and am looking for someone who welcomes mine, too.

I have a 19 year old college student who is home during the summer. He has a summer job with the park district, and I laugh when he tells me that the real world is much different than college. Welcome to Life 101!

My kids are still young and spend every other weekend with their mom. The kids keep me young and smiling and on my toes! I'm looking for someone who appreciates the joy of parenting 2 good kids.

TRAVELING:

I like to travel on both short trips and long. If you call me on Friday afternoon and say, "Let's go to the mountains for a weekend getaway," my response would be..."I'll be ready in 10 minutes!"

BAGGAGE:

I set my baggage down a long time ago, and hope you have, too.

We all have baggage, but I'm looking for someone who travels light.

SEPARATED:

I've been separated for over a year, and the divorce will be final later this year. If you want to know more, just ask because I'm an open book. Plus, it's a funny story which is better told over a nice dinner and a glass of wine. You'll laugh, and you'll laugh some more. If not, dinner's on me. Oh wait, I was going to buy dinner anyway.

I've heard that some women think "separated" men are the best ones to date. I don't know if that's the case, but it sounds reasonable to me! =) I'm not carrying a torch or baggage, and I'm looking forward to meeting someone to share interests and life.

I've been separated for 5 years. We each have our own homes, and there is no chance of reconciliation. We've postponed getting divorced to raise our son jointly and to continue our business relationship (family business). Yes, it's an unusual situation, but my son is growing up happy and healthy with parents who share custody. I'm an open book, so please don't hesitate to be inquisitive.

EXERCISE and DIET:

I'm a vegetarian and while I don't care what you eat, my diet and exercise are important to me. I work out 3-5 times a week so I can enjoy an occasional pizza and a margarita.

I'm not getting older, I'm getting better! Cycling and spinning classes keep me toned and in shape, but some days I think I'm going in circles!

I try to eat healthy most of the time. Haven't gained a pound since college so I guess it's working. Or I got the good genes. While I do watch my diet, I splurge occasionally with a great Italian meal and a fine bottle of wine. As with so many things, it's a balance.

I work out several times a week, and it would be great to have a workout partner. I'm looking for someone who puts the same value I do on a healthy lifestyle as well as what it takes to attain it.

I work out not because I love it, but because I love the feeling when I'm done. Age keeps happening, but I'm hoping to slow it down.

I stay in shape and work out a few times a week, but I don't obsess about it. Eating healthy makes me feel better, but I splurge now and again on a great steak and baked potato with all the fixins.

I like to work out a few times a week. I'm attracted to people who value their fitness and have the discipline to stick to a workout regimen. Yes, it's not easy and it gets harder and harder each year which is why it would be great to have a workout buddy.

ATTRACTIVE AND FIT:

I call myself a young 44, but you can judge for yourself. I am slim and have been since college. I stay in shape by walking a few miles every day and would love for you to join me.

I try to take care of myself, and I hope that my date likes to work out, too. It would be great if you'd join me at the gym a few days a week.

SMARTS:

I enjoy the company of a woman who follows current events.

Easy Questions: (for Ask-A-Question Profile)

- Favorite main course or dessert?
- Favorite non-alcoholic drink?
- Favorite alcoholic drink?
- Do you believe in soul mates? (Answer: Kiss me and I'll see.)
- Do you believe in Chemistry?
- How many times were you married and for how long?
- Describe your clothing style:
- Do you want a date, friend, long term?
- Describe where you'd go for a perfect first date:
- My favorite places to shop for clothes are:
- My decorating style could be described as:
- Are you neat or messy or ?
- Or you organized or unorganized?
- Are you Type A or B?
- What do you like to do for exercise? (Answer: Knitting :D)
- Are you more of an introvert or an extrovert?
- How many nights a week do you go out?
- What do you like to do when you go out?
- What job would you choose if you could have any job? (Answer: Honest U.S. Senator)
- What do you like best about your job?
- If you could travel anywhere in the world, where would you go?
- Are you usually on time for things?
- What did you do last weekend?
- Is physical affection important to you? (Answer: Kiss me and I'll see.)
- What do you usually do for the winter holidays?
- What's your idea of a romantic evening with someone you've dated for several months?
- What simple pleasures in life do you enjoy regularly?

- What are your main staples that you buy at the grocery?
- How good are you on the golf course (or skiing, etc.)?
- What sound do you like the best?

Harder Questions:

- If you won $1000 in the lottery what would you spend it on?
- If someone gave you $500, and you had to spend it in an hour, what would you buy?
- What would entice you to max out your credit card?
- If you didn't go into your current career, what job would you have chosen?
- List 1 or 2 of your biggest accomplishments.
- I like to talk about:
- What's the first thing people notice about you?
- What's the most revealing thing that you dare to share online?
- Do you believe in love at first sight?
- The last volunteer work that I did was:
- If money wasn't an object and you could do anything in the world and go anywhere, where would you go on a first date and what would you do?
- 10 to 15 words that DESCRIBE ME:
- 10 to 15 words that DESCRIBE THE WOMAN I'm looking for:
- What are the 2 or 3 best traits that you offer a partner?
- What are the 2 or 3 most important things you're looking for in a partner?
- What are the 2 or 3 things you think are most important for having a successful relationship?
- How much alone time do you need?
- How much together time do you need?
- What job would you absolutely hate to do?
- Who were your heroes or role models growing up?
- How do you handle disagreement?
- What's your best character trait?

- What's your worst character trait?
- What's your most embarrassing moment**?**
- Who did you vote for and why in the last Presidential election?
- What do your friends know about you that most people don't know?
- What do you wish more people would know about you?
- In 10 to 15 words, describe your kids:
- What are your 2 to 3 biggest date Deal Breakers?
- What are your 2 to 3 biggest date Deal Makers?
- If you had to sing a song which epitomized your life, what song would you sing?
- What's the most adventurous thing you've ever done in your life?
- What's the most adventurous thing you did in the last year?
- What's the most spontaneous thing you've ever done?
- What physical characteristics do you find attractive?
- Who is your best friend and why?
- Other than your physical looks, what do people notice about you first when they meet you?
- What's the last new thing that you "learned"?
- What's the kindest thing you've ever done?
- What's the kindest thing you did in the last year?
- How often do you like to be physically intimate with your partner?
- What's the most fiscally irresponsible thing you ever did?
- What's the most fiscally astute thing you ever did?
- What one thing in your life would you like to do over if you could?
- What are you most thankful for?
- Besides the basics of food, shelter, and clothing, what are some things that you can't live without?
- What type of relationship are you looking for?

APPENDIX: TOP 10 LIST TOPICS

- 10 REASONS WHY YOU SHOULD EMAIL ME NOW

- 10 REASONS WHY YOU SHOULDN'T WASTE YOUR TIME ON THE OTHER MEN

- WHY I DIDN'T DATE THE LADY WHO WAS 10 YEARS YOUNGER

- WHY MY MOTHER/FATHER/SISTER/BROTHER SAYS I'M A REAL CATCH

- WHY MY DOG THINKS I'M THE BEST MAN ON THE PLANET

- WHY YOUR DOG SHOULD DATE MY DOG

- WHY YOUR RHINOCEROUS SHOULD DATE MY RHINOCEROUS

- THE TOP 10 SECRETS YOU SHOULD KNOW ABOUT MEN

- THE TOP 10 GIFTS TO BUY YOUR MAN FOR XMAS

- 10 THINGS NOT TO GET YOUR GUY FOR HIS BIRTHDAY

- THE 10 WEIRDEST THINGS YOU'D FIND IN MY HOUSE

- 10 THINGS I COULDN'T LIVE WITHOUT

- 10 STUPIDEST THINGS I EVER BOUGHT

- 10 BEST THINGS I EVER BOUGHT

- 10 GREAT THINGS I LEARNED IN SCHOOL

- 10 WORTHLESS THINGS I LEARNED IN SCHOOL

- 10 BEST THINGS I LEARNED AT WORK

- 10 WORTHLESS THINGS I LEARNED AT WORK

- 10 GREAT THINGS I LEARNED FROM MY KIDS

- 10 GREAT THINGS I TAUGHT MY KIDS

APPENDIX: QUOTES

- "Gravity is not to blame for two people falling in love. We can blame online dating." (anon)

- "If you think you are beaten you are, if you think you dare not, you don't." (W.D. Wintle)

- "All the world's a stage, and all the men and women merely players." (Shakespeare)

- "Love is a promise, love is a souvenir, once given never forgotten, never let it disappear." (John Lennon)

- "Live the life you've dreamed." (Henry David Thoreau)

- "The spaces between your fingers were created so that another's could fill them in." (anon)

- "Love doesn't make the world go round, love is what makes the ride worthwhile." (Elizabeth B. Browning)

- "The quality of your life is the quality of your relationships." (Anthony Robbins)

- "May the sun always shine on your windowpane; May a rainbow be certain to follow each rain; May the hand of a friend always be near you; May God fill your heart with gladness to cheer you." (Irish Blessing)

- "How do you eat an Elephant? One bite at a time." (Anon)

- "Love is something eternal; the aspect may change, but not the essence." (Vincent Van Gogh)

- "Remember, if you ever need a helping hand, you'll find one at the end of your arm ..." (Audrey Hepburn)

- "In dreams and in love there are no impossibilities." (Janos Arnay)

- "To accomplish great things we must not only act but also dream, not only plan but also believe." (Anatole)

- "He believes that marriage and a career don't mix. So after the wedding, he plans to quit his job." (anon)

- "Among those whom I like or admire, I can find no common denominator, but among those whom I love, I can: all of them make me laugh." (W.H. Auden)

- "Even the gods love jokes." (Plato)

- "If you don't ask, you don't get." (Gandhi)

- "Those who wish to sing, always find a song." (Swedish proverb)

- "Keep a green tree in your heart and perhaps a singing bird will come." (Chinese proverb)

QUOTES TO AMUSE...*NOT* to USE

- "You could talk about same-sex marriage, but people who have been married say, 'It's the same sex all the time'." (Robin Williams)

- [Before opening an envelope for best supporting actress] "I feel like Adam when he said to Eve, ` Back up, I don't know how big this gets'." (Robin Williams)

- "I don't know the question, but sex is definitely the answer." (Woody Allen)

- "A little still she strove, and much repented, and whispering, 'I will ne'er consent' - consented." (Byron)

- "I believe that sex is one of the most beautiful, natural, wholesome things that money can buy." (Steve Martin)

- "I was so naïve as a kid I used to sneak behind the barn and do nothing." (Johnny Carson)

- "I'm looking for Miss Right, or at least, Miss Right Now." (Robin Williams)

GOOD ENDING: I have one housemate...my cat lets me live with her. I think that animals are great judges of character. If you write to me, I'll try and get her to send you a pawthentic, signed testimonial.

GOOD ENDING: I'm looking for my best friend and more. I ask only what I'm willing to bring...kind, affectionate, hard-working, and I have a friendly golden lab who will be your 2nd best friend!

GOOD ENDING: Bye for now. Thanks for stopping by and hope to hear from you soon. I'm a little old-fashioned and confess that I prefer that the woman is the first one to email if she's interested. Oh wait, that was in 2nd grade when Deidre gave me an early Valentine on Feb. 13. If times have changed since then, clue me in, okay?

GOOD ENDING: I believe in karma and also believe we can create our relationship to be any way we want it to be. Yes, it takes chemistry and character, but the beauty of it is that we're in the driver's seat. Let me know if you prefer to drive or be the navigator.

GOOD ENDING: I am the age I say I am, but some days I'm smarter, or sillier, or even younger than my age would indicate. I read Dr. Seuss so I might be too young for you. I've also read "Freud's Interpretation of Dreams" so maybe I'm too old for you. Want to come out and play? Want to find your dream? Email is the key to unlocking the door!

GOOD ENDING: I have been known to think out of the box and color out of the lines. The road less traveled has been my path. Which means I'm a flaming liberal and mesh best with liberal or non-conventional thinkers. Physical chemistry is important for initial attraction, but for it to last, we both need that mental chemistry. Please give me a shout if this sounds like you, but yell REAL loud so I can hear you. If that doesn't work, try an email.

GOOD ENDING: I'm a good emailer and have been known to make people smile. Give me a try and find out. Winks work, too. Eeny, meeny, miny, moe...email or wink, email or wink...??

GOOD ENDING: I wish you the best of luck on this journey and hope that you find the right person... and hope that right person (me) might be getting an email from you.

GOOD ENDING: Does this sound like you? Wow, this must be my lucky day! Travel isn't a problem because at this very second I'm just a click away. Okay, TYI...Tag, you're it!

GOOD ENDING: Are you wondering if I'm like this in person? The answer is "yes". Let's email or chat so you can find out in person. I think it's your turn to go first!

GOOD ENDING: Hope you enjoyed visiting and that you smiled a time or two. If you think we have a lot in common, drop me a line. Since you already know what I look like, please have a picture posted on your profile. Fair is fair!

GOOD ENDING: I'm good at listening when you want to be listened to and supporting and believing in you when you need someone in your corner. I've learned that half of being successful is just showing up. I show up. My actions match my words. I don't have all of life's questions answered, but I've got good answers to many of them. If that's what you're looking for, send me a wink or email.

GOOD ENDING: I'm looking for a match who is kind, caring, romantic, and has a good heart. My match would have a positive outlook on life and enjoy being together at home or on a high seas cruise. If you know that excitement can be that first kiss in the morning or a quick hello on the phone in the middle of the day, let's chat. Isn't it your turn to go first?

GOOD ENDING: Chemistry is great, and integrity, honesty, and communication spell Chemistry to me. I think that is the glue that holds a relationship together. I bring that, and that's what I'm looking for in my partner. If you feel the same way, wink or email.

GOOD ENDING: If it sounds like we'd make good/great/or beautiful music together.....hum my favorite song or send me a quick "hi"....and tell me your favorite song, and I'll tell you mine!

GOOD ENDING: I come with a lifetime warranty of niceness! I look forward to learning about you and having you get to know me. I'm just a click away!

GOOD ENDING: I'm simple and complex (aren't we all). You're complex and simple (aren't you all). Isn't it great that opposites attract! Wink or email if you're interested and within 100 miles of me.

GOOD ENDING: The ride of life is incredible and fantastic, but meeting someone special would make the ride even more enjoyable. I like to spoil the woman in my life and like to be spoiled in return with love and tenderness. I'm not looking for compliments, I'm looking for a complement. If you're ready to see if we might click, click "message" now.

GOOD ENDING: I've been very successful in life and have attained most of my goals but one....I am looking to find that special someone. I believe that material things are wonderful to have and allow you to make choices, but that the best thing in the world is to have someone by your side who cares about you and is there for you. I give as much as I'm asking for, believe in keeping promises, and leaving our world a better place than we found it. I believe it is the duty of parents to help our kids stand on our shoulders. If your interests and values sound similar to mine, please contact me and tell me something about you.

GOOD ENDING: I enjoy the doing as well as the planning and anticipating. I learned a long time ago that the joy in life isn't just the destination, it's the journey. I like sharing. It doubles the fun! If it does for you, too, let me know by wink or email.

GOOD ENDING: What's your favorite first date? Do you like to try a new restaurant? Or do you like to meet at your favorite coffee shop? Maybe you like to do a good workout and then go for coffee? Just one thing.....if you're a better athlete or better kisser than I am, wait till our second date to leave me gasping for air! Send me a wink so I can find out.

GOOD ENDING: Every day is a GIFT. That's why they call it THE PRESENT. Do you get up in the morning knowing you have been given the gift of another day? Do you greet it with a smile? Me, too! Write me, and let's share some smiles and laughter.

GOOD ENDING: Do you want to meet a best friend, partner, and lover? I do, too! Someone who is fun, and healthy, and prefers their trauma/drama on the·movie screen. We all have baggage, but let's leave it on the shelf or carry it to the curb. Life is a wonderful journey, and I'm looking to travel with someone I love. Email so I can confirm your reservation! (NOTE: Be careful using the words "love" and "lover" anywhere in a Profile. It's often too much too soon.)

GOOD ENDING: I like workouts and wine, preferably in that order. I like good conversation with both. We can start to get to know one another with a workout or with wine (or with both). I can't read your mind, so you need to let me know.

GOOD ENDING: I'm looking for my last first date. Qualities that appeal to me are: character, kindness, and making the most of each and every day. I'm happy with my life and am looking for someone who is happy and not done dreaming. I like people who still believe in reaching for the sky and looking for the real thing. I think love is limitless, and speaking of limits....this is a limited time offer. Email if this sounds good to you!

GOOD ENDING: Let's share....dinner, dancing, movies, hiking, museums, traveling, stories, experiences, memories, romance. Let's comfort and laugh, hang out, be wild, be calm and celebrate being on the 3rd rock from the sun. Let's see if our atoms combine like H2O or like dynamite. Wink, write, send up a flare!

GOOD ENDING: I'm a positive person and know that I won the lottery just by being born in this country. I love oxymorons, believe in never saying never, and I am intolerant about intolerance. I will tolerate an email over a non-email. Send me an email and see.

GOOD ENDING: I like bicycles including tandem bikes. I like sharing. I can cook or clean up, wash dishes or dry, your choice. What are you waiting for? Smoke signals are fine (I probably have American Indian ancestors somewhere), but emails are faster.

GOOD ENDING: I love to learn about the world and share. Do you? I think learning never stops. Do you feel the same way? If you enjoyed stopping by, please say hello and tell me a little more about you.

GOOD ENDING: I hope you smiled once or twice while reading my profile. I'm interested in a relationship with one special person. If you are too, send me a short message to let me know you think we have something to explore. Long messages work, too. You choose. Cheers.

GOOD ENDING: Some say that love makes the world go round. To that I'd add a sense of humor, similar values, like goals, and wonderful dreams. Differences make life interesting and let us complement one another. Let's start finding out if our yin and yang are matches. If you click email now, we can start comparing notes.

GOOD ENDING: I'm looking for a best friend, co-conspirator, and life partner. Intelligence and street smarts are turn-ons. If you're the right one and live more than 50 miles away, that isn't a deal breaker, that's a challenge to be overcome. We may be miles apart in geography, but the world is getting smaller every day. Today I'm just a click away.

GOOD ENDING: Wow – I'm not usually this wordy, but I do like to communicate. If my words struck a chord with you send me an email. Let's explore the possibilities.

GOOD ENDING: If you think two is better than one, and dreams are better shared, I hope you will contact me and see if our paths are going in the same direction. It All Starts With A Click of Your Mouse!

GOOD ENDING: Yes, I do respond to "winks", but I don't know if this site has "winks". Would ~.O be a wink? These emoticons are tricky. I'd rather know more about you than a wink can convey, but help me out here....what is the politically correct emoticon to use?

GOOD ENDING: HURRY! Our operators are standing by! Click now for this limited time offer!

GOOD ENDING: I like traveling and sports (both participating and watching). I believe in mutual sharing... sharing of experiences, opinions, decisions, and feelings. Let's start by sharing an email. Do you want to go first or shall I? I think it's your turn...

GOOD ENDING: Wishing you the best of Luck in your search. P.S. – did I tell you I've always been lucky! Email now and maybe your luck will change!

APPENDIX: 1st FLIRT EMAILS & Subject Lines

First Flirt SUBJECT LINES:

- Way to go Chicago…
- Have you figured it out?
- It's the best…
- SURPRISE!
- Trick or Treat…
- Truth or Dare…
- A question for you…
- Hail Citizen…
- The signs are favorable…
- Didn't expect to…
- Which is better…
- Am I too tall or too rich?
- You have the best...
- Why in the world…
- Ok, smarty, answer me this…
- Shall we get married or meet first?
- Apple pie or…
- Which would you choose…
- Maui or ??
- Did I pass your test??
- I ran around the Internet 3 times…

FIRST FLIRTS:

- <u>FIRST FLIRT</u>: HURRAY! Surely you're some sort of throwback to the time of King Arthur? There is no mention of Harley motorcycles, watching DVD's all night, and you like REAL popcorn! Am I dreaming or are you really real?

- <u>FIRST FLIRT</u>: Why did the girl sit on the watch? My 9 yo niece just emailed me that joke. Since you have kids the same age, I figured you'd appreciate it! Answer: Because she wanted to be on time. Care to share the latest "kid" joke in your part of the world?

- FIRST FLIRT: Why did the girl sit on the watch? (NOTE: Use that as your Subject Line). Hi..my 11 yo niece just emailed me that joke. And guess what?? She wouldn't tell me the answer until I wrote back and guessed. My niece is pretty darn smart and cute, so I'm going to see if it works with an older, smarter, attractive woman. Awaiting your answer... :D

- FIRST FLIRT: Hello, Washington..... do you copy? We seem to have a communication failure. Interference, perhaps sunspots. An attractive alien has appeared on my radar screen. She is unlike most that I have encountered. She has an out-of-this-world smile, and says she knows the difference between two and too. I will try to make contact. Please advise.

- FIRST FLIRT: Hi Ms. Texas...I'm far too young for you (I still read Dr. Seuss) and far too old (Freud's Interpretation of Dreams). But I had to at least comment on your lovely bio and great list of reasons I should date you. Maybe I qualify?? (NOTE: This is a very good way to see if the woman is willing to date outside her AGE range. Many are. A Dr. Seuss disclaimer works especially well if you're OLDER than she is. You could also reference Snoopy or Disneyland or any place reminiscent of being a kid.)

- FIRST FLIRT: WOW! What an AWESOME sounding woman!! Not to mention, attractive, and my personal favorite CLASSY! I like theater more than DVD's, too. Care to play "Can I buy you a drink or a cup of coffee"? Oh wait, I think we're already playing! (NOTE: He sorta asks for the coffee date but doesn't. This man knows how to flirt. If she needs more time to get to know him, she'll let him know.)

- FIRST FLIRT: PULITZER PRIZE....of all the hundreds of profiles I've read, yours is the best. You don't say you're funny, you are funny (the line about the convertible was a riot, and I don't even own one). I don't know if we're a match, but see what you think. Bye for now, but if for good, I wish you the best. Some man will be far more fortunate than he might ever dream. P.S. – If you've got your heart set on a convertible, we can always go test drive one!

- FIRST FLIRT: Well...I read and then reread your profile. That's a first for me....it must mean I enjoyed what you had to say and how you say it. Your list of reasons NOT to date you had me hooked by the 3rd one! Shall I send you the top 3 reasons why you should date me?

- FIRST FLIRT: I absolutely loved your profile! I'm still laughing. Most of what you write about I have experienced, and more. I think it would be fun to chat, compare stories, and perhaps meet for coffee. Or are you more a "cup of tea" kind of woman? Pepsi? Wine?

- FIRST FLIRT: Hi, I sure like what you say and how you say it. What you read in my profile is just a sample of this very nice and honest person. You say you don't like "fudge" in profiles. Ditto here. No "fudging" from me. Are you more a Snickers woman or do you prefer M&M's?

- FIRST FLIRT: I'm afraid that I am just a little bit outside your parameters at 5'9" inches tall, but I could dust off my cowboy boots with the stomper heels. That would make me close to 6' and in your upper height range. Plus, in person, I'm much taller than I am on these laptop monitors. I'd be pleased if you read my profile.

- FIRST FLIRT: AWARD! You are the BEST 45 year old I've seen online. Maybe we're enough of a match because: 1) I'm a "darn" liberal and so are you and 2) You sound abnormally normal and so do I! Best! (NOTE: You can substitute any age and any political view to suit you.)

- FIRST FLIRT: Extremely creative and entertaining profile. Love the photo of you in Paris. Now...can you figure out a way to get those mountains nearer the ocean? Have a lovely day and thanks for the smile. Wish you were closer. (NOTE: This is a good way to see if the woman is willing to date outside her mileage range. Many are and will send emails to that effect.)

- FIRST FLIRT: I wish you were closer, but it gives me hope that women like you do exist in my state. Interested in dating outside your mile range? (NOTE: This is a good way to see if the woman is willing to date outside her mileage parameter. Often she is.)

- FIRST FLIRT: I read your profile, and I can say that you know how to express yourself. That is refreshing. Your story about "catching your match" got me smiling and relating. Want to hear my funniest story about being here?

- <u>FIRST FLIRT</u>: Hi, I enjoyed reading your clever profile. We have similar interests, and I match many of your preferences. I would enjoy hearing from you - watching the sunsets with a glass of Napa Valley wine is my idea of a lovely evening, too. Whose vineyard do you favor? Regards,

- <u>FIRST FLIRT</u>: Hi there. We seem to have a lot in common, at least that's what the "Search" criteria is telling me. We're also in the same line of work…health care. I've heard Vitamin MM works well. VIT. MM?? Very Interesting Tell Me More?

- <u>FIRST FLIRT</u>: Just wanted to say hi and compliment you… lovely face and dynamite profile. Your job in government sounds fascinating. If you find my bio of interest, I'd enjoy hearing from you. Are you one of those super-secret-hush-hush agents? Oh wait, if you tell me, are you gonna have to …gulp…make me disappear?

- <u>FIRST FLIRT</u>: Good Morning! Your words are a breath of fresh air….far above the crowd, especially the part about _____. (NOTE: Put in 1 specific thing here). I don't know if we're enough of a match... but wanted to say the one who finds you will be fortunate indeed.

- <u>FIRST FLIRT</u>: I read your profile twice and enjoyed it. Especially what you had to say about making your own way. I'd be pleased if you check out my profile and let me know what you think.

- <u>FIRST FLIRT</u>: Really enjoyed your profile. We'd be perfect for each other except your cat looks smarter than my dog. However, maybe you can overlook that shortcoming since I have so much more going for me. Check with your cat, and let me know what she says! (NOTE: You can substitute any funny thing that makes you "unperfect" such as you like coffee, and I'm a tea drinker.)

- <u>FIRST FLIRT</u>: YOU GOT ME! ;-) …Your wonderful profile popped up, and I felt compelled to touch base and say hello. I see you like to jog. I am heading out for a run, but would enjoy chatting more if you are interested. Take care and have a great day.

- <u>FIRST FLIRT</u>: I really enjoyed your profile. You 1) love to read and 2) love to cook and 3) love your kids (all ways to a man's heart!). I'd enjoy hearing more about you. (NOTE: You can substitute any 2 or 3 things that you find attractive about her.)

338

- <u>FIRST FLIRT:</u> You may be too much of a "wild" woman for me, but years ago I rode a Harley (not as nice as yours). Are you interested in ex-Harley guys who still know the difference between the clutch and the gas?

- <u>FIRST FLIRT:</u> I've always been attracted to smart, witty women. I hope there's some mutual interest. (NOTE: You can substitute "smart, witty" with any 2 words which fit her.)

- <u>FIRST FLIRT:</u> I see you just started to play golf. I'm not nearly as good as I want to be, but I'm getting there. I've played for a whole 12 months. Maybe we can get better together. Check out my profile and see if you're interested in communicating and playing golf.

- <u>FIRST FLIRT:</u> Hi. I enjoyed what you had to say about "blind dates" and the slice of life you shared. Thanks for the grins! What's new in your world today? (NOTE: You can focus on any 1 thing in her Profile that you found outstanding or humorous.)

- <u>FIRST FLIRT:</u> Hi. I enjoyed your whole profile, and especially your reading list. We seem to share the same favorite authors. Anything new you'd recommend?

- <u>FIRST FLIRT:</u> I am impressed with your novel profile….it was almost as long as some novels and riveting. I think I passed your deal maker/deal breaker list, but I could be wrong. But I'm willing to take a chance and see if I can score extra points by saying hi first. Now exactly how many points do I get for going first?

- <u>FIRST FLIRT:</u> Thanks for the compliment of making me a favorite. You write extremely well, have a great smile, and seem amazingly normal for a woman who works out 5 days a week. I only work out 4 days a week. Is that a deal breaker?

- <u>FIRST FLIRT:</u> Hi, I like your profile and photos. We appear to share some common interests. There is a geographic distance between us, but I like to travel and so do you. Besides, what are the odds we'd find our perfect match within 50 miles of one another! (NOTE: This is a good way to see if the woman is willing to date outside her mileage range. Many are.)

- <u>FIRST FLIRT</u>: Hi, what are you doing for the next 2 minutes? Maybe you'll be reading my profile. I thought we had enough in common (skiing, cycling, kids) that I should at least stop by and say hi. I'm not a mind reader (yet), so I'd love to hear what you think.

- <u>FIRST FLIRT</u>: Very funny, very good. But so far away you could be on the moon. On the other hand, I do get to So. CA in the winter to visit family and friends. Ever get out this way?? (NOTE: If you have family or friends where the woman is located, this reply is a good way to approach it.)

- <u>FIRST FLIRT</u>: Wow, I log on and... and there you are. What a treat to read your profile. You say you're wondering "Is there a life beyond online dating or maybe a road map?" I couldn't agree more. Want to compare notes?

- <u>FIRST FLIRT</u>: What a wonderful profile. It's kind of fun to write this to you, in two time zones away. There's a sign on the interstate that says NYC is 722 miles away, but you don't seem that far. Ever get out this way?

- <u>FIRST FLIRT</u>: Loved your list of favorite movies. I'm an outdoors person in the summer, but winter finds me curling up on the sofa and reading the latest bestsellers and watching DVD's. I lend to friends, but only after I've met for coffee, gotten 2 forms of ID and a copy of their birth certificate. Do you think that's enough?

- <u>FIRST FLIRT</u>: Your list of favorite places and fun things is interesting and eclectic. Not sure where you are politically...you list Obama's Audacity of Hope and O'Reilly's book as faves. Are you keeping your friends close and your enemies closer? P.S --yes, I'm a political junkie like you!

- <u>FIRST FLIRT</u>: Hi -- I saw that you looked at my profile, and it said that you stared for at least 3 minutes! I stared at yours for at least 2 minutes....okay, maybe 3. Your Favorite Places looks like my list. Looking forward to getting to know you better...and finding out if you prefer coffee or brunch or dinner for a first date??

- <u>FIRST FLIRT</u>: I enjoyed reading your profile especially reading about all the places you traveled. Yes, I can read minds. My mind says that I am open to trading an email or two. How about you?

- FIRST FLIRT: Wow! Tell me more. I haven't done Origami in years! You also cast the net wide and far?? I do like Oregon and the northwest coast - very beautiful. Look forward to hearing from you. (NOTE: This is a great way to ask the woman why she's able to have such a wide-ranging area for dating. Does she travel a lot for business, vacation, is she independently wealthy, what's the deal?)

- FIRST FLIRT: Coffee is my beverage of choice, but only on days that end in Y. I see that you only cry over spilt coffee, too. If I promise NOT to spill coffee on you in the first email, will you read my profile?

- FIRST FLIRT: I keep trying to make myself look taller on this laptop since you say you like tall men. I'm 6' in person, but on this monitor, it looks like I'm barely 6 inches tall. Is there something wrong with my monitor?? Can you tell from my writing that I'm taller than I look?

- FIRST FLIRT: I give up! I surrender! Your smile is intoxicating. You can spell; you can punctuate. You use multi-syllabic words and use them correctly. I even spotted a semi-colon in there somewhere. I am speechless. What should I write so I have a glimmer of a chance of going out with you?

- FIRST FLIRT: Foul play! Entrapment! You used humor to lure me into your web...uh...I mean profile! You made me smile. You made me laugh out loud. Hmm....maybe I need to rewrite my profile?? But before I do, please tell me if you like it!

- FIRST FLIRT: Since I saw you before you saw me, is it okay if I wink first? I couldn't find the wink button, so I'm using the email to wink. This wink means I like the fact that you said _____.
(NOTE: Put in 1 thing from her Profile that you liked and found winkable.)

APPENDIX: COME BACK FLIRTS
WHEN SHE SAYS "THANKS, BUT NO"

- COME BACK FLIRT: Thanks for your response. I wish you the best, and if that new prince starts turning green and looking like a frog, I'd enjoy hearing from you.

- COME BACK FLIRT: Hi and thanks for your reply. Good luck with your new date. If he doesn't work out, I'd enjoy getting to know you.

- COME BACK FLIRT: I wish you the best of luck. You deserve the best, and if things don't work out, I'd enjoy hearing from you.

- COME BACK FLIRT: Good to hear from you. Your response confirms what a lovely person you are. The man you are dating is very fortunate to have you in his life. Good luck, and if he doesn't work out, wink back my way.

- COME BACK FLIRT: Hi and thanks for the email. Best of luck to you, and if it doesn't work out, I'm just an email away.

- COME BACK FLIRT: You are pure class. I wish you continued happiness. I suspect we might have been quite a couple, and if things don't work out, I'm just a click away. Again, I do wish you happiness wherever it is found. Thank you again for your reply.

- COME BACK FLIRT: That was probably the nicest, most complimentary rejection I have ever received. I'm disappointed now more than ever, but I wish you the very best. You are a class act. If things don't work out with your new date, please know I'd enjoy meeting you.

- There's a great lecture at the college on _____. No admission charge for students and faculty. Care to go?

- There's an art gallery opening I was invited to. Free wine tasting and hors d'oeuvres. Would you like to go?

- Our office is having a Christmas party in 2 weeks. Would you like to be my date?

- The free concert series in the park begins next week. Do you like light rock music?

- The Experimental Theater has a free showing next Tuesday night. Want to go?

- There's an open mike at the Comedy House next Thursday. Want to go and listen?

- Next Thursday night is the "Free Art Walk" through Laguna. I went last Christmas with my family. It's usually a lot of fun.

- I've never been to our new library, and it was built a year ago. Care to explore with me?

- They need volunteers at _____ on Saturday. I've signed up for Saturday morning. Care to keep me company?

- There's a charity garage sale on Sunday put on by _____. Would you like to go?

- Our library is having a special program on _____. Would you like to go?

- Home Depot is having a free class on _____. I've always wanted to learn that.

- I've never been on the free Architectural Tour of the City. Care to go?

- There's a Nutritionist speaking at the health food store next week. Want to go with me?

- There's a speaker on _____ at the Senior Center next Wednesday. Would you like to go?

- Our church is holding a bazaar next Friday and Saturday. Want to go?

- Want to go snowshoeing? I've got an extra pair of shoes.

- Would you like to play tennis next weekend?

- The German Festival is downtown in 2 weeks. Lots of free music and dancing.

- Next Saturday is the free day at the zoo. I've been with the kids before, but I'd love for just us 2 to go. What do you think?

- The Renaissance Festival is this weekend. Want to go?

- The Sawdust Art Festival is next weekend. Would you like to go with me?

- I've never been to Disneyland. Want to pretend we're 12 years old again?

- There's a new, used bookstore downtown. Want to check it out this weekend?

- There's a great Sporting Goods store that's having their end of year sale. Want to go?

- Would you like to play a round of golf on Saturday or Sunday?

- If you like baseball, I have season tickets. Care to go next weekend?

- <u>COME BACK FLIRT to the PAST RELATIONSHIP QUESTION:</u>
We parted because we grew apart. Our biggest problem was that I tried to balance spending and saving, but she loved credit cards. Not that I don't like my credit cards. I love those Frequent Flyer miles, but I also love paying them off every month. Come to think of it, I could use a few more miles. :D   Can I entice you into saying "yes" to coffee or lunch next week?

- <u>COME BACK FLIRT to the PAST RELATIONSHIP QUESTION:</u>
I had a good marriage, but my spouse died of cancer a few years ago. I've dated since then and am looking forward to finding a kind, intelligent person who shares similar core values and likes similar activities. I see you like the theater. Anything you've seen lately that you'd recommend? (NOTE: This is a great way to get her interested in going out with you. You can substitute any activity such as "How's your golf game been this year?" or "Any good books you'd recommend?"   You might find yourself on a date at the theater or golf course or at the bookstore this weekend.)

- <u>COME BACK FLIRT to the PAST RELATIONSHIP QUESTION:</u>
We parted because we had different ideas about fidelity. I believed in it. It's a long story which is better told over a good glass of wine or nice dinner. Same question to you...what worked and didn't in your relationship? (NOTE: You have NOT exactly asked her out. However, you've cleverly given HER the opportunity to accept! Aren't you the sly one!   Alternatively, you can tack on "MY TREAT" and now you have issued the invitation.)

- <u>COME BACK FLIRT to the PAST RELATIONSHIP QUESTION:</u>
She used to accompany me hiking and to the hockey games, but as years went by her idea of having fun was tv, more tv, and partying.

- <u>COME BACK FLIRT to the PAST RELATIONSHIP QUESTION:</u>
Even though I worked full time, I ended up being the one who cared for the house, the kids, the dog, etc.   I was the proverbial spouse who was taken for granted. Two good things happened....I've got great kids, and I became a good cook! I'm also good at choosing restaurants and know a great Italian place for coffee or lunch if you'd care to join me this weekend?

FOR FUN: I love to ski either downhill or cross country. I bike in the summer and have been known to get lost on the winding bike trails in the City. Now I have a compass! I like to garden and raise organic herbs and browse for bargains at REI. I also go to Red Rocks for outdoor concerts.

FOR FUN: I like old classic movies like Casablanca and The Day the Earth Stood Still. I like new movies like Slumdog Millionaire and the Harry Potter series and Avatar (amazing!). Fun is having dinner with friends or with you!

FOR FUN: I'm an amateur photographer (check out 2 of my favorite pictures above). My dog walks me often, and it would be great to have good company who says more than ARF and WOOF.

FOR FUN: I'm not big on garage sales, but estate sales are a whole different animal. I like small home fix-up projects. If you're trying to fix up your desert island, I'll help you move the coconuts! I like the sun and beach, but mostly I like being with someone who enjoys me as much as I enjoy them.

FOR FUN: I never thought I'd enjoy dancing, but I just started taking lessons. It's great fun and great exercise. I like salsa, rock 'n' roll. I'm big on candlelight and one-on-one time.

FOR FUN: Comedy Central, CNN, Anderson Cooper....I think I'm the only one here who is willing to admit they watch TV. When I travel, I enjoy learning about other cultures and their history as well as how they view our country. Care to join me?

FOR FUN: Anything to do with water...waves, oceans, rivers, waterfalls, tide pools. Yes to walking on the beach, yes to sailing, yes to fishing. Maybe I was a porpoise in my last life.

FOR FUN: I like indie movies and foreign films and cuddling in front of the big HDTV. As far as music, hands down it's Rock and Roll. Nirvana is one of my favorites. I like hitting the road and going for a drive in the desert or mountains.

FOR FUN: My work takes me all over the country. When I'm home, I like to stay close to home. I come back with good recipes and love to cook for family and friends. I'm a big fan of comedy: 2 ½ Men, Seinfeld reruns, and some of the British sitcoms.

FOR FUN: I'm the quintessential Californian. I surf, swim, and sail. I like great restaurants and nightlife (plenty to choose from here), and dinner and conversation with candlelight. Yes, I watch TV, too, and am willing to admit it. My faves are comedies and movies.

FOR FUN: I'm always on the lookout for new restaurants to try, and I'd love to have you join me. Having someone to share with always makes it twice as fun. I visited Italy a few years ago and plan to go to Switzerland next year. Is your passport current?

FOR FUN: The most fun times of the year are the holidays: Xmas and Thanksgiving, even the 4th of July and Halloween. I also like the big annual garage sale in my subdivision. I clean out my basement and garage, and yes, I do occasionally find treasures to fill it back up again, but just not quite as full.

FOR FUN: I just started taking flying lessons. Talk about fun! No, I'm not a daredevil and wouldn't think of jumping out of a perfectly good plane, but there is something wonderful about gliding over the earth and seeing it from above.

FOR FUN: Spicy food. Icy smoothies on a hot day. Movies at the theater. Movies at home. Reading the latest bestseller. Photography. Exploring. Being challenged by learning something new. I'll try most anything once...well, probably not bungee jumping.

FOR FUN: I have diverse interests that include: lively conversation, bridge, museums, fine arts, reading, and more. I also play Frisbee with my dog, Yaya, and he's better than I am. I still haven't figured out how to catch it with my teeth.

FOR FUN: I like Birdies. Eagles are even better. Golf and more golf. But no more than once a day. Just kidding, but I do like to play, and am a good teacher if you want to learn. I tried scuba diving once, and I'd do that again in a minute.

FOR FUN: I like to explore out of the way places be it small art galleries, old gold mines, or quaint restaurants. I've been known to kayak and horseback ride. At the end of the day I like a hot shower not a cold, rushing stream.

FOR FUN: I'm on a first name basis at 2 bookstores. I like the endorphin rush of working out and prefer outdoor workouts to the health club. Maybe we can work out together?

FOR FUN: Love miniature golf, fast food in a pinch, great food any time, great wine that's not outrageous in price but sooo good, foreign films, cable TV, MY JOB!, intimate conversation with you.

FOR FUN: You can sleep when you're dead, so let's get moving. Life is too darn short. Let's drive to wine country, go apple picking, hang out at the beach. Do you know what you want to do? Let's do it together.

FOR FUN: Cirque du Soleil, Broadway plays and musicals, Ballet, Opera, Chamber Music, Tennis, Sailing, Chess, Bridge, Cribbage, Scrabble, Mah Jongg, Texas Hold'em. Am I eclectic in my tastes, YES!

FOR FUN: I'm a movie buff and like foreign and quirky films. I also collect old motorcycles and biking memorabilia. Nighttime means a great DVD on a great flat screen with surround sound and real popcorn. Care to exchange DVD's? :-)

FOR FUN: Movies, books, carpentry, football (watching not playing). I like to read about the economy and follow stocks and funds and ETFs. Want to compare notes on our favorite economists and technical gurus?

FOR FUN: Going for a ride on my Harley. Yes, I'm one of those! Love music and driving the car in the summer with the top down. I know it's cliché, but who I'm with is what matters more than what I'm doing. Care to share in my fun? :-)

FOR FUN: Music from Mozart to Rock; art from Monet to Miro. I like museums and hole-in-the-wall places. I like short drives in the city and long drives in the country. The company is the most important thing.

FOR FUN: I have season tickets to the White Sox, season tickets to the theater, and an annual pass to the Botanic Gardens. I enjoy all kinds of museums and outdoor concerts at Ravinia. Want to share in the fun?

MY JOB: Ask me a year in history, and I'll entertain you with a true story. I teach history which is fun and alive if you do it right. It's a great job because I get to work with kids and that keeps me young and on my toes. It's also great to have the summers off because I like to travel to historic places.

MY JOB: Do you need your hard disk replaced or need Windows upgraded? I'm your go-to guy! I do tech support for a large company here in the city.

MY JOB: If you live in Chicago, you've seen some of our work. I work for an architectural firm that specializes in restoring older buildings.

MY JOB: Jobs: in order of importance and fun... First I'm a parent to two great boys, second I'm a volunteer at the Fire Department, and third, I have a real job as an electrician that pays the bills.

MY JOB: Retirement and lots of free time! I'm busier than ever, but my number one priority is finding someone to share good times and good conversation. Care to join me?

MY JOB: I graduate this semester with a managerial job ready for me in Dallas. I'm one of the lucky ones (or I studied hard or both). I'll be new to the city. Care to show me around? I'll buy lunch!

MY JOB: Web developer is my work and my hobby (I freelance for friends). I do programming for a regional airline. Everything from advertising to reservations. It's gratifying to see my work being used by millions of people. Money and success isn't everything, but it does give you choices.

MY JOB: I work as a genetic research lab technician. I can't clone you, but I do get to assist in fascinating research and hear super-intelligent speakers at scientific meetings. If you want to volunteer as a test subject, maybe I could arrange it (kidding...kidding).

MY JOB: On Monday I was the homework expert on 5th grade geography. Last week I was the "show and tell Dad" for the 3rd grade. We made healthy, trail mix snacks. Most days I'm a manager for a telecommunications company. Yes, I wear many hats. (NOTE: If you're a full or part-time dad, pick 2 or 3 DAD JOBS you did this week and SHINE.)

MY JOB: I'm an investigator in D.C. I'm one of those Feds your tax dollars fund. I work just for you! How am I doing? Shall I investigate myself and send you a report? (kidding!)

MY JOB: I love being self-employed. I've been a realtor for 8 years. A lot of my clients are Spanish, and I'm bilingual. However, I just started taking an Italian class. Next summer's vacation is going to be Italy! I've got Hello (Ciao) and Goodbye (Ciao) mastered. Do you think that's enough?

MY JOB: I'm working at managing my investments and playing with the grandkids. Not sure which is more challenging, but both are fun! Sometimes I think I'm grossly overpaid, but don't tell my boss!

MY JOB: I'm a media director for a great company that helps small and medium-sized companies develop their promos, commercials, marketing materials, print ads, etc. I enjoy the creative process and coming up with new ideas and thinking out of the box.

MY JOB: Lots of international travel as a geologist in the oil and gas field. Have been from Austin to Asia and from Minsk to Morocco. I travel a few times a year. Maybe you'd like to join me on the journey?

MY JOB: I'm a park ranger, and I love my work. I never took a "job test" to see what I'd be good at and what I'd enjoy. However, last year I took the one my son was doing, and guess what? It said I'd be good at and enjoy being a forest ranger. Who knew!

MY JOB: I just started working for an alternative energy company whose main focus is solar energy. I like the science part, but the paperwork from Washington is enormous and reads like a foreign language. Good thing I'm bilingual!

MY JOB: I'm a professional photographer and do everything from brochures to print ads to posters and billboards. If it has a picture, we probably do it. I took my own profile photos, and I've posted some of my work on my profile. If you need help with YOUR photos...I know who you can email!

MY JOB: I'm a mathematician who does top secret work for the government. Not really, but I do number crunch (I work for the City Planning Department). Yes there are math geeks in our office, but I promise I'm not and can hold up my end of a conversation. See, I just did. Tag, your turn.

MY JOB: I work as a manager for a coffee company. Yes, I am a morning person, and my favorite coffees are strong, stronger, and strongest. The work is great, the people are perky (bad pun), and I don't bring my work home with me. Well, sometimes I do. Great discounts!

MY JOB: I work for a naturopathic clinic in Boulder as a physician's assistant. We specialize in alternative health remedies and alleviating chronic pain. I love my work and would probably do it for free, but don't tell my boss.

MY JOB: I was blessed with a good voice and do voice-overs on commercials. I've been here almost 7 years, and most days I feel like I won the "job lotto". If you hear me complain, it's because that's what the commercial called for.

MY JOB: I own my own business (that isn't code for unemployed, it's the code for successful entrepreneur...Hooray!). I'm part owner of a small employment agency. One of the best things about working for yourself and having a partner is having flexibility to take time off to smell the roses.

MY JOB: Property manager for a large apartment complex. I'm hiring a 3rd assistant this week! Yeah! Now I'll have time to play more and work less.

MY JOB: I work as a stock broker. I love CNBC and Bloomberg business shows. One guest says one thing, and the next guest contradicts what the last one said. That way they can always say their show got it right! FUNNY!

MY JOB: I did the mega-firm thing, but now work for a boutique firm that specializes in environmental law. Yep, I'm one of those GREEN GUYS. Love feeling like I'm making a difference.

MY JOB: Entrepreneur. No, make that successful entrepreneur. I believe in good preparation and a lot of luck. I successfully started and sold one business. I won't be selling this one (HOA property management). My son wants to take it over after he finishes college.

MY JOB: I am self-employed as a hair stylist, but I have a terrible boss. I tell my boss that if I could finish my work in a 4-hour day, I would. I get most evenings and weekends off, and I'm paid well so maybe I shouldn't complain.

MY JOB: I am employed by a large research firm in Chicago. I used to live in Chicago but moved to Kentucky for the lifestyle. No more wet, windy winters for me. I like Kentucky (and horses) but can work from anywhere I have a good Internet connection.

MY JOB: I'm a CPA and most of my work is for small to medium-sized businesses. Our firm has 8 employees including me. I'm part owner and my "boss" is good about letting me set my own hours.

MY JOB: I process and approve credit applications at a commercial bank. These days all my friends and relatives can't wait to hear the latest economic news and get the "inside" story.

MY JOB: Most days you can find me helping my 2 kids with homework, cruising the grocery aisles for dinner or ordering takeout (yes!). I also do the 1001 other jobs that make up the hardest and best job in the world...parent. My other full time job is as a carpenter who specializes in remodeling kitchens and baths.

MY JOB: I work for an import-export company. Our business specializes in goods from Guatemala and Costa Rica. We deal with textiles from the raw material to the finished product (coats, belts, hats, etc.). Yes, I have a colorful closet! Oh...and I have plenty of FF miles in case you live too far away!

MY JOB: Call me Professor or just Jim (my name). My students tell me I'm not stuffy or boring, and occasionally they look like they're taking notes. The smart ones know I'm a sucker for those apples on my desk. I teach Business Courses, and if I had to do it all over, I would choose this again.

MY JOB: I specialize as an efficiency expert. Yes, there are such things. We're the ones who buy all those closet organizers, desk organizers, and think going to the Container Store is almost as good as going to the movies. ;-)

MY JOB: I do software support for a medium-sized medical company. I'm the one they call when their system is hiccupping. Sometimes it's as simple as forgetting to turn on the printer (true story). I can fix your computer, spell, punctuate, and carry on a conversation.... sometimes at the same time. If you doubt it....there's one sure way to find out.

MY JOB: I have my own house remodeling business. We're "almost" as fast as you see it on those TV home improvement shows. I can find anything I'm looking for on my desk which makes my co-workers and kids think I'm amazing. Please don't tell them otherwise.

MY JOB: I tutor advanced and special needs children. I can't repeat this enough...if you suspect your child is dyslexic (difficulty reading, decoding words), get them tested. Many high IQ kids are dyslexic. The earlier dyslexic kids get help, the better.

APPENDIX: MY ETHNICITY

ETHNICITY: I was born in Minnesota in a small town to German dairy farmers. Dairy work is hard work, but it teaches you a lot about life. These days I love the city and the amenities. Not getting up at 4 a.m. to feed and milk the cows has a lot to say for itself. What? You thought the milk just magically appeared on the grocery store shelves?

ETHNICITY: 31 flavors Baskin Robbins mix. Do you believe in 6 Degrees of Separation? Let's email or get together and see if we can figure out how we're "related". I've lived in 4 states and 2 countries. Give me a week in a new city, and it's home away from home.

ETHNICITY: Norwegian and German with a little bit of French thrown in for good measure. Have good genes on both sides, and if I continue to live healthy and eat healthy, I should have a long life. My granddad is going strong at 82....and has a lady friend!

ETHNICITY: I like to believe that we are all brothers and sisters. It's interesting to know where we were born and where our families came from, but when it comes down to it, we are all one big family living on the same piece of flying ground called EARTH.

ETHNICITY: Grew up in Mexico on a farm, educated in the U.S., and became an American citizen several years ago. Living here makes every day a gift.

ETHNICITY: I think my parents gave me a good acceptance of others, and while I'm proud of my ethnicity (can trace it back to Africa), I like to think of myself as colorblind. Maybe "color-appreciative" would be a better word, but suffice it to say, we're all in this together.

ETHNICITY: My fantastic adoptive parents were from CA, and their grandparents were both from Russia. My real parents were also from CA, but don't know their heritage. I've adopted 1 child of my own, and we're working on doing a family tree.

ETHNICITY: I'm part American Indian, but only a small part...1/32. I only wear war paint on Halloween, and only if I'm the one handing out the candy. I admit to being partial to camping....but only at the Marriott, Sheraton, or Ritz and where there's room service.

ETHNICITY: I am half Dutch, one quarter British, and one quarter Scottish. If I did my math correctly, that adds up to 100% American.

ETHNICITY: My grandparents emigrated here from Russia in the mid-1900's. They came with nothing and were hard-working examples for me to follow. I have a strong work ethic and have had the good fortune to stand on their shoulders.

ETHNICITY: My grandparents were from England, and we have a wee bit of Irish and French thrown in for good measure. My grandparents were long-lived (2 of them over 90), and my parents are doing great. I'm hoping the same is true of me…predisposed to longevity (and smiles).

ETHNICITY: My patients' countries of origin are important to me. Understanding their backgrounds and lifestyles helps me help them with their health care needs. My parents and grandparents are from Puerto Rico.

ETHNICITY: These eyes are French Blue, the fine-tuned, inner chassis was manufactured by German great-grandparents, the chiseled cheekbones are from Italy, and my sense of humor is definitely British.

ETHNICITY: I was born in Quebec, Canada, speak French and English and have a heritage that includes French, English, Spanish, and Scottish relatives. For fun…the world is my sandbox.

ETHNICITY: 4th Generation New Yorker. Part Italian, part German, part Heinz 57. That might explain why I like all kinds of Italian food, bratwurst at ball games, and most ethnic restaurants.

ETHNICITY: I'm a third generation American and am open to dating a good match from any race and any ethnicity. I've got Russian relatives, Italian relatives, Spanish relatives, and probably a few that we are sure had to be adopted!

ETHNICITY: I grew up with a simple life and strong values. My main lineage is from Croatia (it borders Hungary and Serbia and Bosnia). I'm self-sufficient, a hard worker, and am fortunate in my job that I have time to enjoy the fruits of my labor.

ETHNICITY: I'm from the ISLAND. Not the warm, tropical, palm tree islands of the Caribbean, but rather the beautiful wilderness and cosmopolitan flair of Vancouver Island. My relatives hale from all over the world.

ETHNICITY: British British and British. Lots of relatives to visit over here, but sorry to say, none own their own castle. Great fun to visit the relatives and hear family stories over good fish and chips.

ETHNICITY: Grandparents from Italy, Poland, and Russia. Born in New York City, but then moved to Houston a few years ago. I definitely sound "back east", but sometimes that southern Texas drawl creeps in.

ETHNICITY: Scottish, Irish, Portuguese, Welsh, English, Hispanic, Japanese, African, Indian, sheesh...I've lost track − just call it − American.

ETHNICITY: One set of grandparents came from Ireland, the other from Italy. Yes, VERY loud and fun family reunions. Plus great food! I was born in Florida and have lived in Georgia, Colorado, and (of course) Texas. I'm a nice mix of ethnicities!

ETHNICITY: 33% Venezuelan, 33% Italian, and 33% German, 1% ?? Now I'm 100% American. Born in South America but educated in Denver. I've lived here most of my life except for 1 year as an exchange student in Venezuela. Life is Grande!

ETHNICITY: Lots of Japanese which explains my love of Japanese food and their culture. Some Thai (yes, I like Thai cuisine, too), and some Hawaiian. No black sheep that I know of ...or they're hiding under the bigger branches of the family tree.

APPENDIX: MY RELIGION

MY RELIGION: Early every spring the buds open on my forsythia. A few weeks later, my iris start to bloom, and a few weeks after that the roses are budding. This happens every year. Who or what makes it happen, I can't say…but it's miraculous just the same.

MY RELIGION: I go to church regularly. I believe God is everywhere. We just have to look around us. We also have to listen, especially to the quiet voice of our conscience that tells us right from wrong.

MY RELIGION: I believe everyone is capable of goodness although some never find it. I'm more spiritual than religious and believe in the Golden Rule and doing unto others as you would have them do unto you.

MY RELIGION: I think it was Einstein who said….Christianity is great….if people would only practice it! I believe in Einstein.

MY RELIGION: I believe in high ethics and high morality. I live with the belief we are here for a reason, and that we are here to leave the world better than we found it. I live my life to respect all and remember that each day is a gift.

MY RELIGION: Raised Christian, and I go to church regularly. It instilled good principles in me, and I continue to be tolerant of all religions. The principles are good. What's not good is the practice of some religions which insist their religion is more right than their neighbor's.

MY RELIGION: I consider myself open-minded about religion. The only time I have difficulty with someone's religion is if that religion starts insisting they are the only religion and that everyone believe and live their way.

MY RELIGION: Getting in touch with my spiritual side is important to me, but I can find that in nature as easily as I can find it in a formal house of worship.

MY RELIGION: I believe in God and believe it's the duty of organized religion to bring people together and find common ground. How long have the wars in the Middle East been going on? It seems like forever because it has been forever. There has to be a better way.

MY RELIGION: I am more spiritual than religious, and I am optimistic that something awaits us after this life. We all don't have to be crusaders, but we all should give and help others in our own way.

MY RELIGION: In the past I was very active in the Methodist Church. I still attend services, and I've found beauty in all religions.

MY RELIGION: Living a good and caring life is the best religion.

MY RELIGION: I'm most attuned to the Hindu philosophy that we must live life with good Dharma in order to achieve good Karma.

MY RELIGION: I don't belong to a church now, but I think spirituality is important. I have dated people of other faiths (Lutheran, Catholic, Jewish), and I always enjoy learning about other's beliefs and practices.

MY RELIGION: I believe religion is a journey of the soul. God is always right here, in all of us, in all of nature. God is the spirit of love and lives in all of us.

MY RELIGION: I have a Jewish background but was married to a Catholic. I sometimes go to the Unitarian Church in town because I like the social activities, and we have a great, real-world minister.

MY RELIGION: I was raised Roman Catholic, but I'm open to and respect all faiths. There are enough problems in the world without religion being one of them.

MY RELIGION: Sitting quietly and meditating is the best way for me to communicate with my spirituality. I believe in a higher power, and I live my life with a respect for all living things.

MY RELIGION: I believe in God. Anyone who goes to the zoo or to the aquarium can see that things did not just evolve....or did they? If you like to discuss religion and Darwin, I'm your man.

MY RELIGION: I grew up Christian, but my faith now is The Golden Rule with a little bit of Buddhist leanings thrown in for good measure.

MY RELIGION: Each day I remind myself to be grateful for today. It's so easy to focus on what we don't have, we so often forget the many blessings we do have. I'm not a big church goer, but if you want to go, I'll be happy to accompany you.

MY RELIGION: I don't think you need to be on your knees to pray. Sometimes the best prayers are when you are giving a helping hand.

MY RELIGION: Does it count that every time I get online I say, "God please help me"? Or that I always put up the Xmas tree even though I'm Jewish by heritage. Or that I like to dye Easter eggs with my kids?

MY RELIGION: It doesn't matter to me what religion you are or aren't, but it does matter the size of your heart and soul. Getting along with your neighbor or the country across the ocean should be the aim of all religions.

MY RELIGION: Do Unto Others as you would have them do unto you is my first commandment. It's also my 2nd and third, etc.

MY RELIGION: I grew up in a religious home, and I go to church regularly. I like to show my faith through my actions. I volunteer time and donate to worthy causes and the less fortunate.

MY RELIGION: I have never joined a particular religion, but I am a believer. I don't need to see people walking on water to believe we were put here to make this a better place and to help our fellow man.

MY RELIGION: I attend church regularly, and I lead a good life and lead by example for my kids.

MY RELIGION: I'm a Christian, and I believe in freedom of religion. I believe in the separation of church and state. I think that is what makes our country great. Having the freedom to worship is why my ancestors came to the United States.

MY RELIGION: I like the saying...If I stand in my garage, it doesn't mean I'm a car. If I sit in church, it doesn't mean I'm religious. I think religion is in your heart, in your soul, in the deeds you do, in the life you live.

MY RELIGION: My faith is important to me, and I attend services regularly. I think we all find our own spirituality when we are ready to receive it. If you are not a believer, we would not be compatible matches.

MY RELIGION: My favorite religious word is TOLERANCE. If everyone practiced it, wouldn't that be amazing! I give thanks that I live where I can choose my own church and house of worship.

MY RELIGION: I am Christian and believe that God has many different faces. I like an uplifting church service and the music. Our minister's sermons are thought-provoking. They are about the real world and the Bible.

MY RELIGION: My faith is simple – I meditate and seek healing and comfort from nature. Do I know if God created the world or if it was created by the Big Bang? No....but it's miraculous just the same.

MY RELIGION: I'm in the church choir and enjoy Sunday services and especially the Holiday services. It's okay if you're not a regular church goer, but I'd be pleased if you attended especially for the music.

MY RELIGION: I do believe in Santa Claus, the Great Pumpkin, and the Tooth Fairy. I don't like fruitcake, but I do believe in a higher power. I guess you would call me a Catholic who gives out pencils with pumpkin erasers on Halloween.

MY RELIGION: If there was a church of the Golden Rule, I would probably join. But, I'm not a joiner. I like to walk the road less traveled. I seem to learn more and see more that way.

MY RELIGION: If you perform random acts of kindness without expecting payment in return, if you give thanks for what you've been given, if you understand each day of life is a special gift, then we're on the same spiritual page.

MY RELIGION: I always pray when the plane is taking off, and I pray again when it's landing. So far, God has granted my prayers. Now if I could just get His/Her help when I buy that monthly lottery ticket.

MY RELIGION: I'm looking for someone who shares similar religious beliefs. I was born and raised Jewish. I don't keep kosher, but I do go to the synagogue a few times a year and on the High Holidays.

MY RELIGION: I am comfortable in my Christian faith and respect all religions. I think religion is a personal choice, and it's important to live your faith but not impose it on others. Whenever I travel to new cities or countries, I always enjoy visiting historic churches and houses of worship.

MY RELIGION: I strongly believe in GOD. I respect all beliefs and religions that are tolerant of others. I go to his "office" on some Sundays, but I also meet him more informally outdoors in nature.

MY RELIGION: Was it Gandhi who said, "God has no religion"? That makes sense to me. I do believe in a deep connection with GOD, but I don't go to church regularly.

APPENDIX: MY EDUCATION

MY EDUCATION: I enjoyed my college education and feel fortunate that I had parents who encouraged me in my field (lab tech). There are all kinds of quality education. I learn things from my patients every day.

MY EDUCATION: I think we never stop learning. I learned a ton from my parents, kids, friends, colleagues. Who hasn't learned from love relationships? We can all probably write a few chapters on that! Oh yes...I have an Associate's degree from Univ. of Michigan.

MY EDUCATION: Served in the army for 6 years, and now I'm serving an apprenticeship as a carpenter. If you're looking for a Mr. Fix-it guy, woodworking is my trade and my hobby.

MY EDUCATION: If it has a motor, I'm your go-to guy. I've always enjoyed working on cars, and I became a mechanic several years ago. You can't wing it any more...you have to go to classes to know how to work on these complicated machines. BMW's are my specialty, but if you twist my arm, I'll work on any car...even Fords (we call those cars...Fix Or Repair Daily)!

MY EDUCATION: I have a BS in Multi-Media/Communications from the University of Illinois. I actually use my education every day.

MY EDUCATION: I learned a lot in 1) Kindergarten: be nice, share, use scotch tape to fix stuff. 2) in College Statistics 301: Correlation doesn't mean Causation. 3) Work: be nice, share, use scotch tape to fix stuff. (NOTE: You can easily adapt this to your own 3 things that you've learned in grade school, college, and life).

MY EDUCATION: 2 years of college and then started my own business. The School of Life teaches lessons which are as valuable as book learning. I'm encouraging my kids to go to college but know from personal experience there are many paths to success.

MY EDUCATION: I've worked as an administrative assistant for the last few years saving up money for college. Education is important to me. I start college in the fall going for a BA in Hospitality, Travel, and Tourism.

MY EDUCATION: From academia...BS from Arizona State in Business (Resource Management). Degree was good for opening the door to a good job. Still learning the lessons of life and love. Care to compare notes?

MY EDUCATION: Great education at a well-known university. 1 year abroad finishing up. I knew early on I wanted to travel and specialize in International Marketing.

MY EDUCATION: BA and advanced degree from University of Florida. Book learning and real life teach different but equally valuable lessons. I'm now semi-retired and take classes just for fun.

MY EDUCATION: Became a mechanic right out of high school. Love my job and take continuing ed classes all the time to keep current.

MY EDUCATION: BA in Education (early childhood ed is my focus). I'm fascinated by the different ways children learn. One thing I do know…learning never stops!

MY EDUCATION: I have a Bachelor's in Psychology from U of Missouri. Yes, even psychologists get divorced. All I can say is it takes 2 to make a relationship work. It doesn't work if only 1 person is willing to give and share.

MY EDUCATION: I had 1 semester left at Berkeley when I got married. Although I've been successful in business and in raising a family, I'd like to go back and finish just to say, "I did it!"

MY EDUCATION: MD from New York Medical College. Love the acquisition of knowledge and continue to take courses. Medical knowledge is constantly changing. I started out as a teacher, went into private practice, and now do both.

MY EDUCATION: Lots of life experience and 2.5 years of college which I wouldn't trade for anything. I was lured away by a music job in CA. I don't regret it for a minute. When opportunity knocks, you have to answer.

MY EDUCATION: I was raised by working class parents who instilled in me the value of education coupled with life experiences. I graduated from MIT (Massachusetts Institute of Tech.). I value my education and equally value the lessons that life has taught me.

MY EDUCATION: Washington State University and School of Life (advanced degree). Hard work earned me promotions and better life choices. Occasionally take courses from Colorado University.

MY EDUCATION: Degree from Loyola in Chicago. Just enrolled in Online Dating University. Wow, what a school! I haven't dated in years. Can't believe how much I didn't know about Internet dating!

MY EDUCATION: School of Life has taught me much more than I learned in college, but that's probably because I've been in the School of Life longer! College opened my eyes to all the possibilities. BA from Columbia.

MY EDUCATION: Bachelor's in Psychology from University of Delaware and Master's in Education from University of Calif. (Santa Cruz). School is great preparation for what the world throws at you.

MY EDUCATION: I'm the classic kid of a military Dad. I went to a half dozen different grade and high schools. I've had wonderful life experiences, but the world has changed, and I'm adamant about finishing college and going on for an advanced degree.

MY EDUCATION: I am a law school graduate from D.U. here in Colorado. In some ways law school was easier than Online dating. There's less "reading between the lines". Online reality gets creative at times if you know what I mean! ;-)

MY EDUCATION: I believe in the saying that success comes when Preparation meets Opportunity. My academic prep began at U of Miami. Opportunity met preparation when the great tech company I work for now said yes to my application.

MY EDUCATION: The School of Life has been invaluable. I own an antique store but most of my business is now online. I get to meet people from all walks of life and have learned that vintage "things" have stories and lessons to teach us.

MY EDUCATION: I started with a liberal arts education from U. of C. in Los Angeles. That's a good place to start when you don't know what you want to be when you grow up. I plan to work and get some "real world" experience before going for an advanced degree.

MY EDUCATION: Did the formal stuff years ago (Business degree, OSU). My education and degree were invaluable as are the continuing-Ed classes from the "School of Life".

MY EDUCATION: Just finished up my BS from Univ. of Hawaii. The S was for Science not Surfing! Now heading to the mainland to Vet School. Looking forward to meeting new folks and enjoying the next part of the voyage.

MY EDUCATION: My Bachelor's was in English, but when I got out I got interested in sustainable agriculture and organic gardening. My degree has been helpful because there are always reports to write. It helps if I spell the words right!

MY EDUCATION: I thought I was smart with my degree in Marketing. However, online dating has taught me a lot about online marketing and creative license. Disclaimer: My profile and photos are current because I'm not just looking for a date, I'm looking for a mate.

MY EDUCATION: Princeton grad with all that that implies. I respect education and know the value of social connections. The School of Life taught me it's true what they say: WHO you know is as important as WHAT you know.

MY EDUCATION: I received a BA degree from Washington State. What year was that? Probably when Lincoln was President. I enjoy bright people from all walks of life. Young and old have much to teach.

MY EDUCATION: College graduate from Univ. of Connecticut. Got good grades. School taught me to have a good work ethic....but it's what you do after college that makes all the difference.

MY EDUCATION: BS/Advertising and Marketing. I'm half Type A and half Type B. I'm good at details as well as the big picture. The most important thing I've learned: try not to make the same mistake twice.

MY EDUCATION: My alma mater is the Univ. of Wisconsin in Madison. Have a PhD and have the privilege of consulting for Fortune 100 companies. Couldn't have done it without 2 great mentors who encouraged me.

MY EDUCATION: I did well in school (and business), graduating from Cal Tech. Getting good memory genes from Mom and Dad helped! The real world has taught me that social connections have an important place on the totem pole.

MY EDUCATION: Have a BS in Biology from University of Penn. Great degree and a good place to start. Seems like I'm always reading and learning, which is a good thing! Keeps those brain cells from going to sleep. Use it or lose it!

MY EDUCATION: My degree is in Education. I thought college prepared me for teaching......NOT! Real knowledge requires life experiences, and the kids really keep you on your toes. The good news is that I keep them interested and on their toes, too!

APPENDIX: FAVORITE HOT SPOTS

<u>FAVORITE HOT SPOTS:</u> Summertime: by the ocean. Wintertime: Vail or Copper Mountain or Aspen or Steamboat Springs. Anytime: curled up at home with a good book. It's not so much where we are … but the fun we have on the journey.

<u>FAVORITE HOT SPOTS:</u> I love the coast of California. Laguna Beach is the best. I wouldn't want to live in Disneyland, but once every few years with the kids is fun.

<u>FAVORITE HOT SPOTS:</u> I love London but would like to visit my ancestral home in Germany. Not sure we could find it, but it would be fun looking. Bed and Breakfasts are my favorite when traveling for weekend getaways.

<u>FAVORITE HOT SPOTS:</u> I've spent a lot of time in Mexico, Panama, and Costa Rica. I'm bilingual so I make a great tour guide and can ask for directions if we get lost. Multi-cultural festivals are great. Seeking a traveling companion this winter. Ready to pack your things? Let's go...

<u>FAVORITE HOT SPOTS:</u> I speak Spanish, so you can put me on a commuter bus in Mexico City, and I will get us back to the hotel. I like casual places with atmosphere. I have traveled a lot in Mexico, but there are lots of other places I would like to see: Europe, Australia, Africa...

<u>FAVORITE HOT SPOTS:</u> Exotic places have the most appeal to me. And warm...like Tahiti, the Bahamas, Bermuda, and all the Saints...St. Thomas, St. Bart, etc.   I'd like to see London (yes, I know it's not warm), but it is cultural. Care to join me?

<u>FAVORITE HOT SPOTS:</u> I spend most of my time by the water, and that should come as no surprise because it's only 2 miles away. I'd like to go back to Italy (maybe with you??). By far it's been the most beautiful place I have been.

<u>FAVORITE HOT SPOTS:</u> A concert in the park, mountain hot springs, Cafe Kona, Tattered Cover bookstore. I'm not looking for an "Amazing Race" partner, just a partner to go amazing places and have amazing times.

<u>FAVORITE HOT SPOTS:</u>   I'm looking for an "Amazing Race" adventure partner! Someone who isn't afraid to venture into new places. That must be you because Online Dating is a new adventure every day.

FAVORITE HOT SPOTS: Italy, and then Italy, and, of course, Italy. Locally, it's Sunday brunch downtown, any night sitting on my back deck watching the sun set and trying to identify the constellations.

FAVORITE HOT SPOTS: My favorite spot is with someone I care about. That could be Maine in the fall on a foliage tour, Chicago on an architectural tour, or just touring the grocery store trying to decide what we should cook for dinner.

FAVORITE HOT SPOTS: I just moved back here after living in Toronto for almost 10 years. WOW, has the city changed. I'm just starting to get reacquainted and can use all the help I can get. Care to share your knowledge of places to go, things to see, great restaurants?

FAVORITE HOT SPOTS: My all time favorite city in the U.S. is NYC. Overseas it's Paris. I love art museums because the paintings often tell a story about the time and place. If that sounds boring....I'll bet you a Renoir I can change your mind! Oh wait, I don't own a Renoir...how about a Picasso poster?

FAVORITE HOT SPOTS: Concerts at the Botanic Gardens. Red Rocks outdoor concerts are fun and breathtaking....the amphitheater is set between immense red rocks (we're talking dozens of stories high). It's impressive even without music.

FAVORITE HOT SPOTS: Comedy clubs are always fun as is dancing. I just started taking lessons, and while I'm not great, I'm not the worst one in the class. Hanging out with friends is fun, but more fun would be hanging out with a special friend.

FAVORITE HOT SPOTS: Casual or fine dining is my idea of a great night out. Vacations run the gamut: Maui is a favorite especially Lahaina, Kihei, and Kaanapali. Flying over the islands in a helicopter is something I would love to do again with someone special.

FAVORITE HOT SPOTS: Travel is my middle name. I've been to 3 of the 7 continents (Europe, S. America, and, of course, N. America). I'd like to go to the A list places....Africa and Australia and Asia. We can skip Antarctica. Want to get out our traveling map and play a game of darts?

FAVORITE HOT SPOTS: I've been to many countries, Mexico, Japan, Russia, Luxembourg, Austria, Switzerland, Denmark, England, and downtown Los Angeles. Yes, LA! It's the United Nations right in our own backyard.

FAVORITE HOT SPOTS: The authentic Vietnamese food at the Saigon Dragon is wonderful, and there's always Pasta Pasta or Joe's Steakhouse. A wonderful time is more dependent on the person than the place, but a nice atmosphere is always a plus.

FAVORITE HOT SPOTS: First to Café Geisha for tea, then to the Sushi Den for appetizers. Off to the bookstore to browse the travel section. Now it's time to have a yummy Japanese dinner at Wagamama. You see where this is going?

FAVORITE HOT SPOTS: I went to France a few years ago and took cooking lessons. I am going again for the 3rd time this summer. I need someone to break me of this addiction or accompany me. Your choice!

FAVORITE HOT SPOTS: The BIG cities: London and Paris, Chicago and NYC, Rome and Rio. Closer to home is Greenwich. Love that place and the old fish and chip places. I've always wanted to see the pyramids in Egypt. I also like to veg at home and watch a good DVD.

FAVORITE HOT SPOTS: Exploring is fun. Getting lost…not so much fun, but more fun with the right person by your side. I like cookouts with family and friends, as well as live sporting events and theater.

FAVORITE HOT SPOTS: Fenway Park in the summer, a day of sailing on the bay, good theater, good shopping for bargains at the outlet mall, Cape Cod beaches.

FAVORITE HOT SPOTS: St. Bart's and Newport Beach. Both lovely places for vacations, and just as lovely is enjoying a candlelight dinner at home because we can do that any night of the week.

FAVORITE HOT SPOTS: I've traveled to over half of the 50 states, and my 2 favorite cities so far are San Francisco and Chicago. My favorite local restaurants are Samurai House and Fourth Dimension. What are yours?….Send suggestions my way!

FAVORITE HOT SPOTS: Coffee shops, book shops, one-of-a-kind shops. For vacations I sometimes visit family in Minnesota. Hmm….if you have family in Calif., can I borrow them next Xmas? That way I can say we need to go to there rather than head to MN.

FAVORITE HOT SPOTS: Any place where we can hike and have a great picnic. That could be down south to San Diego or up north to wine country. I like the local hangouts (especially seafood places). Being with YOU might become my new favorite hot spot!

FAVORITE HOT SPOTS: Omaha isn't New York City, but it does have The Old Market. I don't vacation in Omaha. I head to Colorado for the mountains and to California or Mexico for the beaches.

FAVORITE HOT SPOTS: Las Vegas is a nice weekend getaway, especially seeing all the new hotels and casinos. Disneyland for adults. My gambling speed is the quarter slots, video poker, and flipping a coin to see if we should walk or take a cab.

FAVORITE HOT SPOTS: So many great places close to home to experience...not just once, but again and again: The Great Sand Dunes, Trail Ridge Road, Estes Park. Lots to see and do. If it sounds good, email me and then look for your winter coat and gloves. It gets cold at 9,000+ feet above sea level.

FAVORITE HOT SPOTS: Anywhere we can get away from the hubbub of the real world. On golf courses, on bike courses, on ski courses. We can take the kids, or I can get the pet sitters (oops...make that babysitters/relatives).

FAVORITE HOT SPOTS: HOME! I travel for a living and love to come home, put my feet up, and go aaaaah. But I wouldn't mind a traveling companion, and I have lots of FF miles if you have the free time. Care to explore the possibilities?

FAVORITE HOT SPOTS: My favorite spots close to home are Barnes and Noble, Borders, and Amazon. I'll be at B and N this Saturday. Can you make it? If so, bring a red rose and a copy of Pride and Prejudice...oh wait, that's Meg Ryan in You've Got Mail. Let's make up our own movie script instead! :D

FAVORITE HOT SPOTS: Let's make our list together. I would move to France, but I can't speak French. I would move to Italy, but I'm even worse in Italian. Switzerland is lovely but too cold. My fireplace works great in the winter. Care to discuss it over a glass of wine?

FAVORITE HOT SPOTS: Coors Field for a Rockies baseball game, Invesco Field for the Broncos (I still miss John Elway). Close to home is Cherry Creek for shop-til-you-drop. Wash Park is great for walking or people watching.

FAVORITE HOT SPOTS: Any place with good food and good wine. I have a preference for cozy places with candlelight (who doesn't). Oh wait... I have a great kitchen, candles, and I love to cook. Yes, my favorite everyday place is home.

FAVORITE HOT SPOTS: My favorite travel destination is the road to LetsFindOut. My favorite traveling companion is SomeoneSpecial. Care to join me?

FAVORITE HOT SPOTS: Sitting on my back deck enjoying my view of the Pacific Ocean is always a special place to me. I feel like I'm on vacation. I do candlelight and piña coladas in the summer, and hot cocoa with teeny marshmallows in the winter. Email now to reserve your table. Seating is limited! :D

FAVORITE HOT SPOTS: Barnes and Noble is my favorite in town place. I like Starbucks, but my favorite coffee shop is 800 miles away in Dana Point, CA on the ocean. My favorite vacation destination...Palm Beach. Great hotels, great beaches, great food, great weather!

FAVORITE HOT SPOTS: The fine dining room in my house when I put on my chef's apron and invite in a group of friends. Walking downtown and window shopping. How do you think I stay in shape to eat my own cooking!

FAVORITE HOT SPOTS: Hopping on the Light Rail and visiting Montrose and Midtown and the Museum District, Spanish Flowers on N. Main (great Mex food and open 24 hours a day for the last 30 yrs). The Galleria...700+ stores so you probably can find what you're looking for. Last time I was there, my sister had to check out the "Purple Store". Yes, you guessed it...everything was some shade of purple!

FAVORITE HOT SPOTS: For the weekend it's Copper Mountain and a cozy mountain chalet. For a vacation, I gravitate to similar kinds of venues...relaxing and romantic. Nice restaurants, nice shops, nice conversation.

FAVORITE HOT SPOTS: I've seen 3 of the eight modern Wonders of the World, and would like to see the other 5. Ready to travel? Let's make plans to check them out!

FAVORITE HOT SPOTS: Last year I volunteered with a group that went to a Mexican village that had no electricity. It was a "vacation" of a lifetime, and I'd like to go back with my kids. It reminds us how lucky we are. Close to home I enjoy theater and museums.

APPENDIX: FAVORITE THINGS

FAVORITE THINGS: People's stories, non-fiction books, laughing with Seinfeld and Comedy Central and Jamie Kennedy and Tyler Perry and Jeff Dunham...and you! Yoga and wine tasting and NOT participating in karaoke!

FAVORITE THINGS: Helping my kids with their homework (but only when I know the answers). Getting a "Thanks, Dad!" Solving world peace....hmmm...maybe you can give me a hand on that one!

FAVORITE THINGS: Laughing and flirting with you, cooking and flirting with you, traveling and flirting with you. Wait....enough about me....let's talk about what YOU like to do!

FAVORITE THINGS: Sightseeing in Rome, scuba diving in Australia, seeing the Great Pyramids in Egypt...of course I've only done 1 of these 3....I've been waiting for you to join me! (NOTE: This works well if you do as he did and combine things you have done with those you'd like to do.)

FAVORITE THINGS: Most kinds of music ranging from the Eagles to New Age. Read (a lot) and watch TV (probably one of the few to actually admit to that). I like the Comedy Channel, especially after watching CNN!

FAVORITE THINGS: My Blackberry, the Internet, my HDTV, my Kindle, anything electronic. Yes, I work "in" the industry and get discounts. And what would YOU like for Christmas this year? And...have you been good?

FAVORITE THINGS: Working out...especially the high when I'm done, cycling, Botanic Gardens, outdoor concerts, chocolate ice cream, anything that has Ben and Jerry on the label.

FAVORITE THINGS: Reading and skiing. Usually not at the same time. Riesling wine and strong coffee.

FAVORITE THINGS: The BIG games: British Open, U.S. Open, and the Super Bowl. Reading books especially Grisham. Learning to salsa dance. Cooking...I'm a good cook, trying to be a great cook!

FAVORITE THINGS: Old stuff...like antiques (and limited edition women)! Going for a drive in the mountains or desert. Watching the sunset from the backyard while sipping an ice-cold glass of homemade lemonade.

FAVORITE THINGS: Saturday mornings taking the dog for a walk. Sunday morning brunch with friends. The "buzz" from a good workout. Eating all kinds of food (I got lucky and got the skinny genes).

FAVORITE THINGS: Monday night football if the Broncos are winning. Golf when the sun is shining (yes, I'm a fair-weather player). Favorite movies – Lord of the Rings and Avatar. Fave chick flick movie is Sleepless in Seattle. Favorite TV show is Bloomberg (stock reports, economy).

FAVORITE THINGS: Love to order pizza in or entertain friends and family with my 5-star HOT homemade chili. Not a big football fan, so is it okay if you watch while I read? LOL! Like good mysteries and enjoyed the H. Potter series. Just started learning to golf. It's a hoot!

FAVORITE THINGS: Really athletic ladies who can chat and work out at the same time (makes the workout go faster). Favorite color is purple, sometimes even when it comes to food. I like purple grapes and purple eggplant parmagian.

FAVORITE THINGS: Going scuba diving when I'm on vacation, shopping at Costco and Home Depot and (gulp) Macy's.

FAVORITE THINGS: Smart women, intelligent women, women who are articulate...I sense a theme here. Favorite flowers are the red roses in my garden. Favorite music is eclectic and then some....runs the gamut from Les Miserables to Celine Dion to Miles Davis.

FAVORITE THINGS: Great restaurants, nightlife in the city, exploring coffeehouses, mentoring inner-city kids, going Xmas shopping on Michigan Avenue, Shedd Aquarium.

FAVORITE THINGS: I hate working out but do it so I can dine with friends; enjoy reading news on the Internet and live theater. I also like having 3-day weekends. I get those every week! I work long hours but then only have to work 4 days a week! Hooray!

FAVORITE THINGS: Seeing new things through my kids' eyes, taking them to the city and country, checking out eBay (I know you do, too!).

FAVORITE THINGS: I like to hold hands, but don't ask me to if you're going skydiving. I'll wave from the ground. I have this "thing" about jumping out of perfectly good airplanes. I'm also into photography, so say CHEESE as you're flying thru the air!

FAVORITE THINGS: Whitewater rafting was my latest adventure which proves I'll try most anything once. I prefer horseback riding to rafting, and there are some great stables with gentle horses less than an hour away. Are you up for a trail ride?

FAVORITE THINGS: I like to surprise people with something they wouldn't get for themselves. I keep my eyes open thru the year looking for that "perfect" Xmas gift (hopefully on sale) that is totally unexpected.

FAVORITE THINGS: Green lights, shopping online for electronic gadgets and bargains, trying new recipes, outdoor cooking on the grill, cleaning house (not really, just wanted to see if you were paying attention), women who pay attention. :D

FAVORITE THINGS: Music, lots of good CDs (Zeppelin, The Who, Rock, Reggae), snowboarding, good books, and my new fave....photography. I'm actually good at it and like it a lot.

FAVORITE THINGS: Good movies (Avatar, Blade Runner, and 'maybe' an occasional chick flick but ONLY if you'll go with me); Good books (Stranger in a Strange Land, Kite Runner); Good company at that chick flick.

FAVORITE THINGS: Talking, laughing, learning. A cat in my lap, Scrabble, crossword puzzles, learning to navigate a new city, women with long legs, cacti when they're blooming,

FAVORITE THINGS: Peanut butter on vanilla ice cream, my pet parrot (who has a pretty good vocab), holding hands just because, all kinds of movies especially those with happy endings, Whole Foods, Trader Joe's.

FAVORITE THINGS: Sleeping late on Sunday, going for a bike ride, family photos, being silly with my kids, someone to share my favorite things.

FAVORITE THINGS: The smell of fresh tomatoes in my garden, a snow day at school, being open to possibilities, watching the light go on when a student gets it, morning espresso, hardback books.

FAVORITE THINGS: Alternative music like Coldplay, my 82 Corvette (it was my dad's, and I always think of him when I drive it), shrimp scampi, gumbo, my neighbor's new golden lab puppy, making a difference.

FAVORITE THINGS: Meeting people who volunteer and being one myself, laughing out loud while watching the Comedy Channel, getting that dynamite digital camera, music from Classical to Golden Oldies to New Age.

FAVORITE THINGS: My kids, business and social networking, reading the Wall Street Journal and local paper, browsing used bookstores, collecting new artists, art fairs, time with my partner.

FAVORITE THINGS: Working out, splurging at Patagonia buying tech gear, light traffic on the way downtown, collecting wine, finding a really great new restaurant, sharing it with someone special. .

FAVORITE THINGS: Getting dressed up and going to the opera, symphony, or theater. Watching Jane Velez Mitchell and Nancy Grace (it's like watching a train wreck....but it's enlightening) and being thankful I can escape the insanity and turn it off!

FAVORITE THINGS: My kids laughing, making pizza from scratch, finding the headset I lost last week, trying to explain to my kids what a "yuppie" is, reading, tweaking my computer to make it run faster, learning something new.

FAVORITE THINGS: The TV remote, thunder and lightning storms, Broadway, living in D.C. and playing tour guide to friends and relatives. Would you like to start at the White House first or the Smithsonian?

FAVORITE THINGS: Shopping at Tommy Bahama for me (or for you). Good wine in front of the fireplace, cruises, mysteries or biographies, learning how to work my new digital camera. I have varied interests and hope you do, too. Looking to share!

FAVORITE THINGS: To eat? Anything. Color? A rainbow. Movies? Anything without subtitles and even a few of those are okay. Music? Rock, Classical, even a little Country. My most favorite...sleeping late on Sunday morning.

FAVORITE THINGS: NPR radio, PBS, fresh-squeezed OJ, Kona coffee, art exhibit at the Met, my Merrill shoes (so comfy and great for slumming), my brown leather boots (comfy and great for hiking).

FAVORITE THINGS: Sunday mornings being lazy, my vintage watch, my collection of books, DVDs and CDs. Another favorite thing would be for you to give me a wink! Or better yet, an email...

FAVORITE THINGS: Fine dining, fine wine, fine women (well...just one fine lady will do), fine books, fine art, finally finishing filling out this profile.

FAVORITE THINGS: Hearing "Love you Dad," a good circle of friends, family photos, getting my hands dirty in the workshop making something out of wood, seeing my forsythia bloom (a sure sign that winter is over and spring is finally here).

FAVORITE THINGS: Music and meditation, writing my profile (it is sorta fun trying to find the words to paint a picture of who you are to someone who has never met you), hugs from my kids, longtime friends, new friends, being close.

FAVORITE THINGS: Discovering new favorite things, undecorating my house and helping friends undecorate theirs (I'm a modern-minimalist), reading Architectural Digest, day hikes, getting to know your favorite things.

FAVORITE THINGS: Spicy food (a few jalapeños on pizza...try it, it's not as hot as you think), Sunday morning with a giant mug of killer coffee, the Sunday paper, going back to bed and cuddling up with a good book.

FAVORITE THINGS: Finding a new yummy vegetarian recipe that my friends will still eat (yes, I'm a veg head). Great sports venues in Houston or on Cable. Flirting with you!

FAVORITE THINGS: GOLF and then there's GOLF. And there's watching the GOLF channel. Practicing my putting (it needs it). Also what everyone else likes...travel, movies, friends, working out, staying in shape for GOLF.

FAVORITE THINGS: Stimulating conversation is a must, stimulating reads (I'm an avid reader), new and used bookstores, limited TV but yes I do watch. Always wanted to learn to speak a foreign language....want to take lessons with me?

FAVORITE THINGS: My motto is....SEEK and ENJOY! I do ask for suggestions from friends and complete strangers on the street. I've learned to (a) pack light & (b) layer. Where do you have in mind for our first adventure? I say let's see what's new downtown...what say you??

FAVORITE THINGS: Heading out "somewhere" to some place we've never been before, anything chocolate, anything that has "bestseller" on the cover, great stores in Dallas and Boston, you kissing me hello.

FAVORITE THINGS: Checking out historic houses (Williamsburg, White House, Hearst Mansion, etc.). Eating out at ethnic restaurants... doesn't have to be expensive or sophisticated though that's okay, too. First it's who I'm with, then it's where we're going.

FAVORITE THINGS: Flea markets, garage sales, foreign films, really short walks in the rain (like running to my car when I forget my umbrella), romantic things like candlelight dinners, travel anywhere and everywhere.

FAVORITE THINGS: Wow, where do I start....so much to do and see in Chicago. Museums, bike riding, people watching, plays, baseball, football. If you can't find it here, we can zip to O'Hare or Midway and get there! What's on your list of things to do and places to see?

FAVORITE THINGS: Simple things like walks in the park. Complex things like planning a trip by car from Colorado to California and making sure we see "everything" but especially the Grand Canyon. My GPS! YES!!!

FAVORITE THINGS: Planning parties with good food where everyone brings 1 of their favorite dishes & the recipe to hand out for us cooking-challenged guys; hearing how my friends met each other and found "the one" (yes, one of my friends married his online date). It IS possible!

FAVORITE THINGS: Someone to root for my TEAMS! Going from biking to the ballroom in 10 minutes flat. I'm a minimalist with "things" but a maximalist with conversation and experiences.

FAVORITE THINGS: Playing Frisbee with Hershey (big playful Chocolate Lab...he thinks he's a lap dog), swimming with dolphins (only did it once but it was remarkable), my TIVO!

FAVORITE THINGS: Splitting a giant Chicken Caesar salad at Romano's so we can indulge and split one of their luscious desserts, cable news shows (CNN, MSNBC), finding a great relationship with a woman who shares similar interests. Care to share that Chicken Caesar salad?

FAVORITE THINGS: Comedy shows (Colbert Report, etc.). Favorite color is light blue....or medium blue...or dark blue....yes, it varies! Favorite food -- pizza. Favorite exercise -- chasing my dog.

FAVORITE THINGS: Ocean breeze and sun on my skin; white sand; smooth blues; strawberry ice cream; old black and white photos; good vino and a roaring fire in winter; my lady smiling at me.

FAVORITE THINGS: "Chillin" at the beach, the smell of coconut sunscreen, going out for seafood (yummm....shrimp scampi), trying not to make a fool of myself on rollerblades, planning our next date...your turn to choose...where to?

APPENDIX: LAST READ

LAST READ: The Siege which is a Stephen White novel. I like many of his books (Privileged Info, The Program, etc.). He's a clinical psychologist in Boulder who writes interesting psychological thrillers. Great airplane or post-skiing books.

LAST READ: I read people all day long... I'm a school psychologist! Multi-tasking is my middle name and in the car and at home I do books on tape. Last one on tape was O'Reilly's Bold Fresh. I enjoyed it AND I'm a liberal! Go figure.

LAST READ: I always have a book handy! Picked up Love in the Time of Cholera (weird title but entertaining book by Nobel Prize author). Many plots: young love, unrequited love, and more.

LAST READ: Magazines (5280, Health) and the local newspaper. Last good but heavy read was America Alone by Mark Steyn about America and the war on terrorism.

LAST READ: Insider's Guide to College (my son and I both thought it was great), 1000 Places to See Before You Die (great calendar with great ideas of travel spots). Care to compare travel lists?

LAST READ: I'm an avid reader: bestsellers, biographies, online news, stock stuff, and yes, I read instruction manuals before I use the new gadget. Really enjoyed A Thousand Splendid Suns.

LAST READ: A Colossal Failure of Common Sense (the collapse of Lehman Brothers). A MUST read if you're interested in Wall Street and what went wrong in the banking collapse. You don't have to be a conspiracy theorist to become spellbound.

LAST READ: Before the holidays I always read Quick and Easy Origami Boxes by Tomoko Fuse. For Xmas, my kids love when I put their gifts in those colorful origami boxes. The box is a gift, and the gift holds the real gift: gift card, earrings, checks, etc.

LAST READ: John Adams (very good look at our real founding fathers); Pillars of the Earth by Ken Follett (great "beach" or airplane book and very engrossing and fun, historical fiction).

LAST READ: Lots of technical reading and journals to keep current at work. Most are helpful, some so-so. For fun, I like Grisham and Ludlum and Robin Cook.

LAST READ: Hot, Flat, and Crowded by Thomas Friedman... and before that his book The World is Flat. He's a Pulitzer Prize author and you learn what's really going on in world economies, energy, etc. You won't be in the dark!

LAST READ: Good Calories, Bad Calories by Taubes. Outstanding! Not a diet book, it's a compilation of scientific studies: why low carb works, why low fat may not, metabolic resistance, and more! Fascinating!

LAST READ: Obama's Audacity of Hope (uplifting), Harry Potter and the Deathly Hallows (come on, I KNOW you liked it, too). I'd say both of these are MUST READS!

LAST READ: Where the Wild Things Are by Sendak. Your little kids or grandkids will love hearing it read to them. On the adult side, I'm a fan of The Far Side by Gary Larson, and NY Times bestsellers, and one of my all time faves was Lord of the Rings Trilogy.

LAST READ: The One-Minute Meditator by Birchard and D. Nichol, MD is a good and easy read on learning to meditate, living in the moment, being mindful. Great for those new to meditation or those looking for a refresher.

LAST READ: I rarely reread books (except Cat in the Hat and Horton Hears a Who), but I recently reread Atlas Shrugged. It was at the beach condo and was as good the second time around as it was the first.

LAST READ: Into Thin Air by Krakauer about a failed Mt. Everest ascent. Take it when you're on a ski trip. Or maybe not...you won't get any skiing in. He makes you feel the wind and cold of Everest. I loaned it to my sister, and she loved it, too!

LAST READ: Angels and Demons (it's even better than the Da Vinci Code in my opinion), David Baldacci's Stone Cold (exciting villain and hero thriller), Sunday NY Times, Newsweek magazine.

LAST READ: "The Dilbert Principle" by Scott Adams – a "business" book, but just as entertaining as his calendars! "The Joy of Cooking" (I rarely make gravy, so I always need the recipe proportions at Thanksgiving time).

LAST READ: 30 Years of Laughs and Lasagna (not a cookbook, a Garfield the Cat book); David Baldacci's Saving Faith.

LAST READ: I mostly like biographies/non-fiction: Truman by McCullough, Perfect Murder Perfect Town (sad but true story that took place in Boulder). Recently read Golden Compass Trilogy and Marley and Me 'cause the kids were reading them. Have a tissue ready!

LAST READ: My 3 favorite authors are S. Turow and the Pattersons (James and R. North). Recently read Midnights with the Mystic (good for seekers and those who love yoga) and The Power of Now.

LAST READ: Lost Symbol by Dan Brown for me. For me and the kids: The Little Prince, The Red Balloon, Goodnight Moon, 1 Fish 2 Fish by Seuss.

LAST READ: A lot of business journals (mostly dry but necessary), We Have Always Lived in the Castle (not my typical read...good but scary), Sunday comics, Art Institute Guidebook.

LAST READ: Pat Conroy (Prince of Tides) is my favorite author. The man writes lyrical words/music. I just started his Lords of Discipline. Even if you don't usually like military themes, you'll like this one. A literary treat!

LAST READ: Moscow Rules, The Defector (both by Silva), The Sweet By and By. Bittersweet and touching, and the author delicately handles the journey we all face.

LAST READ: I like the old classics like Ayn Rand and Animal Farm. I also like new bestsellers like The Girl with the Dragon Tattoo, Last Juror, Lost Symbol.

LAST READ: Midsummer Night's Dream, Othello (Yes, I like Shakespeare a lot and teach it in high school). Ask me to any kind of live theater...I'll say yes!

LAST READ: The Interpretation of Dreams by Freud (yep, that would be Sigmund). Interesting, lots of case studies. I'd read nothing by Freud and had no idea he was such a fascinating author.

LAST READ: Stranger Beside Me by Ann Rule. Scary story of Ted Bundy who Rule personally knew and worked with. I had never heard of Rule, but she's the queen of true crime books. Amazingly told. Get your girl friends and/or daughters to read it. Eye-opener.

LAST READ: My favorite book is usually the one I just finished. I'm an avid reader and just finished enjoying My Sister's Keeper.

LAST READ: Earth The Sequel (gives hope and solutions not gloom and doom). I also subscribe to Architectural Digest and have a pile of remodeling mags on the coffee table (redoing the bath this year).

LAST READ: Really enjoyed The Tipping Point (how little things can make a big difference), very thought-provoking.

LAST READ: Armed Madhouse: Sordid Secrets of a White House Gone Mad (the truth about Bush, why we went to war in Iraq, Lobbyists, etc.). Some say author/reporter Greg Palast is a modern day Thomas Paine. I agree.

LAST READ: Anything "Green": The Green Book (things you can do at home/work to be green), Green for Life (adding healthy stuff to your diet and good juicing recipes).

LAST READ: Death by Black Hole (by Tyson). The Big Bang theory, the origin of the universe. An astrophysicist wrote it, but it reads like a Star Trek adventure. Carl Sagan would have loved it!

LAST READ: I like true stories and my favorite author is Ron Chernow (Rockefeller, The Warburgs). Chernow makes history come alive. You are reading about real people, not just a date or dot on the map.

LAST READ: I never miss Mark Morford's column in the SF Chronicle. Amazing writer! He's witty, offbeat, left, and writes about everything…nothing is off limits.

LAST READ: Nouriel Roubini's website. He's the brilliant economist who predicted the economic mess 2 years before it happened. I have him to thank for getting me out of the market in time.

LAST READ: I like sports books…. Catcher in the Rye, Catch-22, One Flew Over the Cuckoo's Nest. But I still can't figure out why no one scores a home run. Maybe you can explain it to me??

LAST READ: LOVE photography books! My favorite is Colorado 1870 to 2000 by Fielder. He shows you "then" and "now" photos of the same places in Colorado. It's a feast for the eyes and fascinating!

LAST READ: A Wild Sheep Chase and Dance, Dance, Dance by Haruki Murakami (Japanese quirky and brilliant author). If you like quirky and elegant symbolism and characters, try H.M.

LAST READ: The Digital Photography Book by Kelby. I think he gives GREAT suggestions and tips. Let me know…I redid all my profile pics including the ocean one after reading his book.

LAST READ: Jon Stewart and the Daily Show Presents America (on tape). Profane, hilarious, and it made me laugh out loud. You'll learn more about American history than you ever did in school.

APPENDIX: FIRST DATE

FIRST DATE: If you send me a witty email, I will buy you coffee and a Danish. If you send me a witty email and tell me your favorite lawyer joke, please also tell me where you want me to take you to dinner. I like confident ladies who have a great sense of humor.

FIRST DATE: Okay, meet me at the Starbucks at Barnes and Noble after work. I'll be the one with the blue jacket and white carnation, and I'll be sipping a venti Caramel Macchiato. It seems to work in the movies, so it should work here, too, right? This is as real as the movies, right?

FIRST DATE: Let's go to a Magic Show. Everyone is looking for magic, so that way we can be sure we find it! After the show, we can do coffee at Starbucks. Everyone knows that a great first date always includes MAGIC and COFFEE.

FIRST DATE: If you think you know what's going on in the world, you need to meet me. I work for the (super-secret-hush-hush) gubmint. I'm going to be at the Broncos game on Monday night. I'll be the one wearing orange and blue. If you can't find me there, then send me an email, and I'll give you the super-secret code word and the address of my super-secret favorite coffee shop.

FIRST DATE: I'm having dinner, and you're having dinner with me. How does tonight work for you? If that's too soon for you, the Taste of Chicago is next weekend. If you've never been, you can taste everything from hot brats to hot alligators. Alligator tastes sorta like chicken.

FIRST DATE: Well, I think we should meet for an after work drink and dinner. You could tell me how your day went, and I would listen attentively. Then you'd tell me how smart I am, and I could tell you how pretty you are. Then we can get down to serious conversation and talk about life and goals and what makes us energized.

FIRST DATE: Rollerblading or skating....probably not a good idea 'cause I've never done either and don't want to break anything important on the first date. Going stargazing....probably not a good idea because it's not possible to see a black guy in the dark too well, and I'm liable to step off a cliff and break something important. Bungee jumping is probably not a good idea because I don't look good when I'm scared sh*tless of breaking something important. So... what I suggest is this...let's figure it out together and pick a place where we can talk AND keep both feet on the ground at the same time. Candlelight works for me…how about for you?

FIRST DATE: The best first date is one that starts with coffee and biscotti and never ends. We go on to have lunch together and then dinner the next day, and then I invite you to our office Xmas Party, and then you want me to meet your mom and then….(heck, you had me going there….let's start with coffee and that biscotti).

FIRST DATE: A first date? Can't we just skip to the second date and be done with being nervous and smiling for a whole 2 hours? Okay…the 2nd date can be our 1st date….I know this great café in the middle of the Botanic Gardens. It makes you feel like you're in a garden…. hmmm…..maybe 'cause it is a giant garden.

FIRST DATE: Some of my favorite places are walking in City Park when the new plantings are blooming, walking down the pedestrian mall and window shopping or real shopping. I need some new hiking boots…what do you need?

FIRST DATE: Let's run on the beach in the moonlight and roast marshmallows or drink champagne and eat strawberries…oh wait, that's at least the 5th date. Let's see….first date?? Have fun and talk and do what the mood hits us to do. We could have a light lunch or take a walk in Central Park.

FIRST DATE: I like concerts, sporting events, yoga, wall climbing. We could do a river tour or shoot hoops or play tennis. Yes, I'm high energy and looking for someone who enjoys being active with me.

FIRST DATE: Any place with good coffee and good conversation. Starbucks, Whole Foods, Pier Point Coffee Shop in Newport, the ski lifts in Vail, in Maui drinking Maui coffee while we watch the whales breach, in Rome drinking espresso and planning where we'll sightsee for the week. I've done all the above except one…care to join me?

FIRST DATE: My favorite place is this Brazilian restaurant in midtown. Food is fantastic, music is light jazz, not too loud. After dinner we can go upstairs to their rooftop bar and enjoy the sounds and lights of the city.

FIRST DATE: As long as you take the initiative and do the asking first, I am certain the first date would be great whatever we do. Gotcha!…Seriously, if you see me before I see you, ask away. I like confident women, and I know that gentlemen always pay for the 1st date, and the second, and the…….you get the idea. My idea of a great first date is having lunch or dinner on the patio of an outdoor cafe...PERFECT!

FIRST DATE: Coffee, hiking, bicycling, a picnic, Chinese or Vietnamese food, an antique car show....walking around a mall, or a great Festival or Fair! Sharing great conversation. For the most part, it's not what you do, it's who you are with.

FIRST DATE: Meet for a glass of wine or a drink and talk...and laugh! Let's pick some place special. Ya never know...it might be a first date we tell our grandchildren about.

FIRST DATE: Well, how about going for a walk in the Gardens? The mall is great for people watching or shopping (window or real). Or the zoo ...they've got a new baby polar bear, and I've never ridden the train around the park.

FIRST DATE: Lunch is good! A lazy Saturday or Sunday afternoon by the tide pools works for me. I like to play golf, so if you play or even if you don't, being on the course this time of year is always beautiful. We can walk or take the cart. Your choice.

FIRST DATE: Let's go to Paris! Of course I'm referring to Paris, TX. Or am I?? :)

FIRST DATE: This is too much pressure! I'm sorry, you're wonderful, but are you sure you really want to date a nice guy like me? If you're sure you're sure....Let's start off with coffee or brunch at the Eggistential. Best omelets and crepes in town. Then if you're up for a walk, we could cruise the mall looking for holiday bargains or check out the art galleries. I'm not much of a shopper, so ya gotta help me out and point me in the direction of what you'd like for Xmas.

FIRST DATE: Let's go out for ice cream. I'll open the door for you, pull out your chair, help you with your coat. Then let's order the biggest and most decadent 3-scoop banana split with all the toppings. Then let's go for a long walk to work off those calories!

FIRST DATE: Let's get dressed up and go to the theater. We can see a musical or a serious drama. I think Merchant of Venice is coming to the stage next year, but why wait till then? Lots of good plays are passing us by in the meantime!

FIRST DATE: I love exploring nature. Things like caves and old gold mines and searching for geodes is my idea of fun. Just west of here they give a tour of several caves on the weekends, and you get to pan for real gold. If you like to get your feet dirty and go exploring, that would be amazing.

FIRST DATE: Easy now... you're fast, aren't you? You don't even know my favorite color yet! And you expect me to divulge my favorite place for a first date? Well, since you're being nice, I'll give you a hint. It's not downtown. They serve great food, fantastic coffee drinks, and it's open 24/7. Email me, and I'll let you in on a little-known secret of the suburbs.

FIRST DATE: Let's go to OZ. I've never been there, and if you don't like me you can click your heels 3 times and head for home. Alternatively, we can go see the Broadway play "Wicked" which is supposed to be great. It's the pre-Oz story of the witches and the wizard.

FIRST DATE: Well, let's meet at my favorite restaurant (Miguel's) or yours. I can bring my favorite recipe (Swedish Meatballs), and you can bring yours. And if we do hit it off, you can tell our future kids why you love Swedish Meatballs.

FIRST DATE: We could watch the sailboats at the beach, a sunset at the beach, a sunrise at the beach, the surfers at the beach, sip coffee at the beach. Hmm....I live 5 miles from the beach and never tire of the smell of salt air and the warm sun on my face. But dress warm....even in the summer, the cool air off the water can be chilly.

FIRST DATE: We decide to meet. Yay! We have dinner. I try to be funny and entertaining and try not to drop food on me or spill my drink on either of us. You make lots of eye contact and laugh at my jokes. Time goes by WAY too fast. I walk you to your car. I look into your eyes and tell you I had a wonderful time. You step forward and give me a long hug and a kiss on the cheek. You drive away, and I watch your tail lights fade in the distance. I reach into my pocket for my car keys. I find a note you slipped in there while you were hugging me. The note says............... (NOW comes the hard part, what would YOU write on the note?)

FIRST DATE: I'm not into the 'Let's try 15 minutes to see if we click' dates. I think it takes at least 20 minutes to get to know one another! Seriously, I like a leisurely first date where we can have a nice lunch or dinner. If you like something more active, we can walk downtown or go to a museum. Whatever we do, it will be enjoyable and the worst that can happen is that you will meet a very nice guy and have a great day.

FIRST DATE: Something with movement...let's dance or hike or ice skate. I've found that movement stimulates conversation. If you have a dog, we can take yours and mine to the dog park and run them. Or we can go to a flea market or horseback riding or the zoo.

FIRST DATE: Let's go someplace where I can tell you about our second date. On the 2nd date, I would invite you to my lovely backyard deck and cook a fantastic meal for you. Either salmon on the grill or a tenderloin steak cooked to perfection. Salad would be my famous Caesar salad, and I'd add fresh tomatoes from my garden. Dessert would be peach melba or German Chocolate Cake. Okay, while I look for my recipe for German Chocolate Cake, would you please email me and let me know where you'd like to go for our first date.

FIRST DATE: We'd go to my favorite Italian restaurant. We'd split a bottle of wine and start talking. The waiter would be impatient because we'd be so busy talking that we'd forget to look at the menu. You'd order one of the specials, and I'd order one, too. We'd share our meals and feel like we'd known each other for much longer than a few weeks. We'd laugh and talk and talk some more. Good coffee and good dessert would round off a memorable evening.

FIRST DATE: That could mean a trip to the zoo, a trip to the aquarium, the Wild Animal Park, SeaWorld, or ??? You tell me what appeals to you.

FIRST DATE: I am a romantic. Two of my favorite things for a night out are candlelight and fine food. Romantic dates are good for the first date and the second and the third and....you get the idea. It only costs a little more to go first class, and if you can't enjoy the fruits of your labor now, when can we?

FIRST DATE: I'll whisper my plans in your ear. You'll probably hear something like.... Pssst... 1st date, coffee or a nice lunch. 2nd date, dinner, drinks, more conversation. 3rd date, let's take in a movie or dancing and dinner. 4th date, want to work out together and go grocery shopping and make dinner together? 5th date, let's go skiing. 6th date...let's plan a trip to Vegas or ?? 7th date...whoa...I don't think you can plan a relationship, it just happens. But this will give you some ideas of what I see us doing!

FIRST DATE: You made it down this far in my Profile! My karma must be working today. In that case, let's go to a Tarot Card Reading or something non-conventional like that. I've never done that, and I believe everyone should do something really weird at least once a year....or at least once in their lifetime. After that we can go for coffee. I'm pretty sure that caffeine is a mandatory requirement after Tarot Cards.

FIRST DATE: A French film or a trip to a France…...I'm open to suggestions! ;0)

FIRST DATE: Let's go on a camel ride. I'm not sure where we'll find a camel this time of year. We can always wait for the Renaissance Festival. Last year when I went with my nieces they had camels and elephants there. But that's not until Spring. How about a train ride into the city for a movie and dinner while we're waiting for Spring? Or we can go to the zoo and see if we can talk the zookeeper into letting us ride his camel?

FIRST DATE: Let's find a Spencer Gift store (do they still exist?), and you can help me buy something for my brother for his birthday. The funnier the better!

FIRST DATE: Let's go look at the new model houses off of the freeway. One of these years (maybe this year), I'm going to move from a condo to a house. So….I'm interested in a woman's point of view. I don't have dreadful taste, but I tend to go more masculine with lots of wood and granite.

FIRST DATE: Disneyland, Six Flags, the Zoo, SeaWorld, dancing, a concert, or symphony. I'm partial to Bach or Beethoven or Mozart. The theater is always a good choice….let's go to a matinee so we can have dinner downtown, too. Or maybe we can race go-karts. There is no limit to the fun, mischief, and adventure two adult kids can get into.

FIRST DATE: Dinner is always good, but tell me to "dress up" if you want to take me home to meet your mom!

FIRST DATE: Let's chew gum and blow bubbles, or get bubbles and go to the rooftop garden of a tall building and let the bubbles float over the city. Then we could go to the amusement park, ride the rides, and pretend we're 12 again. After a day of that, I'll be ready to act like an adult for the next 12 months. We can conclude our childish day with a Happy Meal at McDonald's or a nice dinner at Morton's. Your choice.

FIRST DATE: Let's walk along the Cape Cod Canal (until it gets too cold), then let's find a cozy place to have dinner. I have one vote and vote for Sushi and Asian food….what's your vote? Oh, you get two votes on the first date.

FIRST DATE: Let's ride around Texas. That should take about a month. If you need to be home before then, let me know, and we'll ride around Dallas checking out the great architecture and shops. I bet you $1 we can find a great restaurant for dinner.

384

FIRST DATE: Let's grab our umbrellas and walk in the rain....but let's make it a really SHORT walk....like from the train to some place that's warm and cozy and serves great coffee or piña coladas! Hmmm....that would be Maui....I don't think there's a train from here to over there. Maybe we'll have to settle for some great, South Seas cuisine.

FIRST DATE: Door #1: We meet for coffee at my favorite café. I'll splurge and take mine with a splash of cream. What can I get for you? My treat. Let's grab that quiet table by the window and sit and talk a while. Door #2: We meet for a drink at the restaurant of your choice. I'd love a glass of red wine, how about you? Maybe we can go shoot some pool later -- best three games out of five; loser buys. OK, OK, I'll buy regardless! Door #3: Your choice. My treat. I'm open to suggestions. What would you like to do?

FIRST DATE: NOT the obligatory "coffee scenario". Puhleeease, anything but that! Here are some other ideas: *Dress up in clown costumes and go out to dinner at McDonald's; *Volunteer at an animal rescue; *Pretend to be artists and do really terrible portraits of people downtown.

FIRST DATE: We are whisked away to a tropical paradise in the Caribbean. We're greeted by our tour guide and driven in a limo to our villa by the ocean. It's surrounded by swaying palm trees and breathtaking ocean views. The air is idyllic and warm, and the water is turquoise blue. We dine on lobster and .....okay, maybe not on our first date. How about for our 2nd date?

FIRST DATE: Let's go see the ice sculptures at the Botanic Gardens or Zoolightful or the holiday decorations downtown. But bundle up....it's cold outside.

FIRST DATE: I'm sitting outdoors at a table for two. I see you walk across the street, and you smile as you recognize me from my photo. You are wearing a leather coat and a mid-length, black skirt. I help you with your coat, and pull out your chair for you. You sit down. Then you scoot your chair closer to me so we can talk. WOW! Whatever happens from there, it's all good.

FIRST DATE: Let's get matching tattoos!!!.... Just kidding!!!.... I don't have a tattoo and don't plan on getting one anytime soon. Small ones can look great on women, but for my own body, I'm partial to the wash-off ones at the Art Festivals. How about a nice lunch or dinner with a glass of wine on the terrace and discuss our favorite tattoos that we won't be getting anytime soon?

FIRST DATE: I am so tired of women who want to use me as a sex toy. ;-) I just want to have fun talking and drinking coffee and getting to know each other. Is that too much to ask? (NOTE: This won't work unless the rest of the Profile is tactfully tongue-in-cheek).

FIRST DATE: We could drive downtown in my Ferrari, but it's in for service. Or, we could cruise to Las Vegas in my Lear Jet, but it's in for service. Wow, this is harder than I thought. Maybe let's just meet for coffee, and you can give me the name of a good mechanic so I can really WOW you on our second date.

FIRST DATE: You are there, and I am here, so one of us is obviously in the wrong place. Meet me at the Starbucks on 2nd Street. Or at the library...we can be outrageous and whisper loudly. Or on the dance floor...we can talk between the songs. Or I'll take you out to dinner.....but you need to tell me where??

APPENDIX: TERRIBLE FIRST DATE

TERRIBLE FIRST DATE: 15 minutes is long enough to decide if you would like to go for a walk and talk more. So let's just meet, check each other out, and go from there.

TERRIBLE FIRST DATE: Who cares? Let's just go out.

TERRIBLE FIRST DATE: Someplace safe. I wouldn't worry for my safety, though my mom likes me to call in to let her know that I got there okay. I can take care of myself, but I wouldn't want to go some place where you would have anxiety over your personal safety. I think the most prudent place would be somewhere where you would be at ease.

TERRIBLE FIRST DATE: I'll fill this out later.

TERRIBLE FIRST DATE: Health clinic to get mutually tested for STDs. Yes, I'm a safety guy.

TERRIBLE FIRST DATE: Let's cross that bridge if it gets to that point.

386

APPENDIX: SEX -- too much hot fire too soon

- I like giving and getting a massage.

- You'll love me stroking your body with my strong hands.

- I am a very sexy and passionate man who enjoys soft porn and am looking for the same in a woman.

- I love to give love over and over.

- I am a woman's dream man! I'll keep you happy and make sure that you are very satisfied in more ways than one!

- I'm a liberated Leo! I'm a real lover, not a fighter.

- I am very tactile. I'm looking for a woman who loves to touch and be touched all over.

- I can't stand yelling! Except when it's accompanied by lots of sweet lovin.

- I am passionate about everything, and I mean everything.

- I am uninhibited sexually and looking for the same in a woman.

- We don't know each other well enough yet, but I must tell you I have a wonderful rooftop Jacuzzi that's just right for 2.

- I like women who thrill me emotionally and satisfy me physically.

- The key to love and happiness is lots of FUN (if you know what I mean, wink wink)!

- Let's have lots of fun together. I'm very sensual and passionate.

- I want intense and powerful chemistry, that strong bond between us.

- I'm looking for an open-minded, sensual, passionate woman.

- To love the bad, sensuous ones is dangerous...and the BEST!

- I'm looking for friendship with FRINGE benefits!

- There is nothing I enjoy more than seeing that loving look in your eyes when we kiss goodnight.

- There's nothing more romantic than feeling your heart beat against mine.

- There's nothing more romantic than curling up with you on the couch on a cold winter day.

- There's nothing more romantic than cuddling with you and watching a great DVD. (NOTE: "Cuddle" is an interesting word. Many women respond to it in Profiles. It seems to work better with women over 45, but often younger women find it appealing if it's used with a light hand or in a humorous way.)

- There is nothing more romantic than going to a private beach where we can run through the waves. (NOTE: You don't have to say "run naked thru the waves". You've set the stage, and women DO have imaginations.)

- When I meet the woman I'm looking for, I'm going to say...Let's kiss and kiss again. I want everyone to know we're happy and enjoy being together.

- I don't think dancing together means we're in-like. I think holding hands says it better.

- I am kind, compassionate, loving, and more. I like romance, and more than that, I like romantic women who appreciate flowers and birthday gifts and Valentines.

- I'm looking for a woman with a warm smile who likes to talk and share. Extra points for liking to kiss and hug.

- You see that spark in my eyes, and I see it in yours.

- A great smile and a great kiss are always a great combination.

- I love to pamper the woman in my life. A great big hug and kiss at the end of the day? ALWAYS!

- I'm looking for a classy woman who likes to plan getaways to romantic destinations.

INDEX

P.S. to you...

One question we were frequently asked in the process of writing this book was:

"Will this book work for women?"

YES...89% of these secrets will work! The secrets to top-notch Photos, awesome Profiles, dynamite First Flirts, great First Dates, and many other secrets work for women, too.

However... *"Awesome Secrets for Women"* is available! There are 2 chapters which aren't in this book. Those are: *What Men Want* and *How To Keep Men Interested* (as if women didn't know). Yes, there are pulse-racing tips to heat up the room.

Message to the Ladies... if you want some great ideas now, *Awesome Secrets for Men* is a good place to start (and you'll learn a lot about men and what they do to attract you). Or get *Awesome Secrets for Women.* Either way... don't forget... most men LOVE it when they get emails from you first.

Ladies... Email the man who caught your eye! Today! If you don't know how, jot down a few 1st Flirts from this book for inspiration. Also, skim the chapters in this book on first-rate photos and how to write a good Profile. It takes all 3 things to achieve online success. *The #1 rule is...if you see him before he sees you, he can't read your mind...he can read your email!*

Happy Journey! :DenverSky5280

Made in the USA
Lexington, KY
13 February 2015